Down Inside

DOWN INSIDE

Thirty Years in Canada's Prison Service

ROBERT CLARK

Edited by Jill Ainsley.
Cover and page design by Julie Scriver.
Cover images: (hands) sakhorn38, iStock.com; (leaf) majorosi, iStock.com.
Printed in Canada.
10 9 8 7 6 5 4 3 2 1

Library and Archives Canada Cataloguing in Publication

Clark, Robert, 1955-, author
  Down inside : thirty years in Canada's prison service / Robert Clark.

Issued in print and electronic formats.
ISBN 978-0-86492-969-3 (softcover).--ISBN 978-0-86492-970-9 (EPUB).--
ISBN 978-0-86492-971-6 (Kindle)

1. Clark, Robert, 1955-. 2. Prison wardens--Ontario--Biography.
3. Criminals--Rehabilitation. I. Title.

HV9505.C63A3 2017   365'.92   C2016-907049-2
                                            C2016-907050-6

We acknowledge the generous support of the Government of Canada, the Canada Council for the Arts, and the Government of New Brunswick.

Goose Lane Editions
500 Beaverbrook Court, Suite 330
Fredericton, New Brunswick
CANADA E3B 5X4
www.gooselane.com

This book is dedicated to my wife, Linda,
and my children, Stephanie and Adam.
If not for their unconditional love and support,
this book would not have been possible.
I love you all more than I can ever express in words.

In my view, if anything emerges from this inquiry,...
it is the realization that the absence of the Rule of Law is
most noticeable at the management level, both within the
prison and at the Regional and National levels. The Rule
of Law has to be imported and integrated, at those levels,
from the other partners in the criminal justice enterprise,
as there is no evidence that it will emerge spontaneously....

Whether prisoners should have certain rights, such as
the right to counsel, the right to effective segregation review,
to family contacts, to exercise, etc., is for Parliament to
decide in compliance with any constitutionally mandated
entitlement. One must resist the temptation to trivialize the
infringement of prisoners' rights as either an insignificant
infringement of rights, or as an infringement of the rights
of people who do not deserve any better. When a right has
been granted by law, it is no less important that such right
be respected because the person entitled to it is a prisoner.

— Justice Louise Arbour, *Commission of Inquiry into
Certain Events at the Prison for Women in Kingston*, 1996

Contents

Introduction

Hell is the state of the soul after death, but it is also the state of the world as seen by an exile whose experience has taught him no longer to trust the world's values.

— John Freccero, Foreword to Dante, *The Inferno*, Robert Pinsky, trans.

One of my earliest memories of growing up in Toronto was my parents telling me, "Lock the door after we leave." As the eldest of three, this instruction became for me and other urban kids of my generation a mantra for personal safety. Locked doors gave our parents peace of mind when they left us alone. When we lock doors, we feel safer. That is what locks are for.

But locks can make things worse. Locked doors can prevent us from seeing what's on the other side. How do we know it's dangerous? What if we're mistaken? And locks can keep out the wrong things, like a chance to explain what really happened to someone who will truly listen. In prison, locks sometimes keep out the hope of being heard at all, of getting a message home, of seeing one's children, of life getting better. Locks can cause people to succumb to resignation over dreams, to rage over co-operation, to death over life. And locking doors is essentially what prison is all about.

If the true goal of prison is to reduce the likelihood of prisoners committing further crimes when released, then it follows that another goal of prison should be to maximize the likelihood of positive change, individually and collectively. This book reveals what really goes on inside Canada's federal prisons as I experienced it first-hand. In telling the stories of my thirty years "down inside," I argue that humane treatment is the most effective way of managing a prison safely and creating conditions to rehabilitate prisoners to become productive members of society. The more humane the environment, the safer for all concerned, prisoners and staff alike; my three decades of experience convince me beyond a doubt that this is true. We must begin by unlocking doors and discovering who and what we are really dealing with.

My career in Canada's federal prison system began in February 1980. I was twenty-four years old and had signed a nine-month contract to work at the Joyceville medium-security prison in Kingston, Ontario, replacing an employee in the gymnasium area. I saw the job as a temporary measure until I could find a teaching job in Toronto, which was my home. As is often the case, however, my plans did not work out the way I expected. I ended up staying with the Canadian federal prison service, and over the next three decades I worked inside seven different federal prisons in Ontario, at all three levels of security, including both of the maximum-security prisons in the Kingston area, Millhaven and the now-defunct Kingston Penitentiary. One reason I moved around so much was that I rose through a series of promotions; the other reason was curiosity.

The vast majority of this thirty-year career was spent working right on the front lines, in the cellblocks and other areas where staff and prisoners interacted face to face every day. I was down inside among prisoners and staff in every facet of prison operations. I locked and unlocked cells, completed prisoner counts, and took prisoners to the hole (solitary confinement) against their will. I took four or five prisoners outside the prison on work details by myself, conducted strip searches, and put out fires on the ranges (hallways of cells) following a murder. At Christmas, I allowed some prisoners phone calls home and declined to release others. I played hockey with the prisoners in a maximum-security prison yard and sat in a tower with a rifle overlooking the same yard. I consoled prisoners when their mothers died. I had a prisoner grab me by the throat, and I had my life threatened more times than I can remember. I had coffee poured for me — and urine thrown at me. I saw a lot of blood.

I met prisoners in maximum security when they carried a shiv (homemade knife) for protection and again in minimum security when they were close to release. Later still, on the outside, I met these same men in grocery stores, and they introduced me to their wives and children. I have interviewed literally hundreds of prisoners in every conceivable scenario, read hundreds of prisoner files, and written hundreds of reports for prisoners to be released, paroled, and sent up to higher security or down to lower security. My reports allowed prisoners to spend time with their families in the community — and I took those men home for the day.

I have never met anyone who has had more diverse experiences in "the belly of the beast" or who knows more about Canada's federal prisons and how they really function. But the strain of working in this type of environment for many years took a heavy toll on my personal life. Looking back, I believe my efforts to cope with the stresses of my job had a deeply negative effect on me and those closest to me. Like so many other Correctional Service of Canada staff, I found the harsh reality of what I experienced inside a federal prison changed me for the worse in ways I cannot fully describe. And like many other CSC staff, I did not talk about it. For thirty years I suffered bouts of personal angst and uncertainty regarding the true nature of prison and its purpose. Many times I considered resigning from the prison service. I experienced innumerable sleepless nights and moments of despondency and resignation, leading to stress leave, alcohol abuse, and divorce.

At the end of my career, I was a deputy warden, where I was second-in-command to the warden and responsible for the safe daily operations of the prison. Around that time, I attended a training session for employees at the warden's level or equivalent. Other higher-ups whom I knew and some of the top people in legal services at national headquarters also participated. During one afternoon session, we were asked to write down three things we would change about the CSC if we could. I wrote the word "culture" three times. The man next to me looked at my paper and shrugged.

Stephen Harper's Conservative government's tough-on-crime agenda helped to prompt my retirement in 2009. When I saw the changes being advanced to make our prison environment more closely resemble the US model — changes I considered unconscionable — I knew I would be unable to participate. I was aghast at how readily the leadership of the CSC embraced these draconian measures, seemingly without any hint of moral conflict.

I decided I had a duty to alert the world to what was going on inside the prison system. Most Canadians would never believe, or want to believe, that a system like this could exist in Canada. Surely, I thought, once Canadians knew the reality, they would demand reforms. I first began to write this book shortly after I retired. I completed about one hundred pages of a polemic when my computer crashed. Having neglected to back up my work, I lost it all. Instead of returning to the keyboard, I backpacked around Thailand, Malaysia, and Laos. Over the next three years, I visited parts of Central America and returned to Southeast Asia, to Vietnam and Cambodia. When I began to write again, late in 2014, I no longer felt I had to prove something or expose wrongdoing. Now sober and happily married to Linda, whom I'd first met as a respected colleague at the Regional Treatment Centre, I simply wanted to write about what my thirty years down inside meant to me.

...

Prison is not as depicted in the movies, full of men with bulging biceps covered in tattoos, who fight all the time. Prison is more like a volatile version of greater society. You can find every kind of person imaginable incarcerated. There are men who spend their days lifting heavy weights, while others paint with watercolours. Some prisoners play bridge while others share dirty syringes, the modern equivalent of drinking moonshine or sniffing rags soaked in paint thinner. Most days in prison are fairly quiet, and everything seems to roll along without much bother.

But prison is a place where violence is often the first recourse to solve a problem, and as I would learn quickly, the level and degree of violence are frightening. During my time, acts of savagery and cruelty occurred that I would not have thought possible. Who would believe that a man would gouge another man's eyes out with a pencil for looking at his girlfriend in the visiting room? Or swing a metal weight-lifting bar at another prisoner and take the top of his head off? A good friend of mine, recently hired, was standing six metres away when this happened; he never got over what he saw and left the prison service shortly after. Another prisoner lost all his teeth to an iron bar for talking on the phone too long; still another had the soles of his feet slashed for walking on a freshly waxed floor. A man on my caseload was stabbed to death while lying on a bench lifting weights on a Sunday morning, possibly in a case of mistaken identity.

It is difficult to understand what would motivate a man sitting in a filthy prison cell to draw with a dirty syringe the infected blood of his male lover and inject it into his own arm as a show of love and commitment, or to strip and cover himself in his own feces before crawling under his bed and refusing to come out. The CSC acknowledges that a large percentage of those incarcerated suffer from one or more diagnosable mental illnesses. This alone makes the environment within a prison difficult to manage; addiction, poor impulse control, mistreatment at the hands of staff, gross negligence, and confinement in a dangerous environment make conditions even worse.

A fact that is less well known is the vast majority of those who are incarcerated for victimizing others have themselves been victims. Having read many prisoner files and conducted many interviews, I say this with certainty. Most of the prisoner files I read contained histories of physical, emotional, and, often, childhood sexual abuse. Their life stories typically follow a similar path through the quagmire of social services, foster homes, training schools, and young offender facilities. These very damaged human beings, these lost souls, have usually suffered unspeakable horrors that began in the earliest years of their existence and left them unable to feel or care about the values on which most of us predicate our lives.

The corrections system employs many fine people, and they deserve great credit for doing their best every day under often impossible circumstances. These gifted staff members include uniformed guards, shop instructors, chaplains, parole officers, nurses, rehabilitation program staff, managers, and school teachers. They are the unsung heroes of Canada's prison service; their presence makes our prisons safer and more humane. Regrettably, they make up a small percentage of a prison's total workforce.

In my opinion, too few prison employees care about the prisoners under their care, other than to make sure they are alive and behaving. Any interest in a prisoner's well-being and their chances for becoming a law-abiding citizen is almost non-existent. Some prison employees seem to regard the prisoners as less than human and feel it is acceptable to mistreat them in myriad ways, ways they would not even consider outside of prison and that they would be ashamed to have their family and friends see. Some employees engage in acts that would be a crime outside the prison walls. Many more of these acts are simply crimes of the conscience: racism, verbal and emotional abuse, intimidation, and so on.

The reality is the harsh and chaotic world inside the walls significantly tests each employee's moral fibre. In many instances, the challenge is too great. I believe a culture of collective indifference toward both the prisoners and CSC's stated higher goals has crept in and become as cemented in place as the stones in the walls of Collins Bay penitentiary. This culture is, in my opinion, largely responsible for most of the problems that occur within our prisons.

Sadly, the organization itself unofficially almost sanctions the mistreatment of prisoners. Many of the people at the top will not risk poor relations with staff or their unions in order to ensure every prisoner's rights are respected. The "blue wall" is perhaps the most disturbing element in this living drama. The term is commonly applied to policing, but it is very much part of the Correctional Service culture. The blue wall is an overdeveloped sense of solidarity, a level of cohesiveness that transcends one's personal values. The unspoken rule is "never rat on a fellow officer, no matter what." The entire group does not subscribe to this way of thinking, but a sufficient percentage does for it to be effective. This unofficial oath of secrecy can be found from the tiniest corner of any prison shop to the highest halls of power in Ottawa, and everywhere in between. And it prevents Canada's penal system from exercising complete control over its prisons. Justice Louise Arbour encountered the blue wall when she led an inquiry in 1996 into practices at the Prison for Women in Kingston. "The deplorable defensive culture that manifested itself during this inquiry has old, established roots within the Correctional Service, and there is nothing to suggest that it emerged at the initiative of the present Commissioner or his senior staff. They are, it would seem, simply entrenched in it," Arbour wrote.

Imagine that you're a new correctional officer, a guard, who has been working at a local prison for three months. You've met many of the staff and are beginning to feel like part of the group. Sometimes you go for a beer with your colleagues after work. Perhaps you're finding working in a prison much more challenging than you originally imagined. One evening, while working in the solitary-confinement unit, you witness an argument between an irate prisoner and a fellow officer. The prisoner is verbally abusive, and the officer, your colleague, is showing increasing signs of frustration. Finally, the officer orders the prisoner back into his cell. As the prisoner turns around to enter the cell, the officer places his hands on the prisoner's back and shoves him from behind. The prisoner, unprepared for the push, stumbles forward into his cell, banging his forehead on the steel door frame. The officer who pushed him did not intend for the man to hit his head; in fact, he may have regretted giving in to his frustration at the moment it happened. But now the cell door is closed and locked, and the prisoner is screaming at the top of his lungs that a staff member has assaulted him. He demands to see the nurse, the unit manager, the warden, his lawyer, and so on.

Having regained some composure, the officer responds, "I didn't push you. You tried to punch me, and you slipped!" With that, he returns to the office.

At some point in the shift, the correctional manager, the most senior person on duty and in charge of the institution for the evening, stops by on his regular rounds. When he hears the yelling, he walks down the range to speak with the irate prisoner. Then he comes to the office where you are sitting with your two colleagues, and he asks about the prisoner's allegation. The officer involved insists the prisoner took a swing at him and slipped, hitting his head on the door frame, and the other officer present supports his version. The correctional manager reminds everyone to submit a written situation report before they leave work. You now find yourself alone in the office with two of your more experienced colleagues. What would you do?

Chances are, at the end of the shift three or four separate reports will be submitted, all giving exactly the same version of events: the prisoner slipped and hurt his head while trying to assault an officer. This version will find its way into many places and many hands, including those of the prisoner's parole officer. The prisoner could be in for a whole different kind of trouble — higher security, a longer sentence, or worse, and the officer responsible for his injury will escape any consequences for an act that, outside prison, could well be a criminal assault. Another brick in the blue wall — the single largest problem, I believe, facing every prison in Canada. The majority of prison employees are like the people in any workplace. Many staff, once immersed in the corrections culture, become loyal to the blue wall. A guard told me that when he started working in Kingston Penitentiary, the other guards told him, "You're not one of us until we have something on you."

I don't doubt that many employees who've adhered to the code have found it tested their conscience at times. So how does this happen? Based on my thirty years of first-hand observation, I blame the job and the environment. Many prison staff, no matter their job and no matter their background, begin to see the prisoners as something less than real people with whole life stories, just like the rest of us, who once were kids and who may still have people who care about them and want them home. Over time, I saw many employees start out eager to make a difference, only to later fall in with the staff who had decided the prisoners under their charge were unworthy of their time and energy. They became indifferent to — even annoyed with — the prisoners' myriad needs. They started to ignore written requests and complaints. They might review unfairly or incompletely a prisoner's eligibility for employment, educational programs, parole, or alternatives to solitary confinement. In its most severe form, verbal abuse and excessive force became routine. The prisoners could have, in turn, responded with anti-social behaviour that only validated the belief they were incapable of change and undeserving of better treatment. Sometimes this thinking gave rise to the conviction that harsher treatment would solve the problem, even if this meant bending or violating the rules governing the treatment of prisoners. Sadly, direct supervisors and some senior managers did not always discourage this response, even though it was clearly illogical and illegal.

The most mentally sophisticated leaders and employees can fall victim to this view, if only in times of extreme stress and competing demands. As a result, the prison system, which fires almost no one, permits itself to mistreat those under its charge if the system deems it necessary. Prisoners languish in solitary confinement for months on end, simply because a better or easier solution isn't readily apparent. Canada's prison system, like most others, is firmly centred in a culture of secure confinement, with rehabilitation a second — and distant — goal. People at the highest levels continue to defend the use of solitary confinement, despite overwhelming evidence that it epitomizes cruel and unusual punishment according to what is now known and understood about its effects.

I once encountered a young and relatively inexperienced parole officer, recently and temporarily promoted from uniformed officer, who recommended a particular prisoner on his caseload receive an order of detention from the National Parole Board (known as the Parole Board of Canada as of February 28, 2013). As a rule, only a very small segment of the prisoner population, the extreme high-risk offenders, receives these orders, which mean they will remain incarcerated until the expiry of their full sentences. Referrals for detention are considered extraordinary action, justified only in cases of extreme violence and/or exceptional circumstances, such as compelling evidence that the prisoner is planning to commit, or likely to commit, an act causing death or serious harm upon release. This particular case did not meet the legal criteria for a detention referral; it was not even close. Not only was there no compelling reason to assume the prisoner would commit an act causing death or serious harm upon release, but also there was no evidence that this prisoner had been involved in significant violence at any time in his history.

I was acting warden at the time, and I declined to support the parole officer's recommendation. At first I put it down to a mistake: a new parole officer had misinterpreted the admittedly complicated legal parameters that govern detention referrals, and, somewhat inexplicably to my mind, the unit manager, the coordinator of case management, and the parole officer's own unit review board all failed to reject the recommendation before it came before me at the detention review board. Had our quality-control system broken down? No. The answer turned out to be much more mundane, and much more frightening. This prisoner didn't meet the detention criteria, but he met and exceeded the pain-in-the-ass criteria; the parole officer had decided he should stay in prison. His unit manager was not trained in risk assessment and was a like-minded former guard and a friend, the two having worked together in uniform earlier in their careers. The coordinator of case management told me she was just "keeping the chair warm" and didn't want to "rock the boat." All of these people were prepared to look the other way while a prisoner potentially had years added to his time behind bars, and it would have been a mistake — a mistake permitted because one employee saw an opportunity to abuse his power and others were unwilling to speak up.

The blue wall endures because prison employees form a tight bond forged by the considerable challenges of their unique work environment. Uniformed staff often see themselves as set apart from the other employee groups, literally as well as figuratively. Security work is unglamorous at best, particularly in comparison to some of the flashier jobs, such as parole officer or rehabilitation program officer. The officers who worked for me at Millhaven, for instance, endured many years of abusive behaviour from the prisoners under their charge. Only another officer can appreciate the anger and frustration one feels when a prisoner throws urine in your face or spits on you or bites you. It can be difficult to take the high road, and when management appears indifferent to the challenges you face, it can understandably seem that only other officers share your feelings.

Perhaps the greatest contributor to the blue wall is a commonly held belief among CSC staff that management cannot be trusted. This doesn't mean my staff didn't trust me; I believe they did, and their trust was never misplaced. Similarly, I worked with many excellent people over the years who taught me a lot and inspired me. To the average employee, "management" meant not the middle managers but those at the top, the wardens and above, and particularly the faceless leaders in Ottawa, who enjoyed the unmitigated contempt of staff and prisoners alike. I certainly had my own experiences with senior managers who apparently neither knew nor cared about what was going on in the prisons they purportedly ran. Once the us-against-them seed is planted, it rarely fails to take root.

One of prison staff's chief complaints was the misperception that the higher-ups routinely and unfailingly gave in to the prisoners. This view was widely held during my time and prevails today, from what I hear. Many employees (and Canadian citizens, for that matter) see prisoners as having too many rights. This is a very tough nut to crack. Logical arguments predicated on an understanding of the Charter do not suffice in this arena. In every prison I worked in, I always tried to make myself available to prisoners who had problems they could not get resolved at lower levels, including prisoners from cellblocks where I did not hold jurisdiction. When I'd ask why they brought their problem to me instead of their unit manager, they'd say, "No one else will help me. A couple of guys said I should ask you. They said you'll tell me straight." I knew this unresponsiveness was probably true, and it caused me untold frustration. I've lost track of how many times I was able, with one phone call, to solve a problem for a prisoner who'd been banging his head against a wall for weeks or months — a symptom of the inertia that pervaded much of the prison system.

I actually enjoyed visits from the prisoners, and I knew it meant a lot to the officers who worked face to face with them and often bore the brunt of the extreme frustration caused by bureaucratic bungling and, in too many cases, the sheer laziness of prison staff. Over the thirty years I worked in prisons, a great many men sat in the visitor's chair, or as I liked to call it, "the chair," in my office. The crimes of some had dominated headlines around the country. Others were wretched, forgotten souls who only wanted to survive their present circumstances. Whoever they were, they came because they believed they needed my help. Such problems could be extremely delicate, especially if a review of the circumstances revealed the prisoner was indeed being mistreated or ignored. That happened a lot, unfortunately.

Some prisoners submitted a complaint and never received a formal response, or, equally frustrating, were told in writing, "Your grievance is denied," when I could clearly see they were right and their grievance should have been upheld. Sometimes prisoners who had submitted applications for things like transfers, temporary absences, and private family visits had their applications ignored. One prisoner from another unit came to me because he had been waiting six months to have private family visits with his wife and daughter. I confronted the parole officer who was ignoring the man's application. Later I learned that same parole officer recommended against the proposed visits, in direct contravention of policy, as payback to the prisoner for complaining to management. I, as acting warden, went into the system and changed the final decision to "approved," diplomatically noting the "incorrect" policy interpretation. These small problems can escalate if they are not corrected. Sometimes I just wanted to shake everybody and say, "Do not forget: they outnumber us four to one."

...

Most Canadians are familiar with the former federal government's position that a tough-on-crime approach is the most likely to reduce crime and deal with those who engage in anti-social acts. Many people argue that if prison is tougher people will stop committing crimes to avoid going back. My experience convinces me otherwise; this argument is extremely flawed and represents an overly simplistic view of the causes of crime. We need look no further than our neighbours to the south. The United States prison system is firmly rooted in a philosophy of longer sentences, secure custody, and harsh treatment, and this approach has been utterly ineffective. In fact, ample evidence suggests it has had the opposite effect. As Henry David Thoreau once wrote, "There are a thousand hacking at the branches of evil to one who strikes at the root."

In my experience, if the staff is humane and reasonable, prisoners are better behaved, and the prisons are generally orderly and stable. Those prisons with the fewest locked doors are also the prisons that experience the fewest problems. Safer environments are the direct result of staff and prisoners interacting face to face regularly. The more often prisoners are exposed to the habits and behaviours of socially adapted people, the more they learn to adopt the same types of behaviour. They see and accept that such interactions are positive and life-affirming. For many prisoners, this is their introduction to a world that is not always negative and dangerous, a world where they may, for the first time in their lives, begin to trust others.

Some of the many victims of crime, their lives permanently changed by terrible events, may not feel sympathetic to my argument for the necessity of humane treatment. The parents of the young girls Paul Bernardo murdered, or the survivors of his numerous sexual assaults, may misconstrue my words as evidence of a casual and sympathetic bias toward the convicted. Nothing could be further from the truth. One of the most difficult periods of my career was the six months I spent as the victim services coordinator at a minimum-security prison, responsible for advising victims of events in prisoners' cases. This assignment put me in direct contact with many victims of crime who, I know, relive every day the fear, pain, anger, and humiliation they felt when a crime was committed against them. Listening to another person describe a terrifying and life-altering event left me so emotionally drained that I was often numb for many hours afterward. Some of my conversations with victims caused me to doubt and question, for the first time, many things I thought I believed in, like redemption and second chances. Although I experienced troubling moments of disillusionment in my career, I remain convinced any government policy that doesn't make rehabilitation the central focus of its prison system is doomed to fail.

In the pages that follow, I try to recreate details and dialogue accurately. I use the techniques of creative non-fiction, sparingly, to convey as closely as possible what actually happened and in what context. As well, I have changed almost all of the names of the prisoners I encountered, and many of my colleagues, in order to afford them a measure of privacy and fairness. The bulk of these stories is based upon my memory of what happened. As such it is possible that I have forgotten certain details in a few instances. At times, I rely more heavily on research to assist me with exact details, times, and dates, as in the escape of Tyrone Conn from Kingston Penitentiary and the murder of a prisoner named John at Joyceville in my second year of service. John's death forever changed my view of my work and the prison environment. I base my account of this event on my recollected experience, but I also draw from the memories of staff who first responded to the murder scene.

The reader will not find many graphic depictions of violence and death. Enough books already exist about the horrors that can happen down inside. While I understand the public interest in such subjects, I believe these acts of extreme anti-social behaviour are symptoms of the culture of collective indifference and the practice of locking doors. Accordingly, I focus on accurately describing the environment inside our federal penitentiaries, this environment's effect on the people who enter it, and how they — all people, including me — adapt to it. With the exception of some instances when I quote or cite others, what follows is my opinion of what currently ails Canada's prison system.

I use the term "prisoner" instead of "inmate" to describe those incarcerated. I believe prisoner more accurately reflects the true nature of the relationship between the keepers and the kept. Similarly, I use the term "solitary confinement" rather than "administrative segregation," the term Correctional Service of Canada prefers — and likely chose for its benign nature. "Administrative segregation" fails to acknowledge the degree of emotional and psychological damage known to occur when people are confined in this way for extended periods. "Solitary confinement" more accurately represents this environment, is plainly understood, and it does not offer the system that applies it so frequently and casually — a system I was a part of and supported — shelter from legal or moral responsibility.

Despite the popular perception that most prisoners are placed in solitary confinement because they pose a risk to the safety of others or as punishment for bad behaviour, the vast majority enter solitary confinement at their own request, out of fear for their personal safety. In essence they are held in protective custody.

The warden or his delegate authorizes all placements in solitary confinement. Within twenty-four hours of a placement, the warden or delegate must review and state in writing that the placement is legal and necessary. The next scheduled formal review takes place three to five working days later. After this review, the prison's solitary-confinement review board assesses the prisoner's case every thirty days. Parole officers and other managers attend, as do the prisoners whose cases are under review. The prisoner has the opportunity to ask questions, and at the end the solitary-confinement manager submits a written recommendation to the warden. According to policy, every prisoner who is maintained in solitary confinement for thirty days or more must see a mental health professional at least once every thirty days. This usually amounts to a short interview. For prisoners who are held in solitary confinement for forty-five days (changed from sixty days) or more, a member of the staff at regional headquarters assesses the case.

These provisions may seem an adequate and reasonable safeguard against the overuse of solitary confinement. In fact, the exact opposite is the case. Having chaired over two hundred solitary-confinement review boards and attended hundreds more, I know these processes typically amount to little more than a rubber stamp. Once a prisoner seeks protective-custody status, they are labelled for life in the eyes of other prisoners and the CSC. Protective-custody prisoners cannot safely be reintegrated into the normal prison population, a return these prisoners are almost always unwilling to attempt. The only option is transfer to a prison that specializes in protective-custody prisoners, like Warkworth or the former Kingston Penitentiary, or one where the prisoner's protective-custody status is unknown, usually out of province.

In short, until a suitable transfer option is identified and approved, there is no end in sight for these prisoners. In almost all cases, the transfer takes months. Other prisons have been known to refuse prisoners with a history of seeking protective custody. In cases where bad behaviour *is* the impetus for placement, such as incurring debts, the options for resolution can become fewer still. This is how most prisoners who end up in solitary confinement remain for dangerously long periods of time. It is also the reason that prisoners often have no idea when solitary confinement might end. This not knowing, in my experience, begins the prisoner's downward spiral into mental and physical illness. Many long-term solitary-confinement prisoners resort to acting out and self-harming as a means to draw attention to their plight. Some take their own lives.

In writing about these issues, I know I will anger people still working in the system who might believe such things are best left unsaid. Out of regard for all those staff hurt by working in this type of environment, I decided to be as open as possible. I suspect a great many prison employees have seen too much and still do not get a good night's sleep. To these people I say, the culture of the organization you work for is far more responsible than you are for the things that go on down inside.

1 First Trip Down Inside

I first glimpsed Kingston, Ontario, in 1978. I was twenty-two and had moved to Kingston to attend Queen's University. Born and raised in Toronto, and having majored in physical education at York, I intended to complete a bachelor of education degree and work as a high school phys ed teacher in Toronto. Kingston sits on the shores of Lake Ontario and boasts some of the best freshwater sailing in the world. It's sometimes called the Limestone City, after the material most of the city's oldest buildings — including city hall, the courthouse, and the university — are built from. The downtown streets are lined with old brownstones, turn-of-the-century houses, and huge oak and maple trees. The Queen's campus is beautiful with its ivy-covered halls, large trees, and abundant greenery.

The most surprising thing about Kingston to me, and likely most of the new arrivals that fall, was the high number of federal prisons located in and around this very small community. In fact, on the day I arrived in town, it was the Prison for Women and Kingston Penitentiary that first caught my attention. The Prison for Women was right across the street from my first stop when I arrived that early September afternoon: the Faculty of Education, or what is commonly called west campus. That same day, I saw Kingston Penitentiary for the very first time, and I remember being awestruck. With its foreboding walls and towers, it looks very much like a prison you might see in an old black-and-white movie. I was amazed that this very famous place, full of the most dangerous men in Canada, was situated right on King Street in the middle of town. A city map I received as part of my Queen's orientation package described Kingston as the "incarceration capital of Canada." I still remember that, probably because for a long time it stared at me from the fridge door, four small magnets holding it in place, like a prisoner shackled to a stone wall.

Our required curriculum at the Faculty of Education included a period of volunteer work in the community, for which we earned a credit toward our degree. I asked to volunteer with the Correctional Service of Canada and was given a name and a phone number: Norm Staples, supervisor of recreation, Millhaven Institution, in Bath, Ontario.

The next day was sunny and cold. I had my first class at nine o'clock, and after that, with the prison phone number in my pocket, I found a pay phone. I hesitated, wondering if this was a good time to call; I had no idea. I put the money in the phone and dialled.

On the third ring a female voice answered. "Good morning, Millhaven Institution. How may I direct your call?"

I asked for Mr. Norm Staples. There was a pause, and then another female voice answered. "Recreation department. Marg speaking."

I repeated my request for Norm Staples.

"I'm sorry, but Norm's down inside right now. I don't expect him back for a while. Can I take a message?"

I faltered momentarily upon hearing the words "down inside." When I regained my wits, I gave Marg my name and the reason for my call. She assured me Norm would be happy to talk to me and advised me to call back in a little while. I hung up feeling both exhilaration and a kind of nervous energy. This was a promising beginning: I was going inside a real live maximum-security prison. Then the phrase Marg had used struck me again; she had said Norm was "down inside." My imagination propelled me into a frightening scene from a movie with huge, rugged, tattooed men too dangerous to live outside the bars, a place where life is cheap, and you can be killed for just a wrong look. That term played on a loop in my mind: he's down inside. I confess now it caused me to momentarily second-guess my decision. I quickly regained my enthusiasm, however, and looked at my watch. I would go back to class and leave halfway through the next one. I sat for twenty-five minutes listening to my professor explain the best ways to teach sex education in a high school setting. He had a woman's bathing cap on his head, which I thought did not make him look any more like a swimming sperm than he did without it. I thought of my own sex education, which I obtained in the form of talk on the school playground. At five minutes to eleven I got up with head bowed, tiptoed up the carpeted stairs, and slipped out. No one was using the nearby pay phone. Good.

This time, a man's voice answered my call. "Recreation. Norm Staples speaking."

As I began to explain who I was, Norm told me he was aware of the community engagement program, having attended the Faculty of Education himself. He said a community volunteer would be a welcome addition to his department, and he suggested I should come out to the institution so we could meet, discuss the specifics of what I might actually do, and tour the recreation department. The longer we talked, the more at ease I felt. As for what I would experience down inside, that remained to be seen.

We set a date for the next week. I anxiously anticipated our meeting, imagining what it would be like inside a real prison — and not just any prison but the infamous maximum-security Millhaven Institution, a twenty-minute drive west of Kingston. I wondered what the prisoners would think of me, and I worried about them sensing my uneasiness, which was growing quickly. What if these guys were the type who killed people on a whim? After all, what possible hope can there be for those in a maximum-security prison? By the time the day arrived, I had made up my mind that these prisoners must be the most violent and dangerous people in all of Canada. I decided all I could do was stay close to Norm and follow his instruction.

To get to Millhaven Institution from Kingston, you drive west on Highway 33. Within a few minutes, you find yourself beside Lake Ontario. It's a beautiful drive, especially on clear days when the sun is on the water and the sailboats are out in full force. When you leave the highway at the Millhaven turnoff, the road bends and divides at the top of a small hill. You drive another few minutes on a service road, passing many signs cautioning that you are on a federal government reserve and all persons and vehicles are subject to search and seizure.

When the prison finally comes into view, you might be genuinely awestruck. I was. Millhaven Institution is a sprawling two-level, brick fortress-like structure. Two chain-link fences, six metres high and about five metres apart, surround it. Both fences have barbed wire at the top as well as razor wire in great unfolding circles. Outside the fences, prison towers stand at intervals around the facility, each with a small glass-walled room at the top for viewing the area below. I looked up at the closest tower, thinking I would see a prison guard with his gun. I saw no one.

I turned into the small lot marked visitor parking. I was a few minutes early, so I sat and looked around. Across the road, a gravel path led to a small brick structure with dark windows and a single door marked ID Building. I knew from Norm's instructions that I was to go in and give my name to the officer. He would be expecting me. I got out of the car and crossed the road toward the path. I noticed this small building was built directly beneath one of the prison towers. I looked up, and this time I did see a uniformed man at the window, looking down at me with seeming interest. Then he turned away and was gone. In my anxious state I thought maybe I had broken a rule. Had I parked in wrong place?

As I entered I saw a counter on the left where two large ledger books sat open, pens placed beside them. Behind the counter a man wearing the prison uniform got to his feet. He was in his thirties, with bright red hair, thinning on top, and a large stomach protruding where his waistline might have once been. His face was round and flushed, and his nose was red, his eyes bloodshot. His uniform looked like he had slept in it, and his sleeves were rolled up, revealing beefy pink forearms and meaty hands with chewed fingernails. His name tag identified him as Geoff.

"Good afternoon," I said. "I'm here to see Norm Staples, the supervisor of recreation."

Geoff looked at a sheet of paper on the desk behind him. While he was busy, I surreptitiously glanced around. The brick walls were painted light green. The tile floor looked old and dirty. In a corner were three or four plastic chairs, and a bulletin board with photocopied sheets tacked to it hung on the wall beside them. A yellow cardboard header read "Visitors Rules."

Geoff was looking at me now. "You know where you're going?"

"No," I said, feeling increasingly apprehensive.

"Go out this door and through those gates." He pointed to another door on the opposite wall. Through the window I saw two very large chain-link gates some distance away.

"When you go through the second gate, there are two trailers before you go inside the prison. Norm is in the one on the right." Geoff pushed one of the ledgers across the counter toward me and handed me the pen. "Here, sign your life away."

I thanked him. The door made a loud buzzing sound as I put my hand on it. Stepping out onto the path, I started toward the gates. A paved walkway continued on the other side and led to a large set of glass doors. On either side of the path were two large trailers. The one on the right had wooden steps leading up to a small porch and a solid door. A large window was in the side of the trailer, overlooking the path. As I walked toward the gates, I noticed two rows of very small windows covered by metal grills around most of the outside of the prison. Some of them were open slightly and had things hanging outside, like T-shirts or shorts. I realized these must be the cells where the prisoners lived. I also realized that meant the prisoners might be looking out at me. I turned to look back up at the tower above me. No one was visible now.

A sign warned me, "Stand clear of moving gates." I did. With a loud electronic noise, the outside gate began to move slowly from right to left. When it opened enough for me to step inside the fenced enclosure, it stopped. It occurred to me that someone looking at me from somewhere must be operating it. I stepped inside the first gate, and it immediately resumed its droning to slowly close behind me. I looked up at the security camera in the upper corner of this cage-like structure to show I had an honest face. Big smile. With the first gate closed behind me, the inner gate began to creep open on its track. Gradually the protective barrier between me and the prison was moving aside. I had a strange sensation of excited vulnerability. I remember feeling as if something was changing for me. Maybe it was the chance to say I had been inside a maximum-security prison. Maybe I thought I would be a more interesting person with my tales of life behind the walls. The gate stopped moving, I stepped through the opening, and walked to the trailer on the right. I knocked on the metal door at the top of the steps, and stepped back a bit. I put my hands in my pockets and looked around as if I knew where I was. The door opened, and a man stood smiling broadly at me, hand on the doorknob.

"Rob Clark, I presume. Please come in." Norm Staples was about thirty-five years old and in good shape. He had reddish, thinning hair and a moustache. He seemed happy to see me and introduced me to Marg. She smiled and reached across her desk to shake my hand. She had pictures on her desk as well as a coffee cup with her name on it. She offered me a coffee; I politely declined.

"So," Norm said, "you're interested in doing your volunteer hours in here."

"Yes, if you think I could help out in some way a couple of days a week."

"I don't see why that would be a problem. We already have a few community volunteers at Millhaven, just not many. We don't have anyone in recreation. The volunteers here are usually John Howard volunteers [John Howard Society is an advocacy group for prisoners' rights in Canada] or sometimes law students assisting prisoners with appeals and things like that."

Norm described the facilities and assured me the prisoners were, for the most part, very cordial when it came to dealing with volunteers. "We just have to get you security cleared, and I'll send out a memo to security about what days you're going to be coming to the institution."

"It's as easy as that?"

"Pretty much."

"Would you like to go down inside and see the area and our facilities?" Norm asked. "I can introduce you to the guys you'll be working with."

"That sounds good," I said, trying to sound like going inside a prison was normal for me.

Marg picked up the phone. "I'll let them know you're coming down."

We stepped out onto the sidewalk. "This way," Norm said, and we turned right toward the set of large glass doors at the top of two wide concrete steps.

Inside the doors was what seemed to be a foyer with cinder block walls. Directly ahead was a large, darkly tinted window. The glass looked very thick and was set in a large steel section of the wall with a round hole in the steel face, directly below the glass window. To the right of the window was a heavy steel door with a very small window. The door was suspended on a metal track, much like the gates I had come through. A sign on the door warned, "Stay back when door moving."

I would later learn that behind the dark glass was an armed control post with banks of switches operating various security doors as well as security monitors by which the officers could observe activities randomly. This was also the place where the firearms were kept, along with many other types of security equipment, such as handcuffs, chemical agents, batons, and shields. I learned that the hole below the glass was the method by which firearms, ammunition, and keys were handed out as required. This round hole also served as a gun port through which the officers inside could fire outside, if necessary.

Norm stepped up to the window and waved at someone inside. The door began to move slowly and noisily along the track, and then we stepped through. The dark heavy glass extended along the left wall for another five metres or so. Norm waved toward the glass, and we walked past the post and into a very long passageway. It was actually two passageways side by side, separated by steel framing and mesh. The floor was black rubber with narrow windows running the length on both sides. As we walked, I could see a large metal barrier at the other end.

Norm pointed out a window to our right. "Those are the small yards, and those are the units where the prisoners live. That is J Unit on this side and E Unit on that side."

I saw what looked like a small area of grass and a picnic table. A metal door in the side of the building near the windows had a sign I could not read. The area was enclosed by the walls with the little security windows I saw on the way in. A softball lay in the long grass.

When we reached the end of the passageway, I could see through the spaces in the steel barrier a sort of fortress-like control post in the middle of a large rotunda. What I had not noticed from the outside is that Millhaven Institution is built in the design of a wheel, and now I was looking at the hub of that wheel, with passageways like the one we were in running off it. This was N area, and almost everyone moving through the institution passed through it daily to get to their destination. Electric barriers at the entranceways of the five passageways, or spokes, branched out from N area. In the middle of the floor was the control post. Here sat the guard who opened and closed the steel barriers leading to various places down inside the prison.

Our turn came, and the barrier slid open with the same, already familiar, mechanical groan. We stepped through, and Norm called out a hello to the two prison guards who appeared to be the security detail for this important area of the prison. Norm also waved at the dark window of the centre control post.

We walked across the black rubber floor to another barrier, where we waited for that barrier to open. As we stood Norm gestured for me to look up. My gaze followed his pointing finger to the yellow wall above us. At first I did not notice anything.

Norm leaned toward me. "See the area where the wall is damaged?"

I noticed chips out of the blocks that showed grey against the yellow paint.

"That's from a shotgun blast a while back. A prisoner was being stabbed in this passageway coming back from the hospital. The officer with the moustache standing over there was on duty. He saw the one guy getting stabbed and got a shotgun from the control. He fired a warning shot up at the ceiling and then pointed the gun at the two prisoners."

I could not resist looking over at the prison guard.

Norm continued, "Anyway, I guess the *kaboom* was so loud that it scared the daylights out of both the prisoners and they stopped."

"Wow," I said, unable to think of anything else to say. My recently discovered bravado was considerably shaken, and I was back to feeling nervous. Fortunately, Norm did not seem to notice. When the barrier opened, we stepped through and walked down another passageway, seemingly going further and further into the prison. As we approached another metal barrier, it made a noise and began to slide open early so as to be ajar when we reached it — *a courtesy in a place like this*, I thought.

Norm waved again at the glass, which was on the other side of this barrier. We were now standing in a small area in front of the control post with three different barriers from which to choose. Norm walked straight ahead, and this barrier also began to move in anticipation. Above the barrier a small sign read "Recreation." We stepped into a wide hallway. Directly to my left was a small gymnasium, and further to the left was another open doorway. Through that door, I saw weights and some mirrors on the wall. Although the gym appeared unoccupied, I heard the unmistakable sounds of men lifting heavy weights in the other room. I kept up with Norm as he walked a few more steps before reaching a wooden door with a large glass window; again I could hear voices. He opened the door and stepped aside for me to pass ahead of him.

The room, something like an office, held about six people that day. Behind a desk with a phone sat a large man in blue jeans and a golf shirt. Another man was also wearing jeans. Four men wore green uniforms: prisoners. All were seated on plastic chairs except for the man behind the desk. He had tipped a wooden chair back against the wall; he dropped it back to the floor as we entered.

It seemed like a friendly conversation had been going on as we entered, and it died away as everyone glanced first at me and then at Norm.

"Hi, guys," Norm said. "This is Rob Clark, the guy from Queen's I was telling you about."

The men all looked right at me.

Norm continued, "Rob has a phys ed background. He's interested in helping out here for part of his school year, and he gets a credit for it at the end." As Norm finished, the man on the wooden chair leaned forward and extended his hand out toward me.

"Nice to meet you, Rob. I'm Bill," he said. I shook his hand, and the smaller man in jeans stepped toward me, his index finger supporting a plastic coffee cup.

"Welcome aboard, Rob. I'm Al."

I shook Al's hand too. I tried to sense from the feeling in the room the right way to speak to the men in the green uniforms. They were clearly maximum-security prisoners, and yet Norm and the other two fellows did not seem to be concerned for their own safety. It was as if they were all on good terms, which I could not quite understand.

As I finished shaking Al's hand, I turned toward the prisoners and said, "Hey guys, how's it going?"

That probably sounded pretty dumb. *How's it going?* They were locked in a maximum-security prison — that's how it was going! But these men got to their feet and said hello to me. I extended my hand because that seemed most natural for me to do. I had no idea how things worked in a prison, and I noticed hesitation on the part of the men as they considered shaking my hand.

The first man that stepped forward and shook my hand was the biggest fellow in the room. He grinned. "I'm Brutus."

I smiled. "I'm Rob. Nice to meet you."

Brutus was about forty years old. I guessed he was about six foot one and weighed in around 230 pounds of solid muscle. He had blue eyes and some of his teeth were missing from his big grin. Brutus hailed from Newfoundland, "an East Coast boy," as he said, and everyone in the prison generally feared him. He was one of those extremely tough men you know you could not hurt with a baseball bat. My hand disappeared into his huge palm, which was attached to a forearm the size of my thigh. His knuckles and hands were covered in jail tattoos, and his forearms showed numerous scars, burns, and other signs of a life lived in battle.

One by one the other guys stepped forward, shook my hand, and said hello, then returned to their chairs. An older-looking prisoner told me to call him King. He was of average height with a thin build, wore glasses, and some grey showed in his hair and in his chin stubble. He was smoking a cigarette right down to the filter with a long ash hanging from the end, and his fingers were stained with nicotine. I later learned he was considered one of the most dangerous men in Millhaven. Supposedly, he had the power to say who was safe and who was not, so great was his reach among the prisoners. In fact, all the prisoners I met that first day were among the most powerful and influential at Millhaven. I learned over time that my new-found acquaintances were precisely the prisoners that many of the others feared.

There was Lenny, nicknamed Snake. I discovered later that Lenny got this name because when he was high on pills, which apparently was most of the time, his mouth got really dry and he darted his tongue in and out. Nicky was a handsome, rugged man in his twenties, with a movie star smile. Another prisoner went by the nickname Hobo, a long-haired young man of about six feet who was enormous from heavy weight lifting. He wore a T-shirt with the sleeves cut off to emphasize his herculean arms. Hobo was covered in jailhouse tattoos, and his arms also bore many burn scars and what looked like unattended injuries that had eventually healed into raised, uneven scars. Despite his imposing physical presence, Hobo gripped my hand lightly upon our introduction and, barely meeting my gaze, muttered, "Hey," in a low voice. Later on, after he knew me better, he would tell me he was serving a life sentence for killing two bikers. Apparently, Hobo had been at a biker clubhouse party somewhere outside of Windsor. He ran afoul of some of the residents, who showed him the door and roughed him up in the process. Hobo returned with a shotgun.

Finally, there was Nathan, a prisoner of Jamaican background. I would have some interesting conversations with this man in the months ahead, because he was always in the recreation area. He was about five feet six inches with very dark skin and very big eyes.

Nathan was a bodybuilder who worked out several times a day. As a result, he had a strong, broad back and powerful legs. The prisoners who lived on Nathan's range supposedly never tasted eggs, because he confiscated them to maintain his habit of eating twelve yolks per day. He insisted the eggs gave him size and definition, which he constantly appraised in the filthy mirrors of the weight room.

Nathan loved the recreation area and loved being outside, no matter the weather. Occasionally he would come into the rec office with Hobo to get coffee. Although he always looked uncomfortable accepting coffee from "coppers" like Al, Bill, and Norm, where I was concerned Nathan had no issues. My knowledge of power lifting made an immediate impression on him, and he would usually say hello or ask me questions about his workouts. He had a big smile, and he would laugh so hard that he would make me laugh; he had the same effect on others. When he was not working out, he could always be found sleeping in his cell, which he called his "crib."

A prison psychologist had told Nathan to prepare himself for the possibility that he would never be released because of his record. Nathan told me in his strong Jamaican accent that he looked the "prison shrink" in the eye and said he would indeed get out someday — and would look him up when he did. "Holy fuck, Rob, I thought he was going to have a fucking heart attack!" Nathan said, before bursting into his hallmark laughter. This earned Nathan a stint in solitary confinement — and the general respect of the prisoner population.

I found out later the guys considered it acceptable to shake my hand only because I was from the "street" and not a "copper." A copper is anyone who works inside a prison, no matter the particular job. I would learn a prisoner, no matter who he is, can never be seen to be too friendly with the coppers. In a place like Millhaven, shaking hands with a copper could be a death sentence. But my introduction seemed to be going well.

"Here, sit down, Rob, and make yourself comfortable," Norm said.

One of the prisoners reached behind him, lifted a plastic chair over his head, and handed it to me. "Here, Rob."

I sat down, and everyone looked my way without looking too long. Bill broke the ice first.

"So, Rob, you're at Queen's, eh? That's good. And you're at the Faculty of Ed? Very good. I went there myself, and you already know Norm did, too, I guess."

I remarked that Norm had told me as much and, unable to think of anything else to say, observed it was a small world.

One of the prisoners stood up from his chair and said, "I'm going for coffee. Who wants one? Rob, do you want a coffee?"

"Oh, uh, sure I guess."

"What do you take in it?"

"Just milk is good." Two more prisoners also got up and, carrying empty Styrofoam cups, followed the first man out the door and to the right. When the coffee arrived, everyone sat down and started talking. Brutus and King brought their chairs over to where I was sitting and asked what I was going to be doing at the prison.

"Rob will be coming in to recreation a couple of afternoons a week," Norm said.

"Recreation" is the name given to the area of the prison that has the gymnasium, weight room, exercise yard, and prisoner canteen. Usually these facilities are attached to a larger department known as social development, which may include things like the chapel, prisoner purchasing, and hobby craft. As we talked, it became apparent the principal leisure activity for most of the prisoners was weight lifting. The only team sports that seemed to be of interest were softball in the summer and, not surprisingly, hockey in the winter. During the warm weather, some prisoners liked jogging, and others preferred just lying in the sun.

Although outwardly I may have appeared relaxed sitting there in the office, holding a coffee cup and talking about hockey, I was feeling energized. I could not believe I was inside a maximum-security prison, talking to real prisoners. My experience on that first day made a powerful impression on me. I felt I was being accepted into a rare and unique group of men, like I was part of something that most people could never imagine in their entire lifetime. Most of all I believed I had something good to offer the prisoners here; and the positive reaction of these very rugged characters stoked my enthusiasm. Norm, Bill, and Al seemed to be nice guys and, like the prisoners, genuinely interested in me becoming involved in their department.

Hobo left the room and returned with a few pictures, which he passed to Brutus to show to me. One was a small grainy Polaroid, in colour, of some men standing around a large trophy placed on the floor. I immediately recognized Nicky and Brutus among them.

"What's the trophy for?" I asked.

Hobo piped up for the first time. "For the ball hockey league we had."

Despite his massive muscles and many tattoos, I could see in his expression and his body language that this man was unsure of himself. I wondered what his life was like and how he had landed here. In time I would come to know this and other things, amazing things, about the men sitting around me. Brutus handed me a couple more Polaroids and explained each picture. The men shared funny tales of being in jail. The afternoon passed quickly. Norm talked to Bill and Al about how I might help out and the necessary steps to permit me to enter the prison. While they talked logistics, I took in my surroundings. Then it hit me: I was down inside.

Norm looked at his watch and then at me, rising from his chair. The noise of several chairs scraping across the floor filled the little room, and a chorus of "goodbye" and "see you later" followed us into the corridor.

"What do you think?" Norm asked as we passed through the barrier and headed back toward the rotunda. "Do you still want to come and do some activities with the men?"

"Yeah, I would really like to do that."

"We'll have to get you security cleared. I'll give you a form to fill out, and they'll have to do a CPIC on you. After that, when you can come in, we'll get you a visitor's ID."

"Sounds great," I said, although I had never heard of a CPIC — a criminal background check. The conversation shifted to more general subjects, such as what I thought of Queen's University and Kingston compared to Toronto. I said I liked Kingston a lot, and today I liked it that much more. A few minutes later, we reached the trailer. Norm and I shook hands and quickly confirmed what each of us would do in the next week. I said goodbye and moved toward the gates as Norm mounted the steps of the trailer. I did not look back, fearing it would look strange. Geoff was standing at the counter in the ID building and a woman was writing in the same book I had signed. "Thanks," she said as she finished writing. "See you tomorrow."

Geoff turned the register turned toward me. I found my name and the time I had signed in. Checking my watch, I printed the time and signed again. "Thanks very much," I said, turning toward the door.

"No problem," he answered. "Have a good one."

I will, I thought.

As I pulled out of the parking lot, I looked again at the front of the prison and the tower rising above it. I looked up at the glass but saw no one. Driving back to Kingston, I replayed the last two hours over and over in my mind. Each hello, every handshake — *did I say anything foolish?* The more I thought about it, the more convinced I became that everything had gone well. The prisoners and the staff seemed genuinely friendly, and I could not think of a reason for them to pretend. I decided the experience I was embarking on was going to be amazing. I thought about the prisoners I had met, imagining what they might be doing. Maybe they were locked in their cells by now.

It was half past three, and the sky had become very dark. To my right, Lake Ontario stretched as far as the eye could see, and the waves were almost black. It started to rain just as I pulled up to the curb in front of my building. Once inside, I turned on the TV for background noise and opened a beer. My window looked out on the parking lot of a funeral home on Clergy Street. Tomorrow I would confirm my volunteer assignment at school and give them Norm's information as the contact person. I sat for a while, watching the rain and mulling over the assignment I was about to take on.

Over the next week and a half, I spoke with Norm a couple of times, providing him with the personal information required to perform a security check and finalize the details concerning my admission to the prison. We agreed I would attend Millhaven two afternoons a week. On my next visit, I would receive a visitor's pass at the ID building, then Marg would greet me at the trailer and call down inside for one of the staff to escort me to the recreation area. I kept remembering the day when I had first observed the inside and felt the peculiar atmosphere that pervades a prison. I felt I was among some of the most dangerous people that ever lived, and yet these same people seemed quite friendly and relaxed when I was in their company. It seemed akin to being related to a member of organized crime or a motorcycle gang member: you know they have hurt people, and you know that many people would be fearful of them, but at the same time you feel immune because you feel accepted as an outsider to the reality they survive in every day.

From October 1978 to March 1979, I was at Millhaven Institution twice a week, becoming more and more at ease in this new environment. In retrospect, I realize those early experiences at Millhaven as a volunteer played a large part in shaping my views of federal prisoners and my treatment of them for the next thirty years. From the moment I entered their world, those prisoners went out of their way to make me feel comfortable and show their gratitude for the time I devoted to them. They told me many prison stories, brought me coffee if they got one for themselves, and included me in their jokes. The fact that I was a volunteer from the street, and not a real copper, meant these guys could talk and joke with me as much as they wanted. I became quite well known to the prisoners, chiefly because I was a new face, which was rare. There was another thing about me that baffled the prisoners: I was not paid to be there.

They saw me as just a university kid who was trying to help them. "He goes to Queen's," I would hear them say. "He's doing it for school or something." I did not carry a badge, a gun, or a key. I was neutral, like Switzerland, and so they treated me like I was one of them to the extent possible. They showed me pictures of their families, and sometimes they told me why they were in prison. Because they took me in their confidence, I never felt the prisoners were a danger to me. In return I always treated them with respect, and I spoke to them no differently than I would have spoken to friends or family. I believe this made a big difference.

At times I saw prisoners become frustrated and even angry, particularly if they felt disrespected or humiliated. This was most evident when we started playing hockey on the outside rink in the prison yard. At least once a week I would come into the prison with my skates, gloves, hockey stick, and a bag of pucks. For two hours we would skate around, and I would show the guys some hockey drills and encourage them to practise stick handling and so on. Near the end of the two hours, we would divide into two teams and have a game, sometimes with prisoner referees. During some of those scrimmages I saw men go from amicable to enraged in an instant. Men who had seemed like friends before we started playing could very easily end up fighting viciously before the others separated them. I imagine some of those fights were finished at a later time and place. Even I learned to be careful about being "too cute" with the puck and to avoid embarrassing another player by scoring too often. It was best to simply stand off to the side and lean against the boards talking to Al or Bill rather than play on the occasions when tension was palpable. After seeing how some of these men could change so dramatically in an instant, I began to understand how they ended up in a maximum-security prison.

I met some of the other prisoners in these months of volunteering. Jeff was about my age. At about five feet seven and 190 pounds, he was a powerfully built young man with blond hair and wide-set green eyes. I noticed he had no whiskers on his face. Jeff was serving a life sentence for second-degree murder. Another man I met, Jesse, was the best friend of Snake. Jesse was a slightly built man of around five feet nine with red frizzy hair. Jailhouse tattoos covered his arms, and he was a chain-smoker. Jesse was serving a life sentence for the second-degree murder of a Toronto cab driver. Jesse and Snake's mutual love of prescription drugs may have been the reason for their friendship. It was rare to see them apart and rarer still to see them without glassy eyes and slow speech. Both guys were close friends with Nicky, forming a crew of three that was usually together.

I moved freely in the recreation area, circulating from the gym to the weight pit to the yard. Sometimes the prisoners would ask me questions about weight lifting or would want me to draw up an exercise plan for them to follow. Most were looking to increase the size of their arms and chest rather than working on an overall improvement in their fitness level. Sleeveless T-shirts and tank tops were popular and much sought after. I played hockey on the outdoor rink with the prisoners once a week, and I even arranged two games between the prisoners and me and my friends from Toronto. The players on my team included my younger brother Ron and my friend Bob Ballantyne. Roughly thirty prisoners stood in the snow that day, cheering on their friends and good naturedly booing our team.

By late February I had already put in about twice the number of volunteer hours required to receive my credit, and my time at Millhaven was coming to an end. Brutus and Hobo resumed lifting huge weights in the outdoor weight pit. Snake and Jesse continued floating through their sentences, one stoned daydream at a time.

When he wasn't working out, Nathan slept the days away in his crib. At the beginning of April 1979, my degree finished, I said what I thought was a final goodbye to Kingston and turned my beat-up VW Beetle west on the 401. I was going home, ready to begin my teaching career.

2 A Change of Plans

For those seeking employment as teachers in Ontario, 1979 proved a bad year. I sent out many résumés and received not one favourable response. In August, I was in a Toronto bar called the Ports of Call; it's not there anymore. I ran into Dave Nichol, a guy I had gone to York with. He was also looking for a teaching job and having no success. I told him I'd been toying with the idea of heading to Alberta to look for work on an oil rig. I suggested that if he did not mind hard work (and I didn't), it was a good way to make money until something more desirable came along. As it happened, in a few days Dave was going to drive first to Edmonton and then to Fort McMurray with a guy named Mike Mariani. He invited me to join them. We clinked glasses to celebrate our plan.

My two travelling companions and I drove to Edmonton and then headed north. The car died in a small northern town called Beaverlodge, just outside of Grande Prairie, forcing our return to Edmonton. While looking for oil-rig jobs, I noticed a CN Rail ad for work outdoors repairing railway tracks and switches. The pay was very generous (we would soon find out why), and meals, accommodation, and transportation were provided. Fortunately the CN office was not far from where we were staying. We were low on money and had no car. We ran.

This turned out to be the most physically demanding job I ever had in my life. We worked in Arctic-like conditions and started before sun-up. We worked with picks, shovels, and sledgehammers specifically designed to hit the tops of railway spikes. We dug up railway ties and replaced broken rails, and occasionally we replaced a switch. Our transportation was a school bus with no heat to speak of and a rear window partially broken from a tool thrown in the back. Exhaust fumes drifted in through the broken window, so we had to keep windows open at the front of the bus to draw out the toxic air.

We ate our meals at truck stops in whatever small town we ended up in. We would sign our name on the back of the bill and give it to the "white hat," our boss. We lived in small motels, usually close to the tracks. To reach remote sections of track we rode on handcars, some electric, some hand-pumped, just like the old days. If it was too far out for these little carts, we would hitch a ride on a real train. Once I got to sit up in the little window of the caboose. Another time we sat in the backs of new Dodge Ram pickup trucks on their way to some dealership. It was beautiful rolling along through the wilderness with the sun just coming up and many deer venturing out of the woods in search of food.

At night we would put on multiple layers and go for a jog around the town we were lodging in. Despite the bitter cold on these nights, the exercise was enjoyable and very invigorating. I still remember the brilliance of the northern lights. Then, just before I flew home for Christmas, I got a phone call from my dad to tell me Norm Staples had called from Kingston. He had a job for me if I wanted it.

I started work at Joyceville Institution, a medium-security prison, on February 19, 1980, hired on a nine-month contract to replace a man who was taking French-language training. I had moved back to Kingston only three days previously, using a car borrowed from my cousin Debbie and with all my clothes jammed in a garbage bag. I had checked into the Holiday Inn downtown and grabbed a *Whig-Standard*, the city newspaper. The next morning, I looked at listings for furnished apartments while having breakfast in a restaurant called Morrison's.

It snowed heavily as I scanned the pages, eventually coming to an advertisement for a one-bedroom furnished apartment, available immediately for $175 a month, on MacDonnell Street. I had no idea where that would be, but I left Morrison's and found a pay phone on Princess Street, Kingston's main drag, to call the number listed in the ad. Within twenty-four hours of my return, I had found a place to live and stocked my new home with food and other bachelor essentials, like paper plates and plastic cutlery.

Joyceville Institution, located northeast of Kingston on Highway 15, was built in the 1950s. The prison shows its age inside and out. Joyceville, a large square structure, looks completely different from Millhaven. The windows of the inside cellblocks face an open-air inner courtyard, a large paved square where prisoners congregate, deal, fight, engage in illegal activities, or just walk, talk, and plan. Around the prison is a pair of tall chain-link fences topped with razor wire. At the back of the prison is an exercise yard that overlooks the Rideau Canal.

I arrived feeling nervous. I was confident about working with the prisoners, but I also knew this was an actual job, and I did not know anybody who worked here. In fact, I no longer knew anybody in Kingston. I got out of my parked car and fell in behind a man heading toward the ID building. Unlike the one I knew at Millhaven, this building had huge chain-link gates that allowed vehicles access to the prison compound and in between the perimeter fences. Three officers were working in this building, two behind large glass windows. The third officer stood at a small counter. I showed him my letter confirming my employment. He read it and then held my letter against the glass. The officer behind the glass looked at my letter, too quickly to read it all, and motioned that I should stand off to the side.

I watched others sign in as I waited. Then a man of about thirty-five, with a big moustache, carrying some shopping bags, rounded the corner. "Karl, here's the guy," said the guard behind the counter.

Karl gave me an enthusiastic handshake and a big grin. "Glad you're here, Rob. C'mon with me."

We entered the prison by a very large steel door with a small security window in it. Inside was quite bleak, like a very old hospital with terrazzo floors and pale green plaster walls. Karl waved as we passed the main security office, which back then was called the keeper's hall. I could hear a voice on a crackling two-way security radio. A very tall, very thin man with sparse grey hair and a large nose sat behind one desk reading something, a cigarette burning between his fingers. Behind him on the wall was a wooden board about one by two metres.

"That's called the count board," Karl explained, "and there's one in the main security office of every prison in Canada. The board is divided into individual units, each unit is divided into its four ranges, and each range shows every cell by number in sequence. It has the name, number, and cell location of every single prisoner in the prison." Every new prisoner arriving at Joyceville had his name and number printed on a small piece of magnetic tape placed adjacent to the corresponding cell location on the board. So important was the count board, Karl told me, no one could touch it without the keeper's authorization.

We turned right and stopped at a large leather-bound book lying open on a windowsill at the end of the hall. Karl wrote his name using the pen attached by a string and handed the pen to me. "We sign in and out every day."

I signed below him. We turned and headed back the way we had come, past the keeper's hall and down a long hallway to a large electric barrier, which opened as we approached. We stepped into a small area dominated by a control post protected by a thick glass window. This was admin control, and it served a similar purpose to N area at Millhaven. Four other electric barriers besides the one we had come through led to different places, including the inner courtyard. The cellblocks were located on the other side of the courtyard, and prisoners passed through this barrier to work, attend medical appointments, see visitors, and so on.

The guard inside admin control opened and closed the barriers as sleepy-looking prisoners trickled through. An officer outside the control post frisked each one and asked them where they were headed. He greeted Karl enthusiastically as we passed on our way to the barrier leading to the recreation corridor. With a loud electrical whine the barrier slid open. We were now in a hallway lined with large windows facing the courtyard. I looked out as we walked along, marvelling at the many cell windows — four levels of them, from what I could see. Karl was making small talk and pointing out different things, but I was not listening. I was thinking about my contract here for the next nine months and wondering if this was what I really wanted to do.

We entered the gym. The dark-green tiled floor was filthy and covered in cigarette burns. A large, raised stage dominated the far wall. In the middle of the stage hung a heavy leather punching bag. Lines on the floor marked courts for volleyball, badminton, and basketball, and basketball hoops were at each end of the gym. Two regulation hockey nets with goalie equipment were in one corner, next to hockey sticks in a battered metal garbage can.

Grey-painted concrete steps faced the stage and ran almost the length of the gym. These served as bleachers; stacked on the steps were at least three hundred metal chairs. Doors next to the stage led to the recreation staff office, the equipment room, and out to the yard. Beside the equipment room was a large opening covered in heavy-duty steel mesh with two small square windows, or wickets, cut into it. A hinged sheet of plywood behind the mesh secured the room. This was the canteen, a prisoner-operated store that sold such items as snacks, pop, cigarettes and cigars, and stamps. To the left of the stage was a room containing a badly damaged washroom stall and toilet — a sink was partially falling off the wall — as well as a punching bag, cloth knuckle-wraps, bag gloves, and skipping ropes. Known only as the bag room, I would learn this little hole in the wall had been the scene of many disputes settled between prisoners. It was out of staff view, and prisoners could have a "six man" (a lookout) standing casually near the door or sitting on the stage, smoking a cigarette, ready to signal if staff came too close; the fight would resume later. Many mornings fresh blood from the night before stained the floor and the sink.

Weight-lifting prisoners had to go down a flight of stairs to the weight pit, a very long room with a bank of narrow windows. Prisoners wrote their workout days and times in marker on the walls beside the filthy cracked and broken mirrors. Weights were strewn everywhere, and cigarette butts and spit littered the floor. Sinks, shower stalls, and toilet stalls occupied the middle of the room. Past the shower area was another room of weights and benches with a number of large homemade dumbbells on the floor. The room stank of sweat and stale air. When I stood in the weight pit that first day, I could not have guessed that, one year later, a prisoner I would become friendly with would be murdered in that exact spot.

By the time Karl and I completed our tour of the area, we had still really only exchanged names and a couple of pleasantries. Karl, unaware of my previous experience in a prison, explained the general operations while I scrutinized my surroundings, not saying much beyond, "Uh-huh." He could easily have assumed I was reacting too casually for the environment.

We went back upstairs and crossed the gym to the staff office. Two other men were already there. One was a member of the panel that had interviewed me: Dennis Bally, a handsome man of about thirty, with a thick black moustache and hair to match. "Hey, Rob!" he said, shaking my hand with great enthusiasm. "Great to finally see you again!"

The other man in the room shook my hand firmly. "Joe Carmichael, glad to meet you." Joe was only about five feet tall, clean-shaven, and built like a bulldog. His silver hair and glasses might have made him seem older except for an unmistakable vitality. I would learn over time that Joe was one of the funniest guys around. In all the time we worked together, he was never stuck for an answer; his quick wit came in handy when prisoners argued with him, and he was an expert at telling jokes. The only member of the group I had yet to meet was Mike Laporte, who was working the late shift. The recreation facilities were open every weeknight, and each of us worked one week of nights every fourth week: the shift ran from two until ten. We also took turns working Saturday and Sunday. The rest of the time we worked Monday to Friday, eight a.m. to four p.m.

I noticed similarities to the recreation office at Millhaven: one old wooden desk covered in papers, a few chairs, and some lockers toward the back window. A washroom stall was conspicuously placed in this already cramped room. Joe made tea for all of us while we got acquainted. The clock on the wall read a quarter past eight.

Karl said, "Well, the prisoners will be down soon."

I heard voices and footsteps coming across the gym. We got to our feet, and Joe grabbed a clipboard from a nail. I recognized it as the workers' roll call. It listed about ten prisoner names, their four-digit prison numbers, and a number and a letter, like 3B, indicating the prisoner's range where he lived. This made it easier for employees when we had to call a unit to ask, for example, where a particular prisoner was.

Three prisoners were in the gym and had taken up places on the stage, smoking cigarettes and drinking coffee out of plastic peanut butter jars, which were very popular in prison at that time. Prisoners could clean out the jars and use them, with the lid on, to carry coffee or sometimes brew (homemade alcohol). Coffee and cigarettes comprised the main diet of most prisoners, and many brought a jar of coffee to work with them. These three prisoners looked sleepy and disinterested; they barely noticed me, the new guy. We exchanged greetings in quiet voices.

"The prisoners come down to work every day, Monday to Friday," Dennis explained. "They call workup just after eight, and all the employed prisoners are released from their ranges to proceed to their respective work locations." Prisoners who worked in the industrial shops, the main kitchen, or the school would go through a large barrier door on the opposite side of the courtyard from the gym. Prisoners who worked in the recreation area, chapel, or library, or who were cleaners in the administrative areas or the visiting area, crossed the courtyard and passed through admin control. At eleven thirty the prisoners returned to the units for lunch and a prisoner count. Once the institutional count was certified as correct, workup was called again at about twelve thirty, and the population moved en masse.

"Holy fuck!" a voice exclaimed as Dennis and I stood talking. "Rob Clark! What the fuck are you doing here?" Walking toward me, smiling broadly, were Hobo and Jeff from Millhaven. The sleepy prisoners sat up, suddenly alert as I shook Hobo's and Jeff's hands. I would later find out other Millhaven acquaintances had also recently arrived at Joyceville: Nicky, Mike, and Snake were here, Jeff told me, and so was Larry, the goalie in our Millhaven hockey games. It must have been confusing to those watching a twenty-four-year-old from Toronto, newly hired and unknown to the staff, appear to be good pals with some of Joyceville's high-profile prisoners.

As it turned out, I would be working the day shift for my first two days. Dennis told me I would work the evening shift the following week, which meant I would manage the department on my own after the others left at four o'clock. I was a bit taken aback but tried not to show it. I doubted I would know everything I needed to know by Monday.

My misgivings began to recede as I became acquainted with my new work environment. The more I paid attention, the more I saw similarities to Millhaven that gave me confidence, things like locking doors and knowing where the prisoners were and who was in the yard. To my eternal gratitude, Dennis wrote out for me everything I had to do on night shifts: important times, where to get keys, what each key was for, et cetera. I carried that piece of paper around for weeks afterwards.

Later that first day, Joe took me to see Lloyd Latimer, the head of social development — in other words, the big boss of the recreation department. Latimer was a tall, balding man in a jacket and tie. He leaned forward to shake my hand as he gestured toward a chair. For the next five minutes he delivered a talk on how to ensure I did not get into trouble. I listened intently, nodding at appropriate times, wondering if this was something all new employees received or if it was because he knew I was friendly with some of the prisoners.

The next two days went very quickly as I learned the routines. Ten prisoners served on the rec gang at Joyceville: four kept the inside areas clean, and four worked in the yard. Another gathered up all the sports equipment each morning and got it ready for that night. The tenth prisoner cleaned the weight pit.

Our job as rec staff was to offer sports and fitness programs and supervise the prisoner-workers assigned to us. Some prisoners, those who worked the early shift that started at five a.m. in the main kitchen or who were off work because their supervisor had phoned in sick that day, were permitted to come down to the gym on weekday afternoons. Sometimes this could add up to as many as one hundred prisoners in the recreation area with only two or even one of us working. Often prisoners were also expecting visits and would pester us to check via phone whether their guests had arrived. It could get pretty hectic if one of us was on our own.

On my second day, Joe took me on a tour of the prison and introduced me around. The visiting room held prisoners and their visitors: old people, wives and girlfriends, and kids of varying ages.

"See these kids?" Joe whispered, playfully poking me with his elbow. "They're just visiting until they're old enough to live here!" Outside the visiting area he jerked his thumb toward the end of the hall. "That's the hole." I noted a heavy steel door with a small glass window. "C'mon," said Joe. "We'll go over to the units and harass the living unit officers."

We headed out and through the barrier to the courtyard. This was my first time seeing it from the inside and at ground level. I looked again at the cell windows, four storeys on three sides. An equal number of windows were on the outside of these same walls. Large, heavy benches were located sparsely around the outer edges of the courtyard, and in two corners steel doors led to the living units.

As we headed for one of these doors, three prisoners came out, all talking at once. They said hi to Joe, and Joe said something that made them laugh. We stepped inside a large tiled vestibule. Two men in street clothes occupied an office directly ahead of us. On either side of this office were the ranges. Huge steel-framed security windows stretched about six metres to the end of the walls and rose almost to the ceiling. At the end of the glass, large steel barriers were closed and locked.

Through the big glass panels directly in front of me was the prisoner common room. Every range had a spacious common room furnished with many square tables where prisoners congregated and ate their meals, brought up on heated carts from the main kitchen three times a day. In the far corner a soap opera played on a black-and-white console TV. Small personal items, like salt and pepper shakers or pens, sat on most of the tables, suggesting the prisoners sat in the same place whenever they were in this room; that probably meant fewer fights. Jackets hung on the backs of some of the chairs. Board games and decks of cards were piled on a small windowsill near the TV. After the gym closed each night, prisoners could use the common room until eleven, when they were locked in their cells and counted.

Cereal boxes and coffee cups were piled near the large metal sink. An older prisoner in a tattered housecoat and slippers shuffled around a hotplate. Behind him was a large coffee urn, a red light glowing above its tap. Every common room had such an urn, and they were heavily used, just like the ashtrays. Another prisoner watched the TV, his feet on the table in front of him. He did not look up as Joe and I went into the office so I could meet the living-unit officers, or LUs, as they were known. One was named Mike, and the other, bigger man was Jack. They greeted Joe like an old friend.

"Well, Joe, who're you dragging around the jail with you?" one of them asked. He stuck his hand out, and I shook it. When Mike and Jack found out I didn't know anyone in Kingston, they said they'd make a point of getting me out for a beer. I met many different people, all very welcoming, as the tour continued. I was beginning to feel like I belonged, and it was only my second day.

When Monday came, the day I would work my first night shift alone, I arrived at a quarter to two in the afternoon. Joe put the kettle on, and he and Karl went over what I should expect. All prisoners returned to their units at a quarter to four for count and supper. At five thirty the keeper announced over the radio the commencement of the recreation period. The LUs simultaneously opened all the range barriers in the prison. Depending on what was going on in the gym or the yard, prisoners started gathering at the barriers at around 5:20, growing increasingly restless as they waited. When the barriers were opened, 350 men poured into the courtyard and stampeded to the door leading to the gym. They flew down the stairs as fast as they could go, anxious to get the best hockey sticks or goalie glove, the only straight pool cue, or to claim the new weight bench. Sometimes people got hurt.

As it turned out, I was never completely on my own in the gym at night. An LU officer from each of the four units was assigned to the recreation area to provide supervision and patrol the various spaces.

These four officers, bringing two radios with them, typically arrived fifteen minutes before the stampede of prisoners began.

At a quarter past five, I would call the keeper's hall and request permission to have the four prisoner-workers for the canteen move from the units to the gym. Then I would call Units 2 and 4 and ask them to send the canteen workers to the recreation area. By the time I had hung up the phone, the LUs' two-way radios would be crackling, and a man's voice would advise all posts that four prisoners were being released to the recreation area. An acknowledgement from other areas of the prison, like "roger" or the name of the post, always followed these radio transmissions. When the canteen workers arrived, I asked one of the LUs to announce over the radio that I was opening the back door and taking the prisoners to the canteen door, which was on the outside of the recreation building, where I would lock them in. Putting this information over the radio drastically reduced the chance of having my head blown off by a tower officer not expecting to see anyone in the outside yard at that time of night.

I soon realized I could tell a prisoner's status in the prison if they worked in the canteen, as this was considered one of the best jobs in the whole prison. Either they were a force to be reckoned with, or they were a foot soldier reporting to someone higher up the food chain. Of the four men who worked in the canteen, one was named Bill. He was a large, muscular man with long dark hair and a conspicuous Fu Manchu moustache. His enormous arms were covered in tattoos, and he had a teardrop tattooed under his right eye. The fact that he was running the canteen meant he had significant status in the prison. The canteen was considered one of the plum jobs because it was easy for the prisoner-workers to defraud the system, such as it was.

Prisoners presented a handwritten slip of paper listing the items they wished to purchase. The canteen workers filled the order, and the prisoner signed a form confirming receipt. The prison would then deduct the cost of the items from each man's savings account. Unfortunately, many vulnerable prisoners would receive only a portion of the items they signed for. A weaker prisoner might sign for two packs of cigarettes and receive one. If he complained he risked a beating — or worse. If their items weren't stolen at the canteen window, these prisoners sometimes handed over their purchases to others on their range to ensure protection from other forms of abuse. Vulnerable prisoners suffered such abuses daily during their time down inside.

A ball hockey game would start in the gym right at five thirty. Joyceville had a four-team league. On my first night shift, Jeff and a prisoner I did not know refereed the game. Although Joyceville, like most prisons, offered evening group meetings — such as Alcoholics Anonymous, Native Brotherhood for Aboriginal prisoners, the Lifers' group, and the John Howard Society — no groups were scheduled on Monday nights. These groups met in two classrooms near the gym, another area that the LUs and I would patrol during the evening. Guests from Kingston often participated in these meetings, and on those evenings we distributed memos to security in advance saying who was coming in, at what time, for how long, et cetera. Security would call me to escort the visitors to the recreation area and deposit them safely at the classroom.

Once activities in the gym were underway, all that remained was to be visible and available. Every now and then two or three of us would take one of the radios and do a wind, a patrol of the area. Once the ball hockey game started, nothing much else would be going on, because the games were so rough. The other prisoners loved to watch from the bleachers or the stage. Seeing their friends trying to kill each other with hockey sticks was very entertaining, and the more fans, the rougher the game. Fights commonly broke out, and many guys had to leave the game early. Depending on how much they were bleeding, I would escort them up to the prison hospital to see the nurse.

Being a goalie was even more dangerous than being a player. If goals went in, the players blamed the goalie first. (In fact, a few years later, a prisoner-goalie at Millhaven had his throat cut from behind with a skate; he bled to death in the snow. (That was the end of the hockey program at Millhaven.)

At nine p.m., the canteen closed. Once the plywood was secured inside the cage, I would ask the LUs to radio security that I was again going out the back door to bring the workers in. My co-workers stressed during my briefing that I would have to make sure no prisoners were hiding in the canteen at the end of the night. A smaller prisoner could take advantage of one of the times when the canteen wasn't under direct observation to slide on his belly through the wicket opening. If he hid successfully, he would have at least until the next prisoner count to attempt to get through the door to the outside. The prisoner-workers knew to leave the light on for me until I had looked inside. Once I was satisfied that no one was hiding, we would turn off the lights and come outside, and I would lock the door.

The prisoners would start trickling back to the units through the courtyard door or toward the barrier at admin control, where the distribution of medication, known as the pill parade, would soon start. By then, we had emptied the recreation area of the last prisoners, and I headed up front with all the keys, ready to make my way home while the LUs moved the crowd in the courtyard toward the units. At ten thirty it was time for an informal count, and at eleven the LUs entered the ranges for the last time that day. The prisoners were locked in their cells for the night, and a formal count took place.

My first night shift at Joyceville followed the usual routine almost perfectly — with one exception. Shortly before nine that night, I was standing near the recreation office door with two of the LUs when I heard a voice behind me. It was Bill, and he was sticking his head through the canteen wicket.

"We're all done in here for tonight, Rob, if you wanna let us out," he said.

My colleagues were already on the radio. I could hear the plywood panel being lowered and locked as I went around to unlock the outside door. When I opened the door, the four prisoners were in front of me on the threshold, standing together so that I could not step inside; behind them the canteen was in complete darkness. I stopped, looking at them. They did not move but simply looked back at me.

"Okay, let's go," Bill said and stepped past me, followed by the other three.

"Hang on, guys. I have to check the canteen," I said. They stopped, and I stepped into the room, which now seemed pitch black. They followed me back inside and one of them pulled the door closed behind us. Now the five of us were standing close together in total darkness. No one said a word. I began to feel around on the wall, even though I had no idea where the light switch might be. In the pitch black, the prisoners were so close to me that I could hear them breathing. Finally, I touched something that fell down and hit what sounded like the counter in front of us.

"Hang on there, Rob," Bill said. "Let me get that for you."

The lights came on. Big boxes of chips and chocolate bars, cases of pop, and cartons of cigarettes were stacked to the ceiling and along the walls. The room was small, and the visual search took all of ten seconds. I turned off the light, and we all paraded out.

One of the LUs, seeing my return, raised his radio and declared, "All clear in the recreation yard."

Bill, who was ahead of me, turned around, and looked at me with a big grin on his face. I was kind of puzzled, but I smiled. He shook his head. "Too much!" he said, laughing. He headed to the courtyard door. "See ya tomorrow!"

As I watched him walking away, it dawned on me: they had been testing me. I played back every moment in my mind, to check if I had tripped up at some point. I decided that I had handled the whole thing as well as possible under the circumstances. Bill's reaction suggested he agreed.

I was right. From that day on, Bill was a faithful ally, at least as far as a prisoner could be. He always had a friendly hello for me no matter who was around. If I had to wade through fifty prisoners to get to admin control when he was around, he would say loudly, "Clear the way, boys, clear the way! Toughest guy in the joint comin' through!" I would roll my eyes at him, and he would give me a big wink. He got a real kick out of doing this. The prisoners who knew me would laugh. These men knew I wasn't a tough guy. Rather, the majority saw me as a good copper, one who tried to help the prisoners. I was always very respectful and friendly in my dealings with them, mostly because that was how I was raised. And even though I could not imagine myself sinking into such a state of degradation as I witnessed in some of these men, I never felt superior to them. I think they knew this, and it made all the difference. Because Joyceville was a medium-security prison, there was not the same level of tension that existed at Millhaven. As well, the introduction of plain-clothes guards (LUs) in the units greatly improved the quality of staff-prisoner relations at Joyceville, even in comparison to other medium-security prisons at that time.

Probably the best part about working nights at Joyceville was movie night on Friday or Saturday. The prisoner committee chose the titles, which we ordered from a film distributor. A massive, electrically controlled movie screen hung at the far end of the gym, and at the opposite end of the gym, on the second level, was a projector room with two sixteen-millimetre film projectors. We — the recreation officer on duty and the two prisoners who served as projectionists — accessed the projector room from the outside. We ascended the concrete steps, bearing leather-strapped cases containing the reels as well as pop and chips.

One of the projectionists was a bank robber named Frank, and the other one was Jeff; being stuck in the projection booth for two hours could have been tiresome, but these were good guys. At around 5:20 we'd open the flaps in front of the projectors and look down on the gym from ceiling height. We watched the LUs below checking their radios and smoking. When the courtyard door flew open at five thirty, the sound of men running filled the room like thunder. The first ones over the threshold charged to the bleachers and grabbed their favourite chairs, four or five at a time, racing to stake out the perfect place on the floor to watch the movie. They'd set up chairs for their friends, placing coats and shirts to mark them as taken. Most prisoners brought pop and snacks to have during the movie. They also smoked a lot of cigarettes.

We would watch them below us, focusing first on this one and then on that one. "He's a fuckin' goof!" someone in the booth would say, and we'd laugh. After about fifteen minutes, we were ready to start the movie. I'd use the phone in the booth to call down to an LU in the recreation office. "All set if you are," I'd say. The LU would go to the breaker panels and flip the switches for the gym lights.

Four LUs and a few hundred prisoners sitting in total darkness, watching a movie: it seems hard to believe now. I remember the first time I witnessed how the reactions of this prison audience differed from an audience in a theatre. Whenever a cop was killed or shot, the prisoners cheered wildly. If the cops killed a bad guy, they booed and hissed. If there was a mean-spirited cop, they cursed and threatened the air around them. Some of the more popular movies we showed were spaghetti westerns like *A Fistful of Dollars* and *Hang 'Em High*. *The French Connection* was well received because the villains appeared superior to the detectives. *Vanishing Point* resonated with the rebellious nature of this audience, and Clint Eastwood's *Dirty Harry* films animated the audience into a roar of verbal threats and abuse toward the rogue cop who exemplified their own perceived mistreatment at the hands of those in authority. Sometimes the prisoners would yell out jokes or sarcastic insults at the LUs who were in the gym, and this always provoked lots of laughter. When the lights finally came back on, the crowd would rouse itself and disperse in different directions.

Frank had been around, as he used to say, and he was very old school. At fifty he looked more like sixty-five. He was thin and frail and had limited movement on the left side of his body. His permed hair contrasted sharply with his otherwise unkempt appearance. His eyes always looked tired, and his thin moustache drooped over the corners of his mouth. He was serving eleven years for a bank robbery.

"Eleven years for one robbery?" Jeff asked, his voice rising in surprise. "What the fuck happened?"

"You wouldn't believe it."

Jeff and I both leaned closer on our chairs.

Frank robbed a bank in London, Ontario, with a gun and a note. As he described it, the first part of the robbery went well. The tellers, although frightened by the gun, co-operated. Then Frank noticed a man standing behind a desk, staring at him. Deciding this must be someone important, Frank pointed his gun and yelled at the man to back away from his desk. The man began to move — but not quickly enough for Frank. He fired.

"I swear to God on my mother's life, I never meant to shoot him," Frank told us. "I really, really didn't mean to." Jeff and I just looked at him. "What I meant to do was put a bullet in the wall over his head. You know: scare the fuckin' shit out of him." Frank took a long drag off his cigarette. When he resumed, he sounded even more tired than usual. "Anyway, I didn't aim too fuckin' good, because I hit the cocksucker in the neck."

Frank ran out of the bank and right into the police. When they saw the gun, they fired. Frank said he was struck multiple times; this, he said, was the source of his partial paralysis. Fortunately for Frank, the man he shot was not critically wounded, and he survived.

However, Frank's problems did not begin in that bank. As with hundreds of other prisoners whose stories I would hear over the next thirty years, Frank's life was a disaster from the time he was born. By age fourteen, he had a heroin addiction and a criminal record. Many of the men I met in prison became wards of the state when they were very young, a process that often started with unstable, alcoholic, and abusive parents; a series of foster homes and social workers fails to halt the onset of truancy and petty crime. These kids "graduate" to young offender facilities and then to provincial institutions, where staff and bigger prisoners invariably abuse them. By the time they reach the federal prison system, many have become hardened to the point where they cannot be reached. Mental illness and serious addictions may have damaged them further, and they usually have an innate distrust of all authority figures. This group is the most dangerous element within a prison, I believe, because it is the group most easily provoked into violence, individually or on a large scale. This group constitutes the majority of the prisoner population.

Over the next few months, I got to know most of the other prison staff and most of the prisoners. I met people around Kingston, and I joined a hockey team. My co-workers Karl MacLaughlin and Mike Laporte invited me to their homes for dinner, and I began to meet some of their friends as well. Two of the LUs I became friends with were Bob MacLean and Keith Speck. Keith helped me to join some of the sports teams he was involved with, and Bob and I became roommates in a two-bedroom apartment in the city. I was beginning to feel like I belonged in Kingston, but my assignment was up in November. Unless I found another job, I would pack up and return to Toronto before Christmas. I began checking daily the CSC job openings posted on a clipboard outside the guards' locker area.

Finally I saw a new posting, the first one in three weeks, advertising for living-unit officers for the Ontario region. The closing date was two weeks away. I photocopied the posting and showed it to Dennis and Karl. We all agreed this was a stroke of luck. Not only would I have help preparing for the competition, but if I passed it, there was only Joyceville and one other prison I could be assigned to, as the other prisons in the area did not operate under the living-unit concept. That meant I had at least a 50 per cent chance of staying at Joyceville with my new friends.

Over the next few days, I talked to some of the LUs about the position. The guys assured me they'd be happy to have me on board, and so I filled in a CSC job application. I was shortlisted and passed the interview, and when the list of successful candidates came out, I placed fifth. Two weeks later, I received a letter saying that I had been assigned to Joyceville. I started as an LU in Unit 3 in late October 1980.

3 Living Unit

The living-unit system was the best paradigm the Correctional Service ever had. Prisons have traditionally relied on static security — barriers, fences, steel bars, and other impersonal measures — to maintain order. Dynamic security recognizes positive interpersonal relations between staff and prisoners as a critical component in operating a successful prison. The living-unit system was introduced at Joyceville in 1976, but when I started in 1980, most prisons still had uniformed guards working in the cellblocks where the prisoners lived. In the living-unit system, plain-clothes officers replaced the uniformed guards. The theory was that if the staff working the units were not in uniform, it would be easier to build rapport and improve staff-prisoner relations.

In addition to wearing plain clothes, the LUs worked only in the units and were assigned a small caseload of prisoners who lived in their particular unit. This casework required living-unit officers and prisoners to regularly review matters like release plans and other issues affecting a prisoner's overall progress. The LUs had access to the case-management files for each prisoner and were expected to review these and complete written reports the National Parole Board could consult when considering release. The warden would also refer to these reports if a prisoner sought a transfer to a lower-security prison. Consequently, prisoners had a vested interest in making a positive impression on their respective LU and all the unit staff. LU officers chose these positions because they wanted to do more than just lock doors or do counts. They wanted to read files and learn how to assess the risks and the possibilities in each man assigned to them. They wanted to feel like they were part of something more meaningful than locking up prisoners. This motivation made a marked difference, and, with a few exceptions, it showed.

Each unit had particular characteristics. One unit might have a reputation for being too soft, while another was thought too strict. Twelve LUs divided into three crews of four worked in each unit; the three crews likewise had reputations as hard or soft, according to the prisoners. We always worked our own unit, and we always worked with the same crew. If we had to hire overtime staff we called LUs from our own unit first. We knew "our" prisoners, and we knew the unique environment of our unit.

One LU officer from each unit assisted with recreation supervision, which was beneficial because some prisoners used the recreation area as a place to deal drugs, gamble, settle debts, beat someone, or just get stoned or drunk. Whatever the prisoners did and whomever they were with stood a good chance of being seen by at least one officer who knew their name and where they lived. As soon as recreation was over and everyone was back in their respective units, the officer would fill out the unit logbook — every unit and most security posts contained a logbook in which staff recorded pertinent information concerning the post or prisoner-related issues. He'd enter a detailed account about which prisoners were involved in what in the gym or the yard that evening. When we started work each day, the first thing we did was consult the logbook to see what had happened since we were last on shift. It was a very effective system of control that created little or no conflict and greatly improved the atmosphere of the institution.

One aspect of the physical design of Joyceville allowed us to keep a close eye on prisoners at all times. It was probably the best form of dynamic security the prison service had, and its use would make all prisons safer and better run: hand-keyed locks on the cell doors and the range barriers in the units. These require regular, daily face-to-face contact between staff and prisoners. A prisoner's request for an officer to open his cell door or to let him on or off the range for some reason affords the officer a chance to observe the prisoner and to speak to him. If the prisoner is known for being under the influence, for example, the officer can look closely at his eyes. Or if a prisoner usually goes to recreation every night to work out but suddenly becomes more withdrawn and starts to stay in his cell, the LUs will notice and record the change in the logbook; other crews will watch him more closely as well. If the behaviour persists, the man's assigned LU, or an LU who has a rapport with him, will call him in to find out what's going on. Although the prisoners were often reluctant to co-operate with such inquiries, the LU would record in the logbook whatever information is gleaned, and we would continue to monitor the situation. Sometimes we'd become aware of a problem between two prisoners living on the same range and would work covertly to separate the two without drawing attention to the problem itself. A range change under the guise of a change of employment or to live closer to friends were a couple of the ways we could accomplish this.

Walking down the range to open a particular cell puts the officer in areas where staff-prisoner interactions are likely to happen. In my experience, the more often the staff engaged with the prisoners, the more often positive rapport occurred. Staff and prisoners became acquainted in a way that normalized conversation about many different subjects. Whenever I was posted as the range officer and prisoners asked for favours, like getting into their cell early, I always opened the cell. It wasn't any trouble, given how much time I spent just sitting and observing, and these small accommodations helped my reputation around the unit.

In the prisons of today, uniformed guards once again staff the units. They typically demonstrate no interest in the evaluation of or release planning for prisoners. These officers rotate through unit posts as well as other posts; consequently, meaningful interactions between staff and prisoners are all but non-existent. As well, ostensibly in the interests of staff safety, prisons are moving increasingly toward technology like cell doors that open and close electronically from inside a closed security post, further reducing contact between prisoners and staff. Not surprisingly, the uniformed officers assigned to work in the recreation area at night sit in a secure control post. They no longer know the prisoners they see through the thick glass windows.

I spent my first two weeks as an LU in Unit 3 tagging along with one of the crews for the eight a.m. to four p.m. shift the first week and the four to midnight shift the next week. Then I joined the crew of Mike Stanford, Anwar (Andy) Aziz, and Fred Takerer. I quickly liked all three very much. We worked well together, and we believed in being fair and not too heavy-handed. The prisoners in our unit knew they could come to us without fear of being snubbed or ignored. If a request or concern seemed legitimate and we could help, we would. During the day, we performed security functions — doing counts and searching cells and unit common areas — and general unit supervision, which included overseeing prisoner-workers and rounding up unemployed prisoners, who were locked in their cells during the day. We sometimes met with prisoners and their parole officers. Although the parole officer had the final say on a man's request for transfer or release, the LUs' observations and opinions about the prisoner's behaviour in the unit factored significantly in the decision.

The evening shift was different. Instead of running the operations, writing reports, and searching, we merely patrolled, conducted counts, and remained observant at all times. The evenings were always a potentially dangerous time, because almost everyone was out of the cells and on the move. If there was going to be trouble, it was most likely to happen at night. All over the prison, prisoners engaged in the art of survival in a very hostile environment. Away from the prying eyes of staff, deals were made and scores were settled. At night time, the drug deals went down, and the drug debts were collected. While all this went on, a large percentage of the prisoners looked to get stoned or drunk, or both. It was not uncommon to catch prisoners trying to sneak back on the range, either under the influence or bleeding. If the drunk was a happy drunk, we might say, "Go in your cell for the night, and we won't charge you." This was considered a huge break and never ceased to win us favour as fair-minded coppers. The other prisoners would even handle the job of getting him to his cell for us; we had only to watch and chuckle.

Angry drunks were taken to the hole. When a volatile prisoner needs to be taken to the hole in the prisons of today, a highly trained tactical squad that the prison service calls the institutional emergency response team, or IERT, removes the prisoner from his cell. These teams employ five officers dressed in helmets, gloves, and elbow pads, plus a camera operator. They carry shields, batons, handcuffs, and pepper spray. They are trained in submission and self-defence techniques. The officers assigned to the unit just sit back and watch.

When we had to take a man to the hole in the eighties, we had no highly trained squad to help us, no specialized training, and no helmets or batons. In fact, we did not even have handcuffs. My own training on "cell extractions" occurred about thirty seconds before the three of us entered the cell of an irate prisoner for the first time and consisted of the following instruction: "Rob, take your watch off. I'll go first, and you guys just grab on to a leg or wrist and don't let go until I say. Normally, I take my glasses off, but I need new ones, so I'm hoping these get broken." With that, the cell door was swung open, and we waited for come what may.

As soon as the door was opened, however, the prisoner sat down on his bed and asked, "Can I bring my smokes?"

I am very proud to say that every time I was involved in taking a man to the hole, he went peacefully. We made this possible by first talking him down for fifteen minutes or more. We spoke loud enough for the rest of the range to hear, saying things to help him save face so that he'd keep his honour if he walked over without fighting us. "We know you can fight," we'd say. "We know we have our hands full with you. That's why we're hoping you'll calm down enough to think this over. If you walk over now, you'll probably get to come back tomorrow when you sober up. But if we have to fight you, there might be charges, and then who knows?"

If the prisoner was too angry to hear us, his pals would start calling out from their cells. "Mikey, listen," they'd say. "Go with these guys!"

The prisoner would usually demand that we permit him to take his cigarettes, and we'd make a show of giving in (we would have let him take them even if he hadn't demanded them). The man would emerge from his cell under his own power. He might yell goodbye to the range. He might even yell something funny that made all of us start laughing, prisoners and staff. By the time we would get to the hole, he would be in a much better mood. He knew that all the men on his range, on the courtyard side at least, watched him walk across the courtyard with three officers, on his own terms. He'd avoided humiliation in front of his peers. He'd submit to a strip search without complaint, and say thanks when his smokes were returned to him. The next day he might not even remember that he threatened us or why. He would, however, remember that we had not embarrassed him or hurt him, and the others would remember that, too. We took great pride back then in being able to manage our prisoners with nothing more than the power of our intellect and the understanding that, in the end, we all just want to be treated with a little respect.

The NHL playoffs further illustrate the difference between prisons now and prisons then. Hockey is a very big deal in prison. Now prisoners have TVs — and much more — in their cells. But back then, the only TV on the range was the big black-and-white set in the unit common room. If the playoffs were on, almost every man in the prison was glued to the TV in the common room. If the game went into overtime, we'd allow the prisoners to stay in the common rooms for fifteen, twenty, even thirty minutes past the usual lockup time. This meant delaying the last formal count of the day, which in turn meant the LUs working the four to midnight shift had to remain on duty to complete the count. The LUs volunteered to delay the end of their shifts so the prisoners could watch the end of the game. That was a pretty big deal.

Looking back, I think being a living-unit officer was one of the most enjoyable jobs I had. When I started as an LU, I was immediately assigned a caseload of ten prisoners on 3D, including Jeff. I had the freedom to interact with the men in a much more meaningful way than had been possible in the recreation department. Now I was involved in writing reports and counselling sessions, not just handing out basketballs. I could use my judgment in how I related to the men. I'd joke with the prisoner-cleaners, and sometimes on a Friday afternoon I would leave open the cell doors of the unemployed guys under my supervision instead of locking them in, as I was supposed to. If they hadn't been in any trouble that week, I wrote them a recreation pass so they could go to the gym and the yard with the early kitchen workers. I found the prisoners fairly easy to work with and reason with most of the time. The respect that guys like Jeff on my range and Nicky and Jesse on 4C showed me in front of the other prisoners, despite the fact that I was now a copper, had a significant impact early on. Over time, however, as I treated everybody with a sense of humour and the same respect I expected from them, I gradually won the guys over on my own, and I earned a good reputation among both prisoners and staff.

Of the two shifts we worked, my favourite was day shift. There was always more going on, and so the time went faster. Three of us would be on duty from eight until four, but one of us worked from seven until three. I preferred these hours; this was always the quietest time of the day. The whole prison would be as still as a cemetery. I would get to the unit at around 6:20 to relieve the guard from the midnight shift and send him on his way, even though he was supposed to stay until a second LU arrived, closer to eight o'clock. Once he was gone, I would draw a cell key for each floor and lock the unit-office door. The first thing I had to do was unlock all the cell doors in the unit by seven a.m.

The cell doors at Joyceville required a large, heavy brass Folger Adam key. The cell-door locks were old and could be noisy to open; the process of unlocking all the doors on a range could wake everybody up. I, however, had a reputation as the quietest LU on early shift, and even a small consideration like this meant a lot to the prisoners. To them it was a show of respect on my part, and to me it was a fun challenge to see if I could do the whole unit without waking up a single person. I would walk quietly to the first range barrier door and slip the huge brass key into the lock, turning it slowly. If I knew that this particular barrier creaked, I opened it in slow motion, listening to the gigantic hinges like a safe-cracker listening for the next tumbler.

As the barrier opened, the odours of the range wafted out. I will never forget that smell — humanity at perhaps its most base level. The smell of thirty-two men living in close quarters: dirty clothes, spoiled food, coffee, and of course cigarettes. With great stealth, I moved down one side of the range and up the other. At each door, I slid the key into the lock like a cat burglar and turned it slowly. I knew every cell-door lock in that unit: which ones were sticky, which ones squeaked, and which ones had to be turned the other way because of improper installation.

In those days, most prisoners hung a small piece of leather on a length of skate lace or bootlace from the handles on the cell doors. Wedged between the unlocked cell door and the frame, this piece of leather kept the door from swinging open. As I opened each man's door, I put the leather strip in place and slid the door closed. After unlocking all the cell doors on one range, I crept back outside the barrier and soundlessly closed and locked it. I moved across the vestibule to the other side and then downstairs to do both ranges down below. By the time the other LUs arrived and the prisoners were stirring, I had coffee brewing in the office and the radio on low.

One morning I was halfway down 3D Range when I felt a tap on my shoulder. I nearly jumped out of my skin, but I did not utter a sound. I turned around to find Louie standing behind me in his housecoat and slippers. Believe me when I say that no one should have to see Louie in his housecoat and slippers; prison is scary enough. He leaned in toward me with his index finger in front of his lips.

"Rob, lock 16 man, he's not in there," he whispered. "He slashed again last night."

With Louie's face over my shoulder, I slowly opened the cell door. The leather fob slipped to the end of its string. The cell bed was soaked in dark reddish stains. Pools of dried blood were all over the floor, and blood spattered the desk and sink. There was so much blood I believed I could actually smell it. The cell was on the courtyard side of the range, and the sun coming in the window illuminated the entire scene. We stood for a few seconds, and then I closed the door and locked it.

Louie shuffled back toward his cell. "I need a cigarette," he said.

This was the cell of Johnny, an angry young man serving a long sentence for a number of very serious assaults. His family had split up when Johnny was small; he went to live with his father, and his brothers went with their mother. Whenever the father got drunk, which was most of the time, he beat Johnny. Eventually Johnny ran away and found his mother in a rough part of downtown Toronto, living in a flophouse. Living with her was just as dangerous as living with his father, so he took to the streets more and more often. One day he came home to find his mother gone.

Johnny told me once that he could not remember when he started cutting himself. By the time I met him, his upper body was a mass of straight, raised lines, almost in rows, like flesh-covered corduroy. Many of these injuries had healed without medical attention, because he often cut himself without anyone knowing. As I recall, an outside hospital treated Johnny for his injuries on this occasion, and he did not return to 3D.

Over the years, I would see more blood than I care to remember.

Of all my responsibilities in this job, I found the casework and release planning the most rewarding. The parole process and consideration of risk factors fascinated me. Of the ten prisoners on my caseload, three were lifers who were far from release planning. Some of the others had been in jail so often that they had no interest in getting out. Prison was home, such as it was. But three men on my caseload had reasonable prospects for early release. One of these three was named John. A big man with long hair and a beard, John was, as I recall, a member of a well-known motorcycle gang. To look at him you might have assumed he was a very violent man serving a long sentence. In fact, his offences were non-violent and his sentence was quite short. He had a young wife and an offer of employment as a truck driver if he could get parole. He certainly had a brighter future than many of the men on the range. I attended a meeting with John and his parole officer in which we agreed to recommend the regional transfer board move him to minimum security. From there, the National Parole Board would review his case. If it granted parole, he might be returned to his wife and the community within months. As the LU, I had to complete a transfer report before the next scheduled transfer board hearing, something I assured John and the parole officer I could easily do.

It was a typical Friday at the end of the next week. I could feel the whole prison gradually slowing down. The weekend was here. At twelve thirty, the keeper called workup, and we opened our barriers. I was standing in the office doorway, watching the men file out and down the stairs. Nicky and Jesse waved on their way by. John came over to me.

"I was just wondering how that report is coming," he said. "Are we still going to make the transfer board?"

"Yes, we will," I said. "Don't give it a second thought." He relaxed visibly. "I'm off for four days, and I come back Wednesday on four to twelve. When I'm on nights next week I'll have lots of time to get it done."

John knew my reputation; he knew I was not bullshitting him. He grinned as he rejoined the flow of humanity heading down the stairs. When the crowd had gone and everything was quiet again, I grabbed a file request form from the cabinet and filled it out with John's name and number. When I returned to work on Wednesday, the files would be waiting for me.

As it turned out, I would not need these files after all, nor would I have to complete a write-up for transfer to minimum security. John's case would never be put before the parole board.

To the best of my knowledge, on the last day of his life, a warm, sunny Sunday, John awoke early. The prison was quiet. He padded down to the common room and filled his cup from the coffee urn. John sat down at the table near the window that he usually shared with two other men. He lit a cigarette. He drank one coffee and, finishing his smoke, rose and went back to his cell. He put on his sweatpants, his running shoes, and his weight belt, loosely buckled. The weight room was sure to be empty now, and he could work out in peace while everybody else slept. He pushed his door closed, the leather fob in place. Taking his coffee cup for water, he left the range and went down the stairs. On the ground level he looked in the LU office as he turned the corner. The LUs were reading the paper and smoking.

John pushed open the barrier and stepped into the warm sun. Seagulls stood in a circle in the middle of the courtyard. John headed across to the courtyard to admin control. The electric barrier opened for him, and he headed to the recreation corridor. He looked in the gym before heading downstairs to the weight room. The gym was empty. The door to the recreation office was open, and two officers sat inside talking, their feet up on the desk; a security radio could be heard. John went down to the weight room. It too was empty.

John headed to the back room, past the shower area, and began to set up his weights on his favourite bench. He enjoyed working out when he had the whole place to himself. Perhaps he planned to shower later, eat something, and then maybe write some letters: a regular Sunday. In the afternoon, he and many other prisoners could go out to the yard and enjoy the sunny summer weather. With any luck, he would be out of here and in a camp (minimum-security prison) within two months. He would work hard to make a good impression, showing that he could be trusted outside the fences. If all went well at the hearing with the parole board, he could be home by Christmas, but he probably dared not hope for too much.

Over in Unit 2, like the rest of the prison that morning, it was as quiet as it gets — almost. Two prisoners were up and moving, and upstairs on the fourth floor another prisoner was also awake.

According to the police investigation that followed, John was lying on a weight bench, preparing to lift the heavily weighted barbell off the steel frame. When he had the bar almost raised, he saw two, possibly three, figures looming over him. One or two of the attackers may have pushed down on the barbell, pinning John to the bench. His assailant stood over him with a raised arm. All John could do was watch. The knife came down right in the middle of his chest. John was stabbed, more than once, by a man he most likely knew but had never had a problem with before. A young prisoner named Brian, coming into the gym to see if the yard was open yet, heard screams and went to the recreation office where the two bleary-eyed LUs struggled to stay awake.

"You should check the weight room!" he told them before hurrying back out.

Brian's voice and the look on his face left no doubt as to the gravity of the situation. Both men leapt to their feet, bolted across the gym floor, and down the stairs. John had managed to crawl from the weight room to the shower area. He was leaning up against the wall, his legs splayed in front of him. He looked up at the officers, his eyes wide with fear. Blood was everywhere.

John died a few seconds later on the shower floor of Joyceville Institution on a beautiful summer Sunday morning.

About this same time, my friend Keith Speck was working the day shift in Unit 2. As is usual on Sunday mornings, the range barriers were unlocked. Prisoners carried the garbage down to the courtyard for pickup on Monday morning, and leaving the barriers open for an hour or two freed the officer from repeatedly opening and closing the barrier. Three prisoners came up the stairs that morning, each separated from the other by only a short gap. Keith went to see who was moving about. As the first prisoner stopped to show Keith his wristwatch, drawing his attention to its smallest details, another prisoner darted into 3B Range. The third man ran past and up to the fourth floor and went straight to the shower. Most prison staff are on the lookout for prisoners' efforts to distract them while another prisoner does something he shouldn't. In this case, the prisoners' efforts were in vain, and police arrested John's killers within ten hours.

As soon as the murder was discovered, every prisoner was locked in his cell — the usual first response to a serious problem. Lockdown gives staff total control of the environment; whatever had occurred or threatened to occur is no longer a threat once everyone is back in his cell. Once all prisoners are locked in their respective cells, a formal count is completed. The formal count means that two staff members visually check every single prisoner. There is always the possibility of a second victim somewhere; a count rules this out. We can make sure the other prisoners are safe and unharmed and identify anyone who is injured, or who shows any signs that arouse suspicion.

In the coming years, I would be involved in more lockdowns than I can count. The anticipated course of events for a lockdown is an initial frenzy of anti-social behaviour from the prisoners. Interestingly, staff morale always temporarily improves, particularly for the uniformed staff. It was as if a crisis brought us back to the core reality of where we were. The security staff felt recognized for the importance of their work that often went unnoticed or unacknowledged. While the uniformed officers directly managed the crisis, other staff handled routine matters. It wasn't uncommon at these times to see parole officers and even clerical staff delivering pre-packaged meals in Styrofoam containers, cell to cell.

At some point, most lockdowns also involve a strip search of each prisoner, and then a search of the contents of their individual cells. A strip search involves removing prisoners from their cells, one at a time. The prisoner is required to completely disrobe at the front of the range, usually the washroom area, in view of two officers. Each article of clothing is inspected as it is removed. Once naked, the prisoner is instructed to open his mouth for visual inspection; dentures are removed. The prisoner is required to run his fingers through his hair, show the bottoms of his feet, and bend over and touch his toes to permit visual inspection of the anal area. While the prisoner is strip-searched, two other officers search his cell. Once the cell search is completed, the prisoner is permitted to get dressed and is locked back inside his cell. Then the next prisoner is removed and the process begins again. Institutional searches cause prisoners to get rid of weapons and drugs before they are searched, and as a result the environment is safer. We often stationed staff members outside the cell windows to watch for prisoners throwing out unauthorized items, including lethal weapons.

While lockdown procedures were carried out on this particular day, I was at home when the phone rang.

"Morning, Rob," said Gerry, an officer I knew well.

"Hello, Gerry," I said. "What's up?"

"You need to come in. We've had a murder."

It took me a minute to register his words. "A murder?"

"Yeah, a guy in your unit actually, on 3D."

I got dressed in a hurry and drove out Highway 15. When I pulled into the prison parking lot, I saw an ambulance and three police cars. People jammed the corridor surrounding the keeper's hall. Two police officers were questioning one of the LUs from Unit 3; apparently he had been one of the two officers in the recreation office that morning.

When I stepped into the courtyard, a loud roar went up from the prisoners whose cells faced the courtyard. The rumour mill had quickly confirmed the reason for the lockdown, and now everyone was joining in to create as much noise and trouble as possible. Prisoners threw flaming paper balls from their cells, starting small fires on the ranges. Prisoners on the courtyard side threw flaming rolls of toilet paper from the cell windows, watching the fireballs drop into the courtyard below. Each time a staff member crossed the courtyard, a clamour erupted from the men. Staff members who the prisoners considered overly harsh provoked a much different chorus than some others.

My crew and some of our other officers were already in the unit. As the prisoners on 3D saw me, another roar went up. They had removed the wooden window plates from the fronts of their cells and angled their little shaving mirrors on the cell doors so they could see everything going on, despite being behind a closed door. Looking down the range I saw a sea of faces I knew, all framed in little mirrors, as if on hand-held television sets. The range floor was covered in garbage, charred paper, some of it still smouldering, and large puddles of water.

John's murder affected me deeply. It brought home with tremendous force the nature of the environment these men lived in all the time. It also brought home to me that, on any given day and when we least expected it, all hell could break loose. This brutal lesson stayed with me for the rest of my career.

4 The Tragic Life of Ty Conn

In 1988 I became a parole officer at Collins Bay Institution. This transfer from Joyceville, the first of many moves in my thirty-year career, brought me into contact with a young man named Tyrone Conn. Our history would prove a long one. I was Conn's parole officer when he escaped while on an escorted temporary absence from Collins Bay. Ten years later our paths crossed again when Conn was transferred to Kingston Penitentiary, where I was a unit manager. Conn became the first prisoner in more than forty years to escape successfully from that maximum-security institution. His escape made international headlines and made Conn the subject of an episode of CBC's *the fifth estate* and a book, both of which seemed to suggest that I bore some personal responsibility for Conn's tragic end. I have regrets about my experience with Ty Conn, but the decision not to recommend him for transfer to a lower-security institution, as he wanted, is not one of them.

I became a parole officer because my interest in that side of the penal system had grown steadily. An eventual vacancy in the ranks gave me the opportunity to be a temporary parole officer at Joyceville, and once I had the chance to acquire skills in the job first-hand, I learned quickly. I worked hard on my reports and took pride in their quality. I competed successfully in a recruitment for parole officers in Ontario, leading to my transfer to Collins Bay. I had heard many stories about this high-medium-security prison. The term "high medium" denoted a security level for prisoners who no longer required the structure of maximum security but were not suited to the relatively open environment of medium-security prisons like Joyceville. This designation made Collins Bay the next stop for most of the prisoners incarcerated at Millhaven, if they moved at all.

Collins Bay's exterior is often compared to the Disneyland castle, but it was reputed to be every bit as tough a joint as Millhaven. After a while, I began to see why. One of the first things I noticed was that many of guards seemed to take a harsher-than-necessary approach when dealing with small problems, more so than the guards I worked with at Joyceville. *Too much testosterone needlessly increasing the tension and creating more conflict*, I thought.

If Collins Bay, at that time, was famous for anything other than its appearance, it would have been for Unit 1, known by staff and prisoners alike as the gladiator school. Prisoners in Ontario who had never been to Collins Bay were aware of its reputation. Some of my colleagues told me that many prisoners at Millhaven who were trying to work their way down to medium security reportedly turned down transfers to Collins Bay simply because they would have to go to Unit 1 first. It was that bad.

When I started at Collins Bay, I was given a caseload of fifty-five prisoners listed by name and number on a sheet of paper. I was also handed a binder almost fifteen centimetres thick. The cover read "Case Management Manual, Correctional Service of Canada," and it was given to every new parole officer. I was also given an office, a key, and a Collins Bay name tag and wished "good luck." This was the basic training for all parole officers in the federal prison system.

Reviewing the list of prisoners assigned to me, I noticed that many had incomplete and long-overdue reports. Apparently, my predecessor had lost interest in the job when he found out he was going to a new one. It would take me a long time to catch up, but at least I had already acted in the job at Joyceville. I started at the top of the list. Each day I reviewed the files in the morning, and I saw prisoners and wrote reports in the afternoon. In those days, we wrote reports by hand and submitted them to the clerical staff for typing. Once the report was typed, I would have the prisoner up to my office and allow him to read it and ask questions.

Interpersonal skills were critical. A man who read something he did not like, something that said he was not yet ready to get out of prison, could become very volatile very quickly. I saw men punch out windows and put holes in walls after leaving a meeting with their parole officer. When this happened, or if the prisoner appeared ready to explode as he was leaving, we'd call his unit to alert them he was on his way back and very upset. We'd also call the keeper's office to let them know we had a potential powder keg walking around and why. If the man's anger appeared to be escalating, they often made the decision to grab him at the four o'clock count, when everyone was confined to their cells, and take him to the hole. By the time the recreation period started at five thirty, the man would be somewhere he could do no harm — for the time being.

Working my way through my caseload, I came to Tyrone Conn's name. I filled out a request for his file and put it in the basket in the general office on my way out that day. I also put out a pass for the prisoner to see me in the afternoon, in preparation for what would be our first encounter. The next morning I picked up the file, headed to my office with it, and began to read.

Ty Conn first entered the federal prison system in 1984 for robbery-with-a-firearm offences. He was sentenced to three years, eight months, and twenty-seven days and placed at Collins Bay. He served two-thirds of his sentence and was released to the community in early 1986 to serve the remainder under supervision. He returned to federal custody less than a year later with a new charge for armed robbery. His federal sentence was now six years, nine months, and twenty-three days. From the mug shots in the file, Conn appeared a clean-cut young man. He looked more like a Boy Scout than a bank robber, and all the reports from work supervisors and unit officers were glowing. Interesting, I thought. I looked forward to meeting him that afternoon.

At one o'clock the phone rang, and I was advised that prisoner Conn was there to see me. I walked up front to the general office to see a very young man in green prison garb. He didn't look old enough to shave. He smiled widely.

"Mr. Clark?" he asked.

When we got to my office, I offered him the chair on the other side of my desk and closed the door before I sat down. Ty looked around the office and then at the blue folders on my desk. "Is that my file?"

"Yes. I read it this morning."

"Pretty bad, I guess, eh?"

"I've seen worse."

We talked for about an hour. My normal practice in an initial interview was to say less than the prisoner. I wanted him to talk, to try to discern a sense of what he was all about. Tyrone Conn turned out to be as nice as his picture looked. He spoke about how foolish his criminal record was and how he knew he had much more potential than the blue folders indicated. I noticed he did not use profanity, as many others did.

Like so many of the prisoners I would meet and work with over this period, Tyrone Conn had himself been a victim from his earliest years. Born in 1967 to a fifteen-year-old girl who abandoned him to his neglectful father, baby Ty ultimately passed into the care of his grandparents. A family in Belleville, Ontario, adopted him when he was three. The father was a psychiatrist named Conn who reputedly meted out excessive punishments for Ty's most trivial childhood missteps. Ty's adoptive mother reportedly suffered from mental illness and was unable to offer Ty any form of emotional security or protection. For eight years Ty languished in an abusive and dysfunctional home before he returned to the charge of the Children's Aid Society. From that point on he was in foster homes, group homes, and youth detention facilities. Not surprisingly, he began to show signs of anti-social behaviour, which would become more extreme over time. His story was disturbingly similar to most of the case histories I read in my career. Of all the prisoners I worked with, I can recall only a few who had not suffered terribly in those formative years. The scars they carried forever changed the ways in which they engaged with a world they had learned to regard as dangerous and untrustworthy.

Ty's file did not mention he had recently reunited with his birth mother; that was something I learned from our interview. She lived in Belleville, and she was now approved to visit him in prison.

Having his mother back was the biggest and best thing that had happened in his whole life, according to Ty. He talked about how he was now ready to abandon his previous ways, and he said the only way to be the person he knew he could be was to focus on his new family and the future. Although I said little, I felt very pleased. Here, among the flotsam and jetsam, was a hidden diamond, I thought, a ray of sunshine in one of the gloomiest places on earth.

After the interview, Ty thanked me for my time. Alone in my office, I opened his file again. In his picture, he looked too young and too innocent to be in a federal prison, especially one like Collins Bay. I wondered if other prisoners were victimizing him because of his youthful appearance. I decided then and there that I would do my best to help this young man turn his life around. We would work together, and over time we would build his case for parole. When the time was right, I would take him before the National Parole Board, where he would be granted a new chance at life. The more I thought about it, the more it seemed right. This is what I had signed up for: to help people.

For several months, I met with Ty every two or three weeks. He would come up to my office, and we would talk about his future and what he wanted to do. One day, I was in my office when the phone rang. It was one of the clerical staff at the front desk.

"Ty Conn is standing here, Rob. He wants to know if you can come up to speak to him for a minute."

"Sure," I said. "I'll be right up."

When I went up front, Ty was watching for me.

"My mom's here for a visit," he said. "I thought maybe you could meet her."

I agreed, and he said he would meet me in the visiting room. He had to be searched and checked in for his visit. I went through the visitors' door, waving to the staff. I saw the usual assortment of young women with kids and, here and there, elderly parents. Ty entered from the other side and pointed to a woman sitting by herself. I extended my hand to her as I sat down. Ty's mother was a small woman with red hair. She seemed very pleasant and thanked me for what I was doing for her son. I told her I was just doing my job and that her son deserved a lot of credit for the effort he was making to turn his life around. I added that I thought their reunion was a major contributing factor to his change of heart and I believed their relationship would help him later on, in the difficult times that were sure to find him as a prisoner on parole.

Ty listened while his mother and I talked. I explained to her that because of his record, we would have to start building credibility for him in stages. I suggested the first stage be a series of four-hour escorted temporary absences (ETAs) to give him the experience of re-socialization outside the prison environment. Once he had completed these successfully, we could apply for an unescorted temporary absence (UTA), which would have him assessed by a halfway house for the supervised accommodation required if he were granted a day-parole release. This was critical to any release plan we were considering. I knew that full parole was out of the question. Ty's mother listened intently and kept looking from me to her son. He placed his hand on hers.

When I returned to my office, I felt very optimistic about this young man's future. He certainly seemed enthralled with his mother, and she with him. Maybe his reappearance was as important to her life as her return was to his. In any event, I felt like I had been handed a slam-dunk as a parole officer. I would experience the sweet taste of success while so many of my colleagues seemed to have bad guys who were content being bad guys.

I met with Ty twice more before making a written submission to the warden for three four-hour ETAs to downtown Kingston, which he approved. I put out a pass for Ty to come to my office the next afternoon. I think he doubted whether the warden would approve my proposal, because he seemed both excited and surprised. There were signatures to be copied and paperwork to follow, but other than these formalities we could schedule the first outing any day after the next two weeks or so.

One of the pieces of paperwork required was an itinerary, so I asked Ty if he had any ideas about how he would like to spend his four hours of freedom. He said he really didn't know Kingston, so I suggested going downtown to the waterfront and starting from there. It was late spring, and the weather was getting nicer by the day. Ty asked if it would be possible for his mother to meet us for coffee, if she could make it down from Belleville. I agreed that it would be perfectly fine.

"In fact," I said, "why not give her the date when we know it, and she can meet us for the whole four hours if she wants to." Ty seemed genuinely excited. I felt glad for him and his mother.

Two weeks later, the big day arrived beautiful and sunny. It was the spring of 1989, I believe. I was at work an hour early. As the escorting officer, I still had to get a gate pass signed and pick up a copy of his photo, his rap sheet, and his ETA permit with all the conditions spelled out. I would carry these with me in case I lost him. If he escaped, I was to call the police first and the prison second. I signed a copy and left it with the keeper. I collected Ty, now in borrowed civilian clothing, and we went out to the front of the institution, where I had a government car waiting. We parked downtown. We had fifteen minutes before we expected to meet Ty's mother. We looked at the boats in the marina and the big steam locomotive behind the old train station. Out in front, on Ontario Street, was the Kingston tour bus, an English trolley–like affair. When Ty's mother arrived, I suggested I could show them around. That way they could visit.

I paid for three tickets on the tour bus and took a seat behind Ty and his mother. For the next hour or so, we toured the Kingston sights. After lunch, we walked farther down Ontario Street so they could see the *Alexander Henry*, a ship converted for use as a floating hotel and a popular tourist destination. Then we visited Kingston's Pump House Steam Museum. I followed at a discreet distance, trying to give them the privacy they needed to get to know each other better.

As they walked through the museum, I had an idea. I stopped and watched them round a corner to look at a display. I waited about two minutes. Then I began to walk again, but slowly. When I could see them up ahead, I turned around and walked back the way I had come to wait out front. About ten minutes later they emerged from the exhibit. When they saw me, Ty's mother looked surprised, but she smiled at me. Ty, on the other hand, looked like he had seen a ghost.

We walked back toward city hall, and Ty said goodbye to his mother. She thanked me for everything, and I sincerely assured her it had been a pleasure. As we drove back to the institution, Ty admitted that my disappearing act freaked him out.

"I thought maybe you were testing me," he said.

"No," I said. "I just think you're trustworthy enough to spend ten minutes alone with your mom without being a danger to the community. You have something to work for now."

He looked intently out the car window, saying nothing.

Ty's next scheduled outing was to his mother's house near Belleville. It was a family celebration of some kind, a birthday, I think. In any event, the date was fixed, and as it turned out, I would not be available that day. Ty suggested the psychology-testing clerk, John Greene, be his escort. Greene was tall with grey hair, glasses, and a slight British accent. He had befriended Ty during his psychology appointments. He was willing to escort Ty, and the warden agreed.

When I left work on that Friday, I stopped in the keeper's office and dropped off the information package for Ty's next outing. The following day he and John Greene drove to Belleville. Ty pointed out they were a bit early and had time to stop for coffee. It was against the rules for Greene to make such a stop because it did not appear on the approved itinerary, but it is also true that he would not have been the first or last escort, including me, to stop for coffee with a prisoner.

Ty suggested a restaurant. Once they sat down, he asked to go to the men's room. Ty leisurely made his way between the tables to the back of the restaurant. That was the last time he was seen for sixty-nine days. During those sixty-nine days he was busy: he committed another robbery using a gun before he was captured, this time in a dramatic police takedown. He returned to prison with his sentence increased to seventeen years, nine months, and twenty-three days. He did not, however, come back to Collins Bay.

When Ty Conn escaped from John Greene in 1989, I had no idea then what lay on the horizon for either one of us. As his parole officer at Collins Bay, I had oversimplified a very complex situation. It was not as easy as sending these men home to their parents, or finding them a job for when they got out of prison. Many prisoners had problems that the support of those around them could not solve. Some had internal issues that caused them to engage in self-destructive acts. A common term in prison back then, "gate fever," described the often paralyzing fear that grips some men as their release date approaches. For all the bravado they might show up to this point, telling their friends and the guards about the amazing things they will do when they finally get out, they would lie awake at night, riddled with anxiety at the prospect of release. In many cases, they had no friends, no family, and no job — nothing and no one waiting for them. When their parole officers asked them their plans after release, they had none. They were not even sure how to answer "What city are you going to?" Some prisoners assaulted other prisoners or even staff to avoid being released. Others broke their release conditions the moment they cleared the door. Sometimes, deep down, we just know what we can handle, and what we cannot. This realization would stay with me for the rest of my career.

During that time, I read everything I could find on case management and parole policy and procedures. I could answer questions from memory for my more experienced colleagues. Then a buzz went through the parole officer ranks about a competition for a position called coordinator, case management. The job would entail serving as the institutional expert on all matters concerning parole, providing professional guidance to all the parole officers, and acting as the functional expert for the warden and the rest of the management team. There would be at least a few openings, because our employer was undergoing a retrofit. A new organizational model of running Canada's prisons was on the horizon: unit management. After some coaxing from my colleagues, and despite my relatively short service as a parole officer, I submitted my name. The way I saw it, this was a no-lose situation. I liked my present job and would be happy to stay exactly where I was, and the competition would be a good learning experience. Three people interviewed me for an hour. When the list of successful candidates was released, I had again placed fifth.

It turned out I would work at Collins Bay for less than three years before accepting a promotion at Millhaven. In the ensuing years, I would find myself back at Joyceville and Collins Bay in management positions, before accepting a position as an investigator at regional headquarters and then eventually moving to Kingston Penitentiary in late 1997, where my path would again cross with Ty Conn's.

As for Ty Conn, in the years that followed, he developed a reputation in prison as an escape artist and a solid con, and he had no trouble gaining the confidence and respect of his fellow prisoners, who marvelled at this young man serving more time than most lifers. From the perspective of staff, he was a polite, clean-shaven young man who seemed anxious to please and repentant of his previous mistakes. There was, however, much more to Tyrone Conn than most people knew. Throughout his many years of incarceration, he was a regular informant to the prison authorities. To be a prison informant is to take one's life in one's hands. It is hard to put into words the prisoners' negative feelings toward the "rats" they know live among them. Four prisoners I knew at Collins Bay used a weight bar to break both legs of one informant.

Ty Conn himself was fond of saying that rats were no better than sex offenders. Yet while he was enjoying a position of status among his fellow prisoners, he was systematically informing on all of those who might be involved in the prison drug trade or other illegal activities. He used this opportunity to gain trust and assistance from the authorities to whom he informed. Over the course of my career, I came to believe that no jailhouse informant, including Ty Conn, was motivated by altruism. They did not inform on other prisoners because they believed in law and order; they wanted only to further their own ends.

Ty Conn provided information to the Belleville and Kingston police about the illegal activities of those who most trusted him. In 1997 while housed at Millhaven, he told security staff he knew where ammunition was hidden in Collins Bay, hoping to win himself a transfer to medium security, where it would be easier for him to escape. Five months later, still at Millhaven, his involvement in another elaborate escape plot came to the attention of security. When confronted, he informed the staff that he had only pretended to be involved in the plot so he could inform on the other prisoners involved in the plan. Unfortunately for him, the prisoners at Millhaven were putting the pieces together and realized who the informant was. For the first time, Ty Conn was in danger and had to be placed in the hole for his own safety, making him a protective-custody prisoner, or PC.

When his safety at Millhaven could no longer be assured, Ty was transferred to Kingston Penitentiary. On arrival in May 1998, he was assigned to upper G Range. Upper G was one of the four ranges at Kingston Pen that make up Unit 3, or the max unit. In 1998 Unit 3 was known as the most dangerous at Kingston Pen because of the maximum-security population: 120 prisoners, many of them violent, all assembled in one place. When Ty arrived at the barrier of upper G, the officer looked him over through the thick glass: a clean-cut man of about thirty, holding a green garbage bag stuffed full of clothes. He smiled at the officer through the glass and gave his name. The officer, who had been expecting him, buzzed the door to open it. "You're in number 18," he said without looking up again.

Ty smiled again and thanked the officer. He entered the range and walked toward his cell, eyes down but taking in all that was around him. One never knew where old enemies might pop up, and he had several new ones back at Millhaven. He probably wondered what news had preceded his arrival at Kingston Pen. Ty went into his cell and threw the bag on the bed. This would be his new home for the foreseeable future. In about two hours, when they opened all the cells for dinner, he would find out what he needed to know. One of his first questions would be the same one many others ask when they arrive: who's the manager in charge of this unit? The answer would take him back almost ten years to Collins Bay and a ride on the Kingston tour bus with his mother: Rob Clark.

The next day, while going through my daily pile of mail, which always contained numerous prisoner requests for interviews, I found a request from Ty Conn, asking to see me. My general practice with some of these prisoner requests was to forward them to the responsible parole officer with a note asking if they knew what the request was about and whether I should get involved. Quite often, prisoner requests could be satisfied at lower levels, and many staff do not appreciate their supervisor interfering in their work unless it's necessary. I forwarded Ty's request to his parole officer with just such a note. The next morning the parole officer came into my office and closed the door. She was a woman of middle age with many years' experience in this type of work. She was all business and knew the directives by heart. We had a mutual respect for each other's knowledge and experience. She plunked herself down in a chair with a mock groan, leaned forward, and placed Ty Conn's request to see me on my desk.

"I had this guy up yesterday, Rob. He wants to see you in the worst way."

"What about?"

"He came from Millhaven protective custody. He says he is supposed to be transferred to Warkworth Institution. Says he was secretly working with the security staff and the cops to stop an escape attempt at Millhaven, where some staff were going to be hurt or killed. He says it has all been arranged, and the staff at Millhaven are going to send us something." But she looked dubious.

"Do you think I should see him?" I asked.

"I don't think you need to. I haven't spoken to anyone at Millhaven yet, but the write-up that got him here refers to what he told me about being an informant, not much beyond that. Until I find out what Millhaven is doing, you won't have much to tell him in terms of answers."

I thought about it and agreed. While she was still seated across from me, I placed the request in my out-box with a note to give it back to me in three days, when either I would know more or Ty would get the answers he wanted from his parole officer.

"What do you make of this?" I asked her.

"I don't know, Rob. Conn says his transfer is all arranged, Millhaven is doing the write-up for his transfer to Warkworth, the police are going to send us something in writing…" Her voice trailed off.

"What? What is it?"

"I'm not sure," she replied. "It's just the write-up that got him here is terrible. A cut-and-paste job with no real details. It's really vague and poorly written. I've looked at his file, and even if Millhaven does do the transfer write-up for Warkworth, I don't see how on earth they could justify making him a medium-security prisoner, with or without support from management. He was in the special handling unit not long ago, and he doesn't even come close to medium security on the scoring tools. I guess we'll see."

After she left, I sat thinking about Ty further. A very cynical thought struck me: maybe this was a dump job, where one prison transfers a prisoner not because it's in the prisoner's best interests but because the prisoner is an inconvenience. Prisoners who were chronically ill and required numerous medical escorts to outside hospitals cost the institution a lot of money in escorts, and some wardens sought to move them on for that reason alone. Prisoners who submit written grievances regularly also make wardens pull their hair out. At that time, the system imposed tight time frames for responses. If a response wasn't completed on time, the complaining prisoner would submit another grievance, objecting to the lack of response to the first grievance. Industrious malcontent prisoners could generate a great deal of work and were often moved around, sometimes on the most questionable of rationales. Fortunately, most of us regarded the dump job as unprofessional.

Now that I considered Ty's case, however, it started to look like a possibility in this instance. For one thing, why not keep Conn in solitary confinement at Millhaven while expediting the approval to Warkworth? The relevant information was at Millhaven, where the staff in charge of the case would, or should, know the details of the incident, including Ty Conn's role and his alleged co-operation with the authorities, which was said to have helped to thwart the escape attempt. A simple phone call between the two wardens was all that was needed, and Conn would have been on his way. The emergency transfer to Kingston Pen meant they had to complete two transfer packages and decisions instead of one.

I agreed with the parole officer that classifying Conn as a medium-security offender would require some very creative writing. They would have to explain why a prisoner who had been legally classified as a maximum-security prisoner just days ago was now legally a medium-security prisoner, contrary to the conventional scoring tools used for this purpose. The write-up would have to explain why and how Conn had managed to reduce his security level simply by becoming a prisoner-informant. Decision-makers might also note that his assistance to authorities began only when he was confronted about his own role in the escape.

I reflected on Ty Conn and Collins Bay and the tour bus. I wondered if he still looked like a kid. I went to the documentation log in my computer and typed in his prisoner number from the request form he had sent me. His name appeared at the top of the screen along with the list of electronic reports generated by various parole officers, most recently at Millhaven. Near the top was the report written to justify his transfer to Kingston Penitentiary. Right above it was the warden's final decision for the transfer to Kingston. I clicked on the parole officer's report to read the details of what had gone on at Millhaven. When the text appeared on the screen, it was immediately apparent that my parole officer was right in her assessment.

Parole officers working in the federal prison system are supposed to adhere to important content guidelines, which ensure reports include the details necessary to make informed, legally binding decisions about the movement of prisoners. If a report doesn't meet the required content guidelines, supervisors are supposed to return it for revision. Looking at this report, I shuddered. It didn't come close to meeting content requirements, and it contained almost no information concerning the alleged escape attempt that had supposedly placed Conn's life in danger and brought him to us. I opened a report from a year earlier and checked the same fields as in the report I had just read. They were identical, the same spelling mistakes in the same sentence in both reports. The whole matter was most puzzling.

The following week, I received Ty's request form back in my mailbox and called his parole officer. I asked if there had been any developments, and she said she was coming up to see me. What did that mean? A few minutes later she appeared, carrying some sheets of paper.

"Good morning," she said brightly. I knew that tone. It meant she had something to tell me that she thought I would not much like. "The report for transfer to Warkworth is done."

"Okay..." I knew something else was coming.

"I can bring it to unit board this week, if you like."

Each week I chaired a unit board meeting at which the parole officers and sometimes a correctional manager affiliated with my unit reviewed the cases of prisoners under consideration for various forms of release or for transfers. There was an opportunity for questions and discussion in order to reach consensus on the right thing to do. Every decision was a balance between the needs of the prisoner and the safety of the public. After hearing from all those present, I decided whether to support the application or deny it. My recommendation went to the warden's office for a final decision. The concurrence rate between my recommendations and the warden's final decisions was about 99.99 per cent in every prison where I worked, so I always tried to be fair and judicious, knowing that a case would not be reviewed in any critical way once it was out of my hands.

"Why are you bringing it to unit board?" I asked, suddenly knowing the answer.

She positively beamed. "They want you to do the decision here! They want this guy sent to Warkworth, but they want you to approve it and sign your name to it! Not only that," she continued, "but wait until you see the write-up for Warkworth. It says almost nothing."

The following week, on Wednesday afternoon, the parole officers for Unit 3 began making their way downstairs to the large conference table that dominated the airy vestibule below the offices. I knew that Ty's case was to be reviewed, and I wanted to encourage lots of dialogue on it, given the sensitive nature of the decision. Basically, Millhaven was proposing to send a maximum-security prisoner to a medium-security prison by overriding the required scoring tools with a written rationale in support of the move. This concept was not without precedent, and presumably someone at Millhaven had thought of it. The real issue would be whether the written rationale was convincing enough that any reasonable person could draw a similar conclusion based upon the facts of the case and the information provided.

We began with an outline of Ty Conn's criminal history: robbery (nine counts); using a firearm while committing (eight counts); escape lawful custody (two counts); theft over; possession of house-breaking instruments; break, enter, and commit; possession of property obtained by crime; theft under; possession of firearm while prohibited (three counts); conspire to commit armed robbery; break, enter with intent; possession of prohibited weapon; disguise with intent; prison breach with intent; and accessory after the fact. Current sentence: forty-seven years, four months, six days. Next scheduled release date: May 2017, unless granted parole. He committed his first armed robbery when he was just seventeen. Of his thirty-three criminal convictions, twenty-two involved weapons and robberies.

We moved on to the prisoner's escape history: he had a long history of escapes and escape attempts from both federal and provincial facilities. He was admitted to Collins Bay in 1984, and officers searching his cell found him in possession of a homemade handcuff key two years later. The officers also found a last will and testament. After his escape from John Greene on an ETA and recapture in 1989, prison authorities received a tip in August 1991 that Ty was planning to escape from one of the family visiting trailers at Collins Bay. Prison authorities decided to grant him his three-day vacation from the chaos and drama of the cellblock, planning to surprise him at the time they believed him most likely to attempt his escape. When the crowd of security officers burst into the trailer, he was quietly watching TV. The officers retreated but not before noticing, and later documenting, that he was dressed all in black. Later that year, Ty used a ladder fashioned from pieces of scrap wood to scale the high stone wall enclosing the entire prison complex. When guards discovered Ty was missing, they searched his cell. A small cork bulletin board hung above each prisoner's desk. Ty had pinned a number of paper items to his, including a small calendar. On the date of his escape, Ty had written, "Gone fishing."

This time he was gone for forty-five days, during which he resumed committing bank robberies, pointing a loaded gun at terrified tellers. During the last robbery, he entered a bank in Ottawa, wearing a ski mask and demanding cash. He got the money without incident and escaped on foot. Later that day, Ottawa police received a tip that the robber they were looking for was hiding in an apartment about a block from the bank. Police and a SWAT team surrounded the building. A few minutes later, Ty Conn emerged on a balcony, carrying a handgun. He climbed to the balcony of the apartment next door. The police watched as he tried to get the door open. When he failed, he shot out the glass. Once he was inside, the police contacted him by phone, and after two hours of negotiation, he gave himself up. This time the criminal justice system dealt Ty Conn a severe blow. His new convictions added to his existing sentence brought the new aggregate to more than forty-seven years.

His return to federal custody was now to maximum-security Millhaven. In November 1992, he and a group of prisoners attempted to cut through the fences in the exercise yard. Ty was approved for transfer to an even higher security facility than Millhaven: the special handling unit (SHU) in the Prairies, Canada's highest level of prison security, housing the most dangerous people we know. Only two SHUs exist: one in Sainte-Anne-des-Plaines, Quebec, and the other in the Saskatchewan Penitentiary in Prince Albert. The SHU in Quebec houses such notable prisoners as Clifford Olson, Allan Legere, and Maurice "Mom" Boucher. In early 1993 during a stop en route to the SHU, at the Ottawa-Carleton Detention Centre, a search revealed a homemade handcuff key in Ty's possession. Ty returned to Millhaven from the SHU two years later, in 1995.

As his parole officer described this most recent escape plan from Millhaven and Ty's version of events, I observed other parole officers around the table raising their eyebrows and exchanging glances. The parole officer explained that another parole officer at Millhaven had completed the transfer package for Ty Conn to be approved for lower-security Warkworth Institution. "The staff at Millhaven want us to approve the transfer to Kingston Penitentiary on their behalf, and send Mr. Conn on his way," she said.

There were many problems with this plan, and I was not the only one at the table to seize on them. The first was the transfer write-up completed at Millhaven: the one document that could carry this thing off had no real analysis of the case-specific factors or the escape-related intelligence that allegedly outweighed all the negatives in the case. The parole officer told us Millhaven had promised to put a detailed account of Conn's participation in the escape investigation in the electronic file in the next few days. The consensus around the table was that Ty Conn, caught planning another escape, negotiated a deal to save his own skin. Not one of us at that table believed him a suitable candidate for transfer to lower security, given his track record and the length of time remaining on his sentence. I advised the group that I wanted to give Millhaven the opportunity to provide us with more information to support their position. I decided to defer a final decision until the next unit board, which would give the parole officer time to follow up with her counterparts at Millhaven. Hopefully, next week we would have enough information to make a final decision.

Next week came and the week after that, but despite repeated calls by us, Millhaven never completed the detailed report and did not provide any new information about Ty Conn. The report sat on my desk. While flipping through it one afternoon, I remembered something that an old warden had said to me when I first entered the management ranks: "Don't ever sign your name to anything you're not prepared to defend in court."

If Ty escaped again — and he could — his actions later could make big headlines. He was considered a high-public-safety-risk prisoner, after all. If I approved the transfer, I had to be able to defend it. I realized what an untenable position I found myself in. Not only that, but I would need to make written comments in support of the transfer and sign my name, stating that I verily believed the prisoner met the criteria for placement at medium security, which I did not. Last but not least, I would be drafting comments for a positive final decision by the warden. In the event that any of this worked out badly, the warden would be responsible as well. I finally concluded this case was not going any further. I wrote out my reasons for denial and sent it to the warden's office with a sticky note on it: "Sorry, but I do not believe this one should be approved. Call if you have questions."

I never heard back, but the warden's final decision appeared on the system several days later: "Transfer denied."

Once I had a final decision, I asked Conn to see me. I looked out the window at Lake Ontario and mulled over what I would say and how. I was used to having talks like this one, where I said no to something very important to someone else. I always hated this part.

Ty refused to see me.

In the months leading up to his escape from Kingston Penitentiary in the spring of 1999, Ty succeeded in doing several things that would assist him in his plan. He went back to informing on his fellow prisoners as a way of ingratiating himself with staff members who could be useful to him. He used his naturally polite demeanour and intellectual cunning to secure a second place of employment, working in the prisoner canteen, which was located down in the recreation area of the prison. What made this particularly clever is that the management of Kingston Pen had placed Ty in the canvas repair shop specifically because they thought it was a safe place to put an escape artist. With his main job in the canvas repair shop, located in another part of the prison, and his second job in the canteen, he was able to move about more than other prisoners, using his employment situation as a cover. He moved regularly back and forth, going from one job to the other, and staff became accustomed to this, but staff could not always be sure where he was. Indeed, even the two work instructors were sometimes confused about which job Ty was supposed to be at from one day to the next, because on some days he worked at both jobs.

His workdays were not wasted. In the canvas repair shop, he prepared several items he would need for his escape, including a grappling hook attached to thirteen metres of canvas strapping. He also fashioned a canvas backpack to hold a fire extinguisher, which he had somehow procured — whether as a defence against a guard dog or its handler, no one will ever know — but he ended up leaving it in the shop. He also had a knife and a bag of cayenne pepper. This escape would not require the manufacture of a homemade ladder; there was an extension ladder right in the shop. He used the staff's confidence in him to acquire valuable information, such as when outside patrols with the dog were made and that the southeast tower did not have an officer in it on the midnight shift.

Ty knew that any escape would have to include a dummy in his cell to delay as long as possible officers' detection of his absence. He took two other prisoners into his confidence and enlisted their help. One of these prisoners lived in the cell right beside Ty's, on the lower floor at the far end of the range, away from the officer's observation post. The prisoners took several steps over the months leading up to the escape. First they introduced a small headboard into the cell, making a clear view of the prisoner's head impossible. Why the officers chose not to remove this unauthorized item I cannot say. The headboard saved Ty from constructing a head for the dummy, the hardest part to make lifelike in appearance. Then Ty began conditioning the officers on his range to see him always in the same position on his bed when they did their patrols or performed institutional counts, and always in the same blue track pants and white running shoes. Each time an officer walked by the cell, he would see the headboard and Ty's lower torso with a leg slung over the side of the bed, a white running shoe suspended in the air. Having got this far, Ty went one step further. He managed to manufacture a microphone with a speaker, which was placed in the cell of his confederate. In the unlikely event that an officer should try to speak to Ty after his escape, the prisoner would respond to the questions from the next cell. No contingency was being overlooked.

On the evening of May 5, 1999, Ty made final preparations. He and his two accomplices assembled the body of the dummy and dressed it in the blue track pants and white running shoes. The small speaker was placed in Ty's cell, and the wire slipped discreetly along the floor into the adjacent cell, a distance of just over a metre. Ty instructed his accomplices to place the dummy on the bed about ten minutes before each institutional count and then to take it apart and hide it behind the bed. This would give the appearance that Ty was going to the recreation area the same as always and coming back now and then like every other night. The trio also decided that because the officers had to make hourly walks on the range, the two accomplices would slip into Ty's cell between patrols to put the dummy back in position and make slight changes to the lighting, TV, et cetera, thus giving the appearance of comings and goings.

Ty reportedly told his accomplices that he did not intend to return to custody — ever. He told them he would either kill himself or force the cops to kill him. Either way, he would not be back.

On the morning of May 6, Ty Conn reported for work at the canvas repair shop. Shortly after the work day started, the shop instructor received a call from the canteen requesting Conn, if he could be spared. Ty was allowed to leave the canvas shop and report to the recreation area where the canteen is located. (If I had been part of the investigation team, I would have been interested to know if it had been Ty's suggestion the day before that he come to work at the canteen that morning.)

Ty worked in the canteen for most of the morning and returned to the canvas shop shortly before lunch, where he remained until returning to the cellblock for lunch with the other prisoners. After the midday meal and the twelve o'clock count, Ty said a final goodbye to his two friends. He thanked them and told them they would not be seeing him again. He made his way back down to the recreation area and asked if he was needed to work that afternoon. The staff member said no, and Ty headed for the canvas repair shop. By reporting to the recreation area first, knowing he was not needed, he created a scenario where he would arrive at the canvas shop after the shop instructor had observed the other prisoner-workers enter. When Ty arrived fifteen minutes later, he slipped into the shop unnoticed. Once inside, seeing that the instructor was busy, he ducked inside a large security cage used to hold sewing machines that were in need of repair. The cage was in an out-of-bounds area of the shop; Ty was one of the few prisoners with permission to be in it. He needed to hide somewhere inside so the shop instructor couldn't see him, because he knew at the end of the workday, the instructor would lock the cage. He moved in behind the sewing machines, ducked down, and waited.

At about 3:05, the shop instructor told the prisoners to start cleaning up and locked up the various tools and equipment. As expected, he went to the back of the shop and closed the cage's wire-mesh door. He took the padlock off the mesh where it hung when not in use, locked the cage, and came out to the front of the shop. He opened the door to let the prisoners out, and a few see ya's were exchanged. Ten minutes later, the shop was cleared and locked. Ty was still inside. It did not matter that he was locked in the cage because it had no top on it. It was used to secure items that could not be lifted over the sides, and so someone had decided a top was unnecessary.

Eventually the staff and the two prison guards who oversaw the industrial shop areas disappeared. Just another day in jail. Ty waited until he was sure that everyone was gone before climbing over the top of the cage, taking the ladder with him. He hid in the shop for approximately twelve hours. Only Ty could have said how he spent those hours, watching it get dark, listening for every sound, charged with adrenalin, his senses on their highest possible alert.

His first big risk of detection would come at four p.m. when the guards entered the ranges to complete a formal stand-up count of all prisoners. A guard would look into Ty's cell for the purposes of confirming the presence of a live, breathing body. If the officer was doing his job as he was trained, he would require each prisoner to stand up as he was counted; Ty knew he stood a good chance of getting caught before he even started. Perhaps an officer had spoken to the dummy in the cell, maybe something had gone wrong, maybe his accomplices were scared and had bailed out, or maybe they were in the hole right now, spilling their guts. Maybe the security team was coming for him. They would have firearms, he knew. Maybe that was how it would end.

Whatever his thoughts were, Ty spent this time making preparations. The canvas repair shop was located on the second floor of the shop dome at Kingston Penitentiary. As a precaution Ty placed big canvas bags on the floor to muffle the noise when he walked around. He also hung two large canvas panels over the loading-dock doors, which looked down on the small wooden guards' shack in the yard, where officers assigned to patrol outside went to get warm, dry off, use the phone, and so on. He had cut eye-level slits in the canvas panels, which permitted Ty to work on the lock and chain securing the doors while observing the area outside, including the movements of the yard officer. At sunset the yard was closed and prisoners and staff went back inside.

Sometime after three a.m., Ty opened the loading-dock doors. It was five metres down to the ground from where he stood, listening and looking for any signs of movement. He climbed down, using the ladder from the shop, and he had his grappling hook with him. Nothing stirred. He moved quickly along the wall of the building and traversed the roughly one hundred metres to the exercise yard. He reached the gate, which should have been locked, slipped past, and quickly crossed the grassy area toward the southeast corner of the yard. An empty tower overlooked the dark void inside the wall. He placed the ladder against the wall at the lowest point and climbed. All was quiet. The only sound would have been his own breathing.

At the top of the wall, he secured his hook, threw the canvas strapping over, and climbed down the strapping. It was now around three thirty a.m. No one is sure what happened next. It is believed that Ty had acquired some knowledge about the area around the prison as part of the planning. He managed to get his bearings and headed for the adjacent neighbourhood called Alwington Place, just moments on foot from the east wall. Further speculation is that Ty was to meet an accomplice with a car on that quiet street, lights and motor off.

At 7:05 the morning of May 7, the grappling hook attached to a length of canvas strapping was found hanging outside the east wall. A ladder was found against the inside of the east wall, near the southeast tower and opposite the grappling hook. Within fifteen minutes an institutional head count had been completed, and Ty's cell was found to contain a dummy on the bed. Prison guards had counted the dummy three times, including during one supposed stand-up count.

Approximately two weeks later, Ty Conn's life came to a dramatic end in a Toronto basement apartment, surrounded by police and a SWAT team. At the time, he was speaking on the phone to a CBC

News correspondent named Theresa Burke, one of the hosts of the television program *the fifth estate* television program. His other hand balanced a sawed-off shotgun pointed at his chest, in case a police officer or SWAT team member attempted to intervene. The room was dark, filthy, and cramped. He was not feeling well, and the police around him pressured him to surrender. It is generally believed the gun went off by accident that night, although suicide remains a possibility.

A red-faced Correctional Service of Canada launched a high-profile internal investigation. A number of prisoners who knew Ty Conn or who had worked with him were interviewed. Each testified that Ty had decided to escape from the moment he set foot in Kingston Pen and had talked about it openly in front of the other prisoners from the beginning. Apparently no one took him seriously because of the unlikelihood he'd succeed in such a challenging task. After exhaustive interviews with many staff and prisoners, the investigation team pieced together the elaborate plan that allowed him to be the first prisoner to escape successfully from Kingston Penitentiary in over forty years.

During his lengthy incarceration, Ty had a great deal of contact with prison psychologists. The investigation team sent by Ottawa was able to access these records and learned that in therapy sessions, Ty had revealed his tremendous difficulty in accepting his lengthy sentence — a sentence he often told others was longer than any lifer would serve. He admitted more than once to an obsession with the idea of escaping from prison. Apparently, he fantasized daily about escaping; the notion dominated his thoughts. At the time of his escape, he was still looking at serving nineteen more years, unless he persuaded the National Parole Board to grant him parole, which was unlikely given his record of weapon offences and escapes. His many years of manipulating others had put him in a most untenable situation.

The investigation's findings, titled "Board of Investigation into the Escape of Inmate from Kingston Penitentiary on May 7, 1999," were highly critical of many aspects of the operations at Kingston Penitentiary, and justifiably so. Three conclusions in particular meant more to me than all the others combined, however, because they vindicated my concerns with Millhaven's management of the case and confirmed that a maximum-security classification was correct in the case of Ty Conn. The Correctional Service's Board of Investigation concluded that Ty Conn was "appropriately placed at Kingston Penitentiary," that the reports completed for his transfer to medium-security Warkworth "lacked in-depth analysis," and that many of the reports in his file "contained information that was simply 'cut and paste' from other reports without validating it."

Ty Conn's story did not end there. His escape and subsequent death became the focus of a television documentary and, later, a book. CBC journalist Linden MacIntyre and his associate Theresa Burke had befriended Conn after he saw a *fifth estate* episode that resonated with his own childhood and troubled past and wrote to MacIntyre. After Conn died, *the fifth estate* devoted an episode to his story. Conn's mother spoke in her interview about the day pass to Kingston and how much it had meant. My voice could be heard in the background explaining how that came about. Later, in the same episode, when the story got to Kingston Pen, and that Conn's hopes of transfer to Warkworth were defeated, I appeared in a short on-camera interview explaining why the transfer to a lower-security institution was denied.

I realize now that I was not completely candid or forthright in front of the camera about all the concerns that led to my final decision. I knew that no one would want me to pin this on others in the service, certainly not other wardens and their staff. So when I was interviewed and given every opportunity to tell my side of the story, I chose to give short, sometimes clipped, politically correct responses that focused only on his potential risk for escape. I did not say anything that was untrue, but I failed to reveal things that would have helped to provide a well-rounded picture. In retrospect, I regret that I did not meet Ty's request to see me on that first day he came to Kingston Penitentiary. If I had, I might have been able to better understand his position and to give him enough hope to carry on until he could legitimately earn a transfer to lower security. Perhaps I would have learned something from Ty that would have caused me to dig deeper into Millhaven's handling of the case. And perhaps that particular episode of *the fifth estate* would have ended differently.

5 Creation of the Millhaven Assessment Unit

I was promoted to the new position at Millhaven at the same time as my personal life also seemed to be flourishing. In 1986, some four years previous, I went on a blind date with a young woman named Elaine. We hit it off and, after a few months of getting to know each other, we began living together in my house on Victoria Street. Our relationship progressed happily to the point that we got married. Our daughter, Stephanie, arrived on October 10, 1987, and our son, Adam, was born on June 16, 1990, as I began my new posting at Millhaven. This promotion placed me among the ranks of management in the Correctional Service of Canada, and I recall taking pride in achieving so much so quickly. I would be the on-site case-management and parole expert for twelve parole officers and the supervisor in charge of the sentence administration department — which calculates prisoners' sentences, release dates, et cetera — and the three support staff who typed the various reports for the parole officers. My new title was coordinator, case management. It seemed I had everything that made life worth living: a wonderful family and a good job.

As a new manager I really had no idea what to it meant to supervise other people, and Millhaven proved a steep and harsh learning curve. I arrived just as Millhaven received a brand-new warden and deputy warden; the latter would be my direct supervisor. The warden was a tall, rugged-looking man who had worked his way up through the system from uniformed guard. The new deputy warden came from a finance background.

Under the new organizational structure of unit management, each prison unit had a dedicated staff of uniformed correctional officers (guards), uniformed correctional managers (keepers), approximately four parole officers, and a unit clerk for clerical support. These employees were responsible only for the prisoners who lived within their specific unit, approximately 120 prisoners, spread over four ranges. The three unit managers were in charge of the individual units and, like me, reported to the deputy warden, who reported to the warden. Wardens in turn reported to the regional deputy commissioner, who reported to the commissioner in Ottawa.

The unit-management system required uniformed guards to carry a small caseload of prisoners and to meet with these prisoners regularly and write brief reports on their progress. This may sound like the living-unit model, but that is where the similarity ends. The vast majority of uniformed staff wanted nothing to do with counselling sessions or release planning for prisoners and vehemently resisted taking on these tasks. The guards' union successfully negotiated a significant pay raise for officers to take on case management, but the guards never embraced this work, locally or nationally.

The reorganization also created some staffing dilemmas. On the one hand, the Correctional Service added a middle manager to each unit in every federal prison in the country, consequently reducing the need for some of the most senior uniformed supervisors in the system. Senior supervisors whose jobs were phased out moved into the ranks of the new unit manager positions. Along with a hefty raise and a chance to wear civilian clothing to work, these senior guards were now in charge of parole officers as well as security officers and signed off on risk-assessment reports headed for the National Parole Board and other places. Some of the best managers I have worked with started in uniform, but any management model that places security staff in charge of its parole officers and has guard-managers as the quality-control agents takes a big risk. If a rookie parole officer supports the wrong prisoner and no one catches it, a member of the community could end up dead. In my view, the unit-management system failed miserably. (Years later, at Kingston Pen, Ty Conn's case demonstrated the problem of guard-managers who didn't read prisoner reports and had no understanding about case-management content guidelines or risk assessment.)

As the CCM, one of my responsibilities that I had not antici-pated was hosting the regional transfer board, which met at Millhaven once a month. The board included my counterparts from the other prisons around the province, as well as the regional transfer officer, who had the final authority on all transfers in the Ontario region. Representatives from the medium- and maximum-security institu-tions brought forward cases for possible transfer to another prison. Some transfers included men who were presently in solitary con-finement at medium security and were being recommended for involuntary transfer to maximum security. Conversely, we had men in Millhaven who deserved a chance at medium security.

I found these meetings very productive and enjoyed them. Each of us had the authority to accept or reject cases based on our best professional judgment, and we did not hesitate to use this power. The presence of the regional transfer officer, Joe Hudacin, made the group even stronger. Joe was confident in his decisions. In fact, many times when two of the institutional reps assembled would debate a case, Joe would raise his hand and say, "I've already decided. He's going." The argument would cease. Joe often stayed for a few minutes at the end of a meeting, and we would sit in the boardroom, finishing our coffee while he wrote out draft decisions. During these times, I talked about other prisoners at Millhaven who should move or guys coming to us who were not, to my mind, maximum-security material. These discussions often bore fruit, and to this day I have the greatest respect for Joe and the job he did back then.

Another new duty I had was in relation to Millhaven's unique set-up and split population. Maximum-security prisoners occupied part of the prison, and prisoners new to the system occupied the other part, called reception. Prisoners in reception were processed and sent to other prisons to begin serving out their sentences. The penitentiary placement board, composed of the Millhaven parole officers who processed the newcomers and me as chair, met to discuss each prisoner and the parole officers' recommendations for placement. We always considered factors such as violence versus non-violence and the length of criminal history. Did he make bail? Did he have support in the community? Once the discussions were over, I rendered a decision to be recorded and prepared for the warden's signature.

My decisions were communicated, in writing, to the prisoner, and prisoners had five days in which to appeal the decision if they wished. Even once a final decision was made, many of these men could sit in twenty-three-hour lockup for days, weeks, and even months, waiting for transfer to their new parent institution. Part of the problem lay with bed-space shortages at the receiving institutions, and in other cases it was escort availability. At that time, all prisons had their own officers deliver prisoners from one institution to another. Various reasons, sometimes financial, could delay these transfers. While prisoners waited, nothing was done on their files; they were doing dead time. For those waiting to get to Warkworth Institution (a protective-custody facility), these transfers could take as much as four to six months.

In the fall of 1990, I was part of a contingent of Millhaven staff that travelled to the Regional Reception Centre at Sainte-Anne-des-Plaines, Quebec, to see how that facility dealt with prisoner admissions. I was impressed. They made use of the time they held these prisoners; we did not. While we in Ontario told new prisoners where they were going and to be patient, in Quebec they evaluated new arrivals in a number of useful ways. And while newcomer prisoners in Ontario languished under twenty-three-hour lockup, each new prisoner in Quebec was put through a series of academic and vocational aptitude tests that assisted staff at the next institution in guiding the prisoner's time and energy. I observed a number of other differences I was sure would tremendously improve Millhaven. One of these was the regional escort team made up of dedicated officers who handled all prisoner transfers for Quebec, no matter who or where. Prisoners' names were added to the list, and each week the regional escort team arrived to pick them up.

The regional file depot was another innovation. This might sound dull, but parole officers and the CCM depended on prisoner files, so a great file room was like a dream come true to me. The regional file depot maintained all the files for newcomer prisoners in the facility. Millhaven's file room staff didn't have the resources for this. Any documentation that came to Millhaven for prisoners in reception went to the attending parole officer and then to the receiving institution for that prisoner, even if the prisoner had not yet been transferred. The regional file depot in Quebec kept two banks of files for thirty days after a prisoner transferred to a new institution. They had discovered, as I had at Millhaven, that documents continued to arrive after the transfer, usually in the first month. After thirty days, the regional file centre forwarded the additional updated file to the prisoner's institution. I thought the system was quite brilliant. Everywhere I looked, they were managing this process better than we were.

When we returned to Millhaven and I shared my impressions, the deputy warden told me to write up what I'd learned for the regional management committee, a monthly meeting of all wardens and high-ranking officials at regional headquarters. I wrote a five-and-a-half page report, complete with recommendations for changes that would mirror the best practices I'd seen in Quebec, and delivered it to the deputy warden's office. My report was not only circulated to the regional management committee but also forwarded to Ottawa. Two weeks later, the deputy warden excitedly informed me that I would be temporarily relieved of my duties as CCM while I put together a presentation for the regional management committee to identify the resource implications of my proposal and show how my recommendations could be adopted. When I asked who was taking over my job, the answer was, "Pick someone."

I started working in the warden's boardroom, where I could work uninterrupted and have access to a phone and a computer. I reported to the assistant warden of correctional programs, Bob MacLean, who was overseeing the project and was a friend outside of work. Bob had made it clear that I would focus on case management, risk assessment, and parole issues; others on the project would consider things like schooling and rehabilitation programming options. This was a perfect fit for my case-management experience and comprehensive knowledge of all the policy manuals. I went to work reviewing the preliminary case-management matters required before the system can begin to do anything with a prisoner that might lead to him leaving jail a better person, and earlier than expected.

It seemed to me that under perfect circumstances, every prisoner would be gainfully occupied from the moment he stepped onto penitentiary property. From a case-management perspective, this would mean a parole officer would have to do more than see the prisoner twice and write up a placement report. The parole officer would have to maintain responsibility for the case, just as if the prisoner had made it to his home institution, and just as I did at Collins Bay. If the prisoner had to wait four months for transfer, the parole officer at Millhaven could do the initial interviews and complete a treatment plan and treatment program referrals. Prisoners doing three years or less would come up for their first parole reviews six months after the start of their sentence, unless they waived it. If Millhaven had sufficient parole officers, I argued, it could handle some of the easier cases or at least do a lot of the preliminary work, like helping the prisoners to contact halfway houses to secure accommodation if granted parole. These changes would represent a significant improvement over what was presently occurring, which was almost nothing.

That December Bob MacLean and I attended the regional management committee meeting in the gym at Millhaven to present our plan, which we titled the Millhaven Assessment Program. I do not remember much about our presentation except that Bob and I spoke with heartfelt conviction, having seen first-hand what Quebec was doing. We proposed to take the best lessons from Quebec and improve upon their model by adding other required functions, such as additional literacy testing and psychological pre-screening. Further, we would prepare all cases for early parole review and obtain whatever police and court documents the National Parole Board would require while these cases were at Millhaven, awaiting transfer. As Bob finished his closing comments, I was standing at the back. The deputy commissioner was sitting right at the front, as was our warden. Bob stepped off to the side amid applause from the audience. I was thinking that we really could not have done much better. When the applause died away, the deputy commissioner rose from his chair and faced the assembled group. He smiled slightly and said, "There's been some very good work here, and some very good thinking that has gone in to this proposal."

Shortly after our presentation, I received a call from regional headquarters. I had been chosen to assist in rewriting the existing case-management manual. One person from each of the five regions would join a group of other subject-matter experts from Corrections Canada headquarters. I would represent Ontario. We'd spend five days working in a rented lodge in Mont-Tremblant, Quebec.

Parole officers and others around the region were asked to contribute their recommendations for policy changes. We assembled a considerable list of possible improvements. Once the group convened at the lodge, we sat down at the dining-room table and decided to start at the front and work our way through. When I got back to Kingston five days later, I was beat but happy. The proposed changes submitted by the Ontario region exceeded some of the other regions and the majority of these were adopted. I received a congratulatory call from a friend at headquarters and, a week after that, a personal thank-you note from the deputy commissioner.

Then I got another call from national headquarters. The commissioner had decided to have a team of knowledgeable people review the centralized reception practices around the country. Following this review, the team would assess the best practices in place at particular sites, with a view to creating a standardized national process for the reception of federal prisoners that would be called front-end assessment. I ended up flying all over the country on this assignment, researching and comparing notes with colleagues from coast to coast. It gave me a much broader perspective on the issues. I learned that what might be a big problem in Ontario was not necessarily a problem anywhere else, and vice versa. This was the case with prisoner transfers, which were problematic in Ontario but not in Quebec, where I had witnessed the use of a dedicated regional transfer team that served all prisons in the area. Another example of this discrepancy concerned the collection of important court documents such as police reports, Crown briefs, and judges' reasons for sentencing. In Ontario at that time, we were struggling to acquire these reports in a timely fashion and failing miserably. When I raised it as a major concern, some of my colleagues appeared surprised. I would later learn the acquisition of these reports was not nearly as problematic in other parts of the country. In fact, the Pacific region was regularly receiving these documents before they had actually received the prisoner into their custody.

Eventually these exciting opportunities came to an end, and I headed back to the familiar territory of Millhaven and my nice, quiet office. I was in my office with the door closed, reviewing reports headed for the National Parole Board.

There was a knock on my door. "It's me," my assistant said.

"C'mon in. It's open."

"I just thought you might want to know that there's a unit manager competition out now," she said. "The poster is in the lounge, if you are interested."

 E Unit

I entered the unit manager competition and came fifth — again. I hadn't had much time to think about promotions. Changes were afoot to turn Millhaven into something more than a holding centre. The file depot and regional escort team ideas were proceeding, and we were to receive additional parole officers, although the deputy warden wasn't pleased at some of the names put forward for consideration. "That guy's useless!" he would rail.

My name came up on the unit manager eligibility list at the same time that a position opened in Millhaven's E Unit, and I accepted. One of three units at Millhaven (A and J were the two others), E Unit was designed and built in 1977 to be the special handling unit for Ontario. As the unit for prisoners deemed too dangerous for maximum security, E Unit's physical design was slightly different from its two counterparts. For one thing, E Unit had its own highly secured exercise yard (such as it was). It also had back-door access to the solitary-confinement unit. In 1984 Millhaven's SHU closed, following the establishment of a Canada-wide SHU in Quebec and one in Saskatchewan.

When you work in the SHU, you risk injury every day you go to work, and you learn very quickly security is paramount. The same people who worked in E Unit when it had been a SHU were still there when I became unit manager. The officers were the most rugged bunch of characters I ever saw, and I realized that testosterone was waist-deep everywhere. These officers were used to being threatened, spit on, and bitten. They'd had urine and feces thrown at them, and more than a few had been the victims of prisoner assaults. Perhaps not surpisingly, one of the many union stewards in my unit used to tell me, "I just treat them all like they're doing a hundred years for rape!" Few had any interest in helping prisoners by taking part in interviews, counselling sessions, or report writing. The uniformed staff in E Unit included the most prominent and anti-management members of the guards' union executive.

I was well aware of the situation going in. Having been at Mill-haven for about two years, I knew the environment. At around the time I was appointed, the deputy warden and I were working late in his office one night on the Millhaven Assessment Program, which was progressing well. I remember our exchange like it was yesterday. He was sitting on his couch, and he said to me, "Do you think you can handle those guys down there?" His question was reasonable. I had no experience supervising prison guards and their uniformed supervisors. I thought carefully before I responded.

"That depends on whether you are happy with how it is running now," I finally said. "If you are happy with how it is running now, then I have no concerns."

This was true. I knew the man I would be replacing. He was a tough old bird who had come into the system as a guard back in the days when guards routinely "wrestled the cons," as he would say. He was also as nice a guy as you could meet. He would do anything for you if he could, and he had some memorable one-liners as well. Over the years he was promoted, and when unit management came in, he was among those guards who became managers. But he had signed up to be a guard, and it was on those terms that the prison service had taken him and then promoted him. He was still in the habit of playing cards at lunch with the guards who reported to him, just as he had throughout his career. If the deputy warden thought everything was fine, then that would afford me some breathing room while I attempted to bring positive changes to the daily operations of this very negative environment — a challenge that, in the end, nearly cost me my sanity.

The deputy warden smiled. "Yes, I'm happy with it now."

I smiled back. "Then I'm okay, too."

When I took over, E Unit was functioning as a reception centre for new prisoners who were in protective custody and would not be safe among the general population; A Unit accommodated the rest of the reception prisoners. When you passed through the barrier between N area and E Unit, you stepped into a long corridor with a black rubber floor. Offices with metal security screens over the windows lay to the right and left. Further down on the right was the servery, where the reception prisoners would come with their trays three times a day to get their meals. Across from the servery was the security office, a long room with numerous plastic chairs, a desk and phone, a logbook and radio, and, of course, the all-important coffee maker. The unit's count board was on the wall.

Every morning in E Unit, the coffee maker was working overtime, and when I went in to get coffee, seven or eight guards would be standing around talking. Aside from the four unit officers working the day shift were the officers assigned to outside escorts, who had some time on their hands before they had to leave. An officer from the hole and any other officer who could slip away for a minute or two usually joined them. As soon as I entered, the talking would stop, and the union reps would verbally accost me, usually with raised voices and much profanity, about whatever new decisions the warden or deputy warden was handing down. I suspected it had something to do with the supportive audience of guards in attendance. Eventually I came to look forward to these morning sparring matches, because I realized that, most of the time, my interlocutors weren't genuinely concerned about the issues they were raising, despite the shouting, obscenities, and doom-and-gloom predictions. They were bored, and fighting with me was a brief respite in an otherwise long, dull day.

I also realized that I could not always defend the actions of the people at the top. Every now and then, the union guys would seize on a decision that defied logic, and I found myself bringing a knife to a gunfight, as they say, if I tried to argue the point; so I did not. An example of this was the deputy warden's idea to reduce overtime by using shop instructors to replace guards who booked off sick during the weekdays, instead of hiring other guards on overtime. This scheme had to be abandoned after a week because the shop instructors booked off sick, too. They didn't want to sit in a tower or go on patrol, and removing an instructor from his shop meant those prisoners had to stay locked up in the unit instead of going to work. This made the maximum-security prisoners very irate, and the unit staff would do nothing to alleviate their tension. The result was disgruntled staff, increased sick leave, and more grievances from the guards, shop instructors, and prisoners. Decisions like that one led to the management team's collective downfall in my opinion.

In my first week in E Unit, as I observed the prisoners coming to the servery to get their lunch, I knew something was wrong. At first, I could not put my finger on what it was, but I eventually realized the prisoners did not raise their eyes as they passed through the meal line. There was no small talk with the prisoners serving them, not even one asking another for a smoke for later on, which was very odd. These were protective-custody prisoners who probably feared for their lives, given that they were in the infamous Millhaven Institution, albeit temporarily, but something more was at play. I began to look more closely at the prisoners serving the food.

"Where do our servery guys come from?" I asked a guard.

"They're all J Unit guys," he said.

That explained it. A few years before I got to Millhaven, a murder took place in J Unit, one of many over the years. The victim was a protective-custody prisoner who had arrived from medium-security

Warkworth. In those days, pedophiles, rapists, Crown witnesses, and so on usually went straight to Warkworth, because it was their only chance of survival. Niki Rivard was a protective-custody sex offender and most prisoners at Warkworth lived in fear of him. Rivard proved too unmanageable for a medium-security institution after he stabbed a fellow prisoner in the face, and in a rare move Warkworth sent him to Millhaven instead of Kingston Penitentiary, the maximum-security prison of choice for protective-custody prisoners.

When he arrived at Millhaven, Rivard was warned the J Unit prisoners would likely give him a negative reception, given his offences. Rivard, in a show of bravado, replied that he had no concerns for his safety and offered to sign something to that effect. After Rivard signed this piece of paper, he was given a cell in J Unit. He lasted long enough to make it down to the gymnasium and make a speech, warning that he would kill anybody who tried to kill him. Within six hours of entering J Unit, he was dead. J Unit officers found him in his cell with approximately sixty stab wounds.

When I had assembled the pieces of the puzzle, I understood why these guys looked like they were headed for the gallows. In order to get their food, they had to come downstairs and walk a gauntlet of former SHU guards and then file past a group of J Unit prisoners, who put extremely small portions on their plates. Every face they saw had the same expression of unmitigated contempt. And I am sure I was not the only one present who wondered if these maximum-security prisoners had done anything disgusting to the food. It wasn't unheard of for prisoners to add urine and feces to the food they served. I felt sure that sooner or later, a J Unit prisoner would attack a protective-custody prisoner.

As it turned out, only days after I took over E Unit, the chief of food services contacted me to discuss long-standing problems with the servery in my unit. The main problem was the amount of food E Unit consumed. Some items — cereal, for instance, and butter and eggs — were depleted in E Unit at an unprecedented rate. In the end, we concluded the J Unit workers stole food and took it back to their ranges. The chief replaced the J Unit prisoners with E Unit reception prisoners waiting for transfers, with my thanks.

This staffing shuffle had a significant impact. First, any reception prisoner lucky enough to get a job in the unit and thus out of his cell for part of the day was always on his best behaviour for fear of losing such a coveted position. Accordingly, the E Unit officers found these prisoner-workers quite compliant compared to what they were used to. The chief stopped losing so much food. What concerned me about the original arrangement was that not one of the guard managers had thought it dangerous to have the two populations mixing.

My job also involved managing the solitary-confinement unit, the hole, and providing operational assistance to the prison hospital. The hole at Millhaven housed some of the most dangerous men in the system. One of these was a young man named MacDonald with a history of assaults on both prisoners and staff. He was in solitary confinement awaiting transfer to the SHU in Quebec for a late-night escape attempt in which he got as far as the top of the inner perimeter fence. Closed-circuit security cameras captured him trying to climb between the large loops of razor wire at the top of the fence. He tried to jump, but one foot caught in the wire. He belly-flopped to the ground. The footage became an instant hit. The following day, a TV and VCR were set up in the entrance to the officer's mess. I heard laughter, shouts, and loud groans as I headed to lunch. I found the staff watching the security footage of MacDonald's botched escape and laughing so hard they could barely stand. Some held a buddy's shoulder for support. Even the secretaries were laughing and dabbing their eyes with tissues. The guard with the remote kept hitting reverse and then forward, making it appear as if MacDonald flew back up to the top of the fence and jumped again, over and over.

One day, officers took MacDonald out of his solitary-confinement cell to escort him to the shower. The process was two officers opened the cell's food slot. The prisoner turned and backed up to the slot and then placed both his hands outside through the food slot for handcuffing. The two officers escorted the prisoner to the secure shower stall, a phone booth–like affair with wire security mesh. It also had a slot, and once the prisoner was locked inside, his cuffs were removed. The process was reversed at the end of the shower.

On this day, however, a breach of the protocol nearly cost a man his life. MacDonald's hands were cuffed in the front instead of behind him, perhaps because he feigned pain in his shoulder from a previous tussle with guards. In any event, once cuffed he drew his hands back inside the shower stall and stealthily reached up to the small steel ledge above the slot. Sitting on the ledge was a piece of a razor blade he had broken away from the disposable razor given to him to use during his shower. He gripped the blade between his thumb and forefinger as the guards opened the stall door.

The shorter of the two guards was well known at Millhaven for all the wrong reasons, and MacDonald was apparently determined to repay him for some of the rough treatment he'd experienced at this officer's hands. Once the door opened, MacDonald stepped forward and brought his hands up, slashing at the officer's throat with the blade. The other officer wrestled MacDonald to the floor, and the injured officer held his neck in an attempt to staunch the bleeding. An ambulance rushed him to hospital and he survived his injuries, but he never returned to his job at Millhaven, nor did he wear the uniform again. Now this prisoner was my problem. He was already approved for transfer to the SHU, as were some others, but we had to deal with him until his transfer.

Another prisoner who found his way to solitary confinement was a man named Sikes. Sikes was infamous around the prison system for being able to make and use zip guns — homemade guns that can fire a projectile. Generally, zip guns are constructed using a heavy metal tube, and I have seen a large number of match heads packed tightly in tinfoil to serve as gunpowder. Sikes had previously been to the SHU, and he found his way to E Unit as part of a return trip to that same institution. At the very moment he arrived on our doorstep, we received information that he might be in possession of a zip gun, probably secreted in a body cavity where it would remain undetected during a strip search. If this sounds impossible, believe me, it is not.

The guards' union threatened to withdraw services under the "dangerous conditions" clause of the Labour Relations Act. Management tried to find out from Ottawa, or anybody in authority, what it could do. Among the solutions considered was leaving Sikes handcuffed and "dry celled" — meaning the water to his cell would be shut off, preventing him from flushing the toilet — until he had a bowel movement. This solution is not foolproof, however. Some prisoners have been known to manage their bodily functions — waiting until three a.m., when officers are less attentive to the monitors, for example — and without getting caught return the contraband to its hiding place. Another suggestion was to get his consent to an X-ray or body cavity search. He refused both, and the law didn't give us the authority to force him. In the end, Sikes was placed in a solitary-confinement cell at the front of the range with the hope that making him more visible to staff would make him less of a risk.

I used to speak regularly to the solitary-confinement prisoners in the interview room or through the food slots in their cell doors. This was not the case with this particular prisoner. I addressed Sikes with a raised voice directed at the monstrous steel door that separated us. I could see his face through the small thick glass window. And Sikes was just as unpopular with the prisoners as he was with the staff, although I cannot recall precisely why. It may have been that he was housed on the protective-custody side of the solitary-confinement unit at the time. Whatever their motivation, other prisoners in the hole berated and threatened him routinely, yelling from their cells.

The prisoner-cleaner also had an ongoing dispute with Sikes, and those two threatened each other daily. Over time, however, the excitement Sikes's arrival generated did fade, and the guard staff began to relax. They were so relaxed that they had time to decide the prisoner-cleaner was becoming a pain in the ass, so they fired him, prompting him to hurl verbal abuse at them. He earned himself an institutional charge for disrespect and was returned to his cell without his feet touching the floor.

Three weeks later, the former cleaner was sitting on a small concrete ledge on the wall outside the door to the institutional courtroom, which was located at the front of the solitary-confinement area, near the cell that Sikes occupied. The former cleaner was waiting his turn to appear in front of the prison judge, charged with being disrespectful to the solitary-confinement officers. When Sikes heard voices outside his cell, he put his eye to the half-inch crack between the steel door and its frame; he recognized his adversary's voice.

How events unfolded after that only Sikes could say for sure. But he stepped back from the crack in the door and moved to the small window that overlooked the open area fronting the solitary-confinement cells. The new prisoner-cleaner had collected all the lunch trays, and the officers were in the office reading newspapers and relaxing, as they did every day at this time. Other than fetching prisoners for court, there was no work to do. Once it looked like the guards were occupied, Sikes pulled down his pants. As it turned out, he really did have a handmade gun hidden in his rectum. The weapon was made from an eight-centimetre-long lead plug, the type used in a concrete wall to hold a very large bolt and support a heavy load. One end was closed with black electrical tape, and a wad of match heads was set to fire the homemade bullet.

The prisoner on the ledge was presumably engrossed in his own thoughts. Sikes retrieved his weapon from where it had remained hidden, on and off, for more than four weeks. He returned to the space in the door. His target was still there, about three metres away. He could not waste time, because there was no way of knowing how long the other prisoner would remain in sight. Placing the end of his gun against the space in the door, he managed to light the fuse.

The explosion was heard in the office, and the guards all jumped up. Smoke and a strong smell of sulphur filled the air. Sikes's quarry was on his feet, yelling for all he was worth. He was not bleeding, because he had not been hit. By the time the officers figured out what he was yelling about, Sikes's cell emergency buzzer had gone off in the office. Looking in the window, through the smoke, a guard saw Sikes holding up what looked like a severely injured hand. The officer opened the food slot. Smoke poured out as Sikes wailed in pain and yelled for a doctor. The floor was covered in blood and the door and the walls near the door jamb were sprayed with red. It turned out the explosion that fired the bullet also caused the gun to blow up in Sikes's hand. I did not see his injury, and from what I heard, I'm glad that I missed it. Sikes's bullet had missed his target by about fifteen centimetres, hitting the wall and taking a large chip out of the painted cinder block. If the bullet had found its mark, it might have been fatal. After that incident, Sikes's transfer to the SHU was expedited.

Sikes had finally moved on, but MacDonald had not. On another occasion involving the latter, we were in the warden's boardroom for one of our regularly scheduled management meetings. It was about two on a winter afternoon. We heard a sudden loud bang and then four or five more in succession. We all recognized the sound: the officer in Tower 1 was firing his rifle at something or someone, and he was emptying his clip to do it. We jumped up simultaneously and went to the window. We could see the officer on the catwalk, rifle raised and shooting. The mobile patrols raced past the pedestrian gates, toward the west side of the prison. We followed the warden into the front entrance area. Several security radios squawked loudly. The words hit like a fist: "Two prisoners escaped! Repeat, two prisoners escaped! They cut through the seg fence! Over!"

The barrier at T control was now open, and uniformed guards poured out through this door. Each was handed a rifle through the gun port as he went. It was one of the most incredible things I had ever seen. One of the guards was a man from my unit. As he pulled a rifle out of the gun port, he turned to me. "Rob, should I use my four-by-four?"

It took me a second to register the question. "What's that, Gary?"

"Should I take my four-by-four?" he repeated anxiously.

I realized he was asking permission to use his own truck during the chase. Fields and low brush surrounded Millhaven. Once they cleared the fences, the two prisoners would have very few places to hide. There were no large tracts of deep forest nor a community close enough where the prisoners could lay low.

If I said yes and Gary damaged his truck, was the government on the hook? I knew what the union would say. If I said no and the prisoners escaped, would the resulting investigation show that I had thwarted a maximum response to a very dangerous situation? Two prisoners from Millhaven would be prepared to hurt people in the course of their escape. I answered, "No, I think it's best to stick to what we have available."

I am glad I did. Millhaven's prison guards were not very ambitious when it came to the more mundane aspects of their job, but they were among the very best when it came to security. Officers recaptured the two escapees using the prison's snowmobiles, and they did it in less than an hour. I was standing in N area when the two culprits were marched through on their way back to the hole. As it turned out, one of the two escapees was none other than MacDonald. He and the other prisoner had been in the solitary-confinement yard down in E Unit, as per usual afternoon routine. Unbeknownst to the guards, however, they had with them a large set of heavy-duty bolt cutters almost a metre long. How these got into the yard past all the guards was beyond my comprehension.

Once in the yard and out of handcuffs, the two prisoners went to work on the first of two fences they would have to cut through to escape. Their activity went undetected until the guard in Tower 1 spied movement between the two perimeter fences. He immediately radioed the situation to all posts, grabbed his AR-15 rifle, flipped the safety off, and ran out to the catwalk. He fired seven or eight times without hitting the prisoners, who continued to cut furiously at the outside fence. In seconds, they were through and started sprinting across the fields.

When they came back through N area with the officers, MacDonald was wearing only a T-shirt and pants, and he had snowmobile tread marks on his upper torso. Other than that, both prisoners appeared no worse for wear, and what had been a somewhat dreary afternoon at Millhaven had within minutes become charged with a tense kind of positive energy among the staff.

As time went on, staff-management relations at Millhaven became completely untenable. Over the next two years, we endured two strikes, two murders, stabbings and suicides, and just about every other problem you might imagine could occur down inside. I noticed a change in the tone of our meetings. The people sitting around the table with me were taking the conflicts with the employee unions personally, and they were very upset. Some of my operational colleagues began looking for weaknesses and slips in the tactics of their perceived enemy. My disdain for double-talk and trickery over taking the high road and setting a good example must have been obvious. Secret meetings in the deputy warden's office that used to include me now went on in my absence, with the door closed. (It was at just such a meeting that the scheme to force shop instructors to work in security posts had been concocted.)

I found myself trapped between two opposing armies, a soldier of neither. If my strained relationship with the rest of the operational management team was known among unionized staff, it did not change my status as "one of them." The union attempted to disrupt operations by encouraging all officers to submit employee grievances about anything they could think of. When a prison employee submitted a written grievance, the process required the manager to interview the employee; the employee could have union presence at the hearing. The staff's shift work impeded the procedure, which was especially difficult when the officers knew that if deadlines weren't met, follow-up grievances could be initiated. This action from the staff was one of the first signs that the basic fabric of the prison was starting to tear. A maximum-security prison is no place to have an all-out war between guards and their bosses, but that was what had begun.

One day Donna Monahan, my assistant at the time, came in from the unit security office, where she had been picking up my mail. She closed the door behind her and looked at me angrily. "Do you know what the officers are doing down there right now? Three of them? Take a guess!" she demanded.

"I don't know. What?"

"They're sitting down there with a stack of grievance forms in front of them, and they're going through the contract page by page, looking for things they can use to put grievances in on you!"

One day shortly thereafter, I was walking past the officers' lounge, the same place I used to put on hockey equipment and where the officers played cards for money every day at lunchtime in full view of the warden and deputy warden. Two guards with outstanding grievances against me were sitting side by side playing cards. I had an idea. I went back to my office, and I pulled out my copy of the guard's contract. I flipped to "Hours of Work."

The next day I entered the lounge and walked over to the same two guys. "How's it going?" I asked.

"Good, Rob. How about you?"

"Great. I was just thinking that this would be a good time to deal with your grievance, since you're not busy until twelve thirty."

They all stopped and looked up at me. One spoke up. "We're on lunch right now, Rob."

"Not technically." Now guards at other tables were listening. "If

I'm not mistaken, you're off after today and won't be back in until Wednesday evening. If we don't handle your grievance today, I'll miss the time frame." I spoke with great sincerity, poker-faced.

The guards were getting annoyed now. "We don't have a union rep."

"Sure you do. Bill here can be your rep, and you can be his."

"I don't want Bill for my union rep."

Bill piped up, "Besides, I'm busy. I'm on lunch!"

So far, everything had gone just as I had expected.

"Okay."

Our exchange had gone the way they had planned — the way it always went with these guys. Everyone in the room had heard our conversation and watched me turn to leave, despite pretending to be focused on the best card hand they'd had in years. It was time to drop the other shoe.

I turned around. "Here's what I think I should do," I said. "I'm going to write up a response for you without the interview. Otherwise I'll miss the time frame, which is not fair to you." Knowing that a formal response without the interview would be another grievance, the officers merely smiled. "When I do the response," I continued, "I'll explain that you were playing cards in the staff lounge and advised me that you didn't wish to participate in the grievance interview process, despite the presence of an available union rep beside you."

"You can't put that on the grievance response!" he bellowed.

"It doesn't say anywhere that I can't. It just says I have to answer your grievance. Someone else will decide whether they wish to consider any other relevant information I choose to add."

I left. Ten minutes later, the two guards appeared at my door.

"Okay, Rob, let's get this bullshit over with so we can get back to lunch!"

"Let's do that," I said.

The number of staff grievances submitted in E Unit began to drop dramatically after that.

I learned many counter tactics very quickly, because almost the entire union executive was in E Unit. Among them was a large man who was the executive vice-president of the guards union for Ontario. The licence plate on his car read "Mr. Big." He once told me, "I have had a lot of bosses, Rob, but I have never had a superior." I liked this line and told him so.

At one point, the Correctional Service of Canada decided that to meet a Health Canada concern for government employees who might be required to use emergency oxygen tanks with a mask, all officers must be clean-shaven to ensure a proper seal on the mask. This presented a huge problem at Millhaven, where many of these men had beards, and Mr. Big was no exception. The managers had to run around trying to catch officers who might come on duty with facial hair. If they did, we had to order them to report to the prison hospital and shave. One day I was walking toward T control and encountered Mr. Big reporting to E Unit for the three-to-eleven shift. Lo and behold, contrary to regulation, he still had his beard. I groaned inwardly as we got closer to each other, and his defiant expression told me he had rehearsed his part in the scene that was about to unfold.

"Hi," I said. "How's it going?" He didn't answer me, but he stopped walking. "I'm sorry to have to do this, but I have to ask that you go to the hospital and shave before you take over your post." He just looked at me. "If you refuse, I have orders to deny you your shift today and send you home." He was not the only one who had prepared.

He stood sizing me up for a moment more and then said, "Okay, Rob, I'll go shave." I was not sure I'd heard him right, and he knew it. "The only reason I am going to go down there and shave is because you had the balls to tell me. You should know that I just passed the warden and then the deputy warden on my way down here, and neither of them had the guts to say a fucking word!"

In the end, Mr. Big and the union at Millhaven won out over the warden and the management team. In an unprecedented show of non-confidence, the deputy commissioner replaced most of the management team. The warden, the deputy warden, and most of the unit managers went in different directions, and a new warden, deputy warden, associate deputy warden, and new unit managers arrived. In my case, I had no idea I was being moved. A friend reported to me that everyone at Joyceville had been told that Rob Clark was coming as a unit manager. I was dumbstruck. How could I be transferred to another job without anyone even speaking to me? I fared better than my colleague Bob MacLean. He later returned from holidays to find someone else sitting in his office, his personal items boxed up for him.

"Didn't they speak to you?" the new occupant simply asked.

Many years later, I was working at regional headquarters on a lay-over between postings at Collins Bay and Kingston Penitentiary. I was doing security investigations for regional headquarters on a full-time basis. Some of these investigations, by their nature, required the prison service to add a community board member to the investigation team to ensure impartiality. I was assigned an investigation at Beaver Creek Institution in Gravenhurst, Ontario. The community board member to accompany me on the three-day assignment was my former warden from Millhaven, who was by now retired but had been retained on contract.

The two of us left Kingston one cold fall morning, and with my former boss driving, we headed out on the 401. The trip would be about three hours one way if we were lucky. As we drove, sipping coffee and glancing at Lake Ontario to the left, we talked about small things. Eventually we came around to our time together at Millhaven. I had some things I wanted him to know, about my loyalty and respect for his position at the time. I felt we had left there unceremoniously, and I wanted him to know that despite all else, I thought he had been mistreated. However, I got to say very little. What followed was a six-hour monologue, round trip, about everything that had happened to him. He spoke with great feeling at times, his voice rising at key points as he laid bare his most private thoughts concerning how he had been undone as the warden of Millhaven. He talked about the members of his management team and showed greater insight into the truth of things than he had publicly declared at the time. He spoke about the people higher up who were making political moves this way and that way in their bids to supplant others and feather their own nests.

When we got home three days later, he pulled into his driveway and turned the engine off. It was dark.

"Well, Rob," he said, "I guess I kind of talked your ear off there. I am sorry about that…I guess I had a lot of things still inside of me about that whole thing."

I told him I thought he handled the situation at Millhaven as well as anyone could under the circumstances. It was, after all, a crazy place. We parted company, shaking hands. I think we both understood each other better after that road trip. He knew why I had been estranged from my peer group, and I knew why he had not fit in with his. Both of us had become *persona non grata* among our own. In the end, though, it did not really matter.

7 Discipline and Punish

I returned to Joyceville in 1993 as manager of Unit 1, which occupied the lower two floors of the southwest corner of the prison and had traditionally been the most docile unit. Most of its prisoners were older or infirm, and my colleagues sometimes joked that I ran a geriatric ward. Not only was I blessed with the easiest unit to run in the prison, but also two of the CSC's very best correctional managers (the new term for keepers), Keith Dickson and Hugh Nelson, were on my team. Each of the parole officers was extremely knowledgeable and efficient, some who are high-ranking officials in the prison service today. After my time at Millhaven, it was as if I had won the lottery.

Soon after my return to Joyceville, however, the prison experienced higher than usual racial tension among the prisoners. These sorts of incidents often started as a skirmish between two men. Supporters gathered on both sides, and skin colour or race quickly surged to the forefront if it was available as a consideration, whether or not it actually contributed to the original conflict. Observant officers could spot the early signs of escalation. A prisoner who usually ran down the stairs when the barriers opened would start waiting for his friend, there being safety in numbers. Prisoners might wear winter parkas, regardless of the temperature, because parkas can readily conceal weapons or, conversely, slow down a metal blade destined for the kidneys or belly. Some of the prisoners at Millhaven used to wear two weight belts to recreation if they were expecting to fight with knives, one turned backwards so the wide supportive section covered the stomach, while the other belt protected the lower back.

That spring, Joyceville found itself in just such a situation. Management increased the number of officers on duty and ensured that oncoming staff received pre-shift briefings on the present mood of the institution. We watched and waited and hoped for the brewing conflict to blow over.

One day amid the mounting strife I received a written report from Terry, one of the prison's correctional managers, informing me that a uniformed officer had declared, in a pre-shift briefing and for all to hear, that he hoped "the fuckin' niggers kill all the Indians!" One of the officers present, Terry advised, was Stephen, who happened to be black and was relatively new to Joyceville. I groaned inwardly. I slumped in my chair and reread the report a few more times.

At 8:25 my faithful assistant, Brenda, stuck her head in my office. "Ops meeting, boss!"

I got up, taking the observation report with me. Everyone else was already at the meeting, including the warden. When it came to the round-table discussion I waited as my colleagues shared their views on issues affecting the smooth operation of the prison.

When my turn came, I placed the report on the table in front of me. "I have an observation report from Terry, from last night," I said. "Has anyone else seen it?"

I began to read it aloud. When I finished, the deputy warden looked like she had swallowed a cricket. The faces around the table sensed the import of this, and the warden, too, wore a grave expression. We eventually concluded, as I knew we would, that a formal investigation would have to take place, and if the officer indeed said what he was alleged to have said, discipline would follow. I would handle the investigation and the discipline.

Returning to my office, I went to a long line of white binders assembled on the bookcase. These binders, called the commissioner's directives, were the operational and administrative bibles for the prison service. Every topic imaginable was covered, including disciplinary investigations and their consequences. I expected the guard to deny the allegations against him. If he did, I fully expected to come up against the blue wall.

The officers' unofficial motto — "You never rat on a fellow officer, no matter what" — is deeply ingrained, and it prevents the CSC from having complete control over its prisons. This misplaced allegiance is further complicated when some of the front-line staff who embrace this view are promoted to supervisors and managers — or much higher — and do not forget where they came from. I'm aware of many instances in which the highest-ranking person on the scene denied any wrongdoing by the staff, despite overwhelming evidence to the contrary.

I embarked on this investigation with some confidence. Nothing at Joyceville could come close to what I had dealt with at Millhaven, after all. I decided the first thing to do was to speak to Terry, the correctional manager who filed the report. We met in my office when he came on shift. He said he had heard the words very clearly. This gave me a more neutral and reliable witness than might be possible if I were to seek out others who were present. I had already decided not to interview Stephen unless it was absolutely necessary. I did not want to place him, of all people, in the position of informing on fellow officers. When I updated the warden and deputy warden, the former told me he'd alerted the deputy commissioner of the Correctional Service to the situation. This communication suggested to me that the case not only indicated a serious problem in the ranks but was also considered politically sensitive by the higher-ups.

I decided the next person I would speak to would be the accused officer; he could have a union rep present for the interview if he wished. I scheduled the meeting for the next afternoon. I knew from reading the commissioner's directives that I, too, should have a witness present, a member of the management team. Bob Boucher, the manager from Unit 3, agreed to sit in and take notes.

The next day at three p.m. sharp we met in my office. I handed everyone copies of the observation report and pointed out that the use of the racial term in question was a serious violation of the code of conduct, which was provided to all employees. I opened the interview with, "I guess the best place to start, unless anybody has objections, is to just ask you if this happened and if you said what is written in this report."

My fellow unit manager looked over at me and then at our guests. I wondered if he was trying to signal me that I was bungling the interview. Then the officer under investigation broke the silence.

"Yes, I said it, and I fuckin' meant it, too!"

We all looked at him, including his union representative, who now looked like a defence lawyer who wasn't expecting to hear his client confess. "He doesn't mean that!" the union rep interjected. "He's just angry!"

"I wanted to see a riot so it would blow up management's overtime budget!" the officer shouted.

The union rep tried in vain to silence him, but he went on railing about management. By the time it was over, all parties had agreed the statement in question had indeed been uttered. That was all I really needed. After the officer and the union rep left, Bob and I looked at each other. "Wow," he said.

The focus of discipline was, first, to correct a behaviour, or so the white binder told me. The sanction needed to consider such things as previous performance of duty, any previous incidents of disciplinary action, and so on. I knew any formal discipline must be measured and defensible. The seriousness of the infraction also needed consideration: stealing photocopy paper is far different than stealing the photocopier. In this case, it appeared the infraction fell well within the bounds of the serious category and was worthy of a serious consequence.

Over the next few days, I consulted with some of the more experienced managers about the approach I might take. Every one of them told me the same thing: none of them had ever been involved in handing out formal discipline. This was a jarring insight not only into my fellow managers but also the culture I worked in. The decision I came to, on my own, was to impose a financial penalty of one day's pay. Although I believed the infraction to be deserving of a more severe penalty, I had no frame of reference for such things, and I decided I should err on the side of encouraging repentance. I drafted the required notifications and placed them in my out-box, all except one, which I hand-delivered to the officer. The warden congratulated me on how I handled what he described as a sensitive and difficult assignment. I just felt relieved to be done with it. As it turned out, however, I was not done.

The following Monday, Hugh Nelson came into my office just before the morning operations meeting. "Guess what?" he asked, grinning broadly. "They're not giving money!"

"Not giving who money?"

"Him! To pay his fine! Nobody's giving!"

Hugh was talking about an age-old custom among the uniformed staff. In the rare instance that a guard had to pay a financial penalty, the other guards reached into their own pockets to give donations toward the officer's fine. This time, however, the other officers were not impressed with their colleague. Officers who might have chipped in were saying in effect, "Not this time."

It was obvious to the uniformed staff that the officer's remark was wrong and offensive but not, apparently, to national headquarters in Ottawa. About six months later I received a phone call to inform me the union was arguing the discipline I had imposed was "too harsh," and headquarters wondered if I'd reduce the sanction to a written reprimand. This was something I'd considered at the time, but I had abandoned the idea after the interview in which the officer ranted about starting a prison riot. I explained this, and the call ended.

A month later, my phone rang again. I was advised an arbitration hearing would be held about the case and given a date and time to report to the Napanee courthouse to present my side. On the appointed day, I made the twenty-minute trip to Napanee, a small village perhaps best known now as the hometown of the musician Avril Lavigne. The only other person who turned up for the scheduled hearing was a Joyceville colleague.

"I don't get it," I said. "Is it cancelled? Maybe we're at the wrong place."

"No, we're not at the wrong place. If I had to guess, I'd say they settled it instead of going to the trouble of holding a hearing." He stepped on the cigarette he'd been smoking and shook his head. "See ya tomorrow." He walked away.

I suspect the sanction was reduced to avoid further unpleasantness with the union, and, not surprisingly, those with the authority forgot to include the underlings in their decision and save us a wasted trip to the Napanee courthouse.

About a year and a half after I returned to Joyceville, we faced another very serious problem: overcrowding in the solitary-confinement unit. The unit's very competent manager had left to become an instructor at the CSC staff college, and a man from regional headquarters took his place. His nickname was Dr. Doom.

At over six feet tall, clean-shaven with a bald pate, Dr. Doom was one of the nicest, most well-intentioned people I met during my career. Unfortunately, he was also a consummate bureaucrat, and he earned his nickname because his remarks on almost any subject, at any time, were filled with doom and gloom. He could find something to worry about in any circumstance. To that point, he'd had very little operational experience, and working in a prison is much different from working at regional headquarters. Some managers' lack of hands-on experience is exposed in how they deal with, or fail to deal with, staff in uniform. I experienced it myself at Millhaven, where managing the staff and prisoner population after coordinating case management and reviewing parole reports was, at first, intimidating. This challenge is not such a bad thing in and of itself, unless you fail to learn from it to your advantage.

It was unfortunate timing that the previous manager of the hole left when tensions were running high and more and more prisoners were seeking the protection of solitary confinement. The numbers in the hole began to grow because if the prisoner or his parole officer was even remotely resistant to the idea of a transfer, the new manager would put the case aside for further review, and sometimes urgently needed decisions were not made. His thoroughness inadvertently kept prisoners in solitary confinement longer than was necessary. There are times, in the prison system especially, when you must take action or risk creating an even bigger problem than the one you are trying to solve. Some of these prisoners should have been prepared for transfer when it was first known that Joyceville was no longer safe for them. In the end, worrying and ruminating prevented Dr. Doom from making timely decisions. As a result, the numbers in solitary confinement climbed higher than anyone could remember. When the numbers peaked and exceeded the hole's capacity, we tripled-bunked prisoners in the prison hospital cells.

Every morning when he arrived at work, Dr. Doom would go straight to the count board. He cared about only one number. He looked for it every single day: the number of prisoners segregated in solitary confinement. Did the number go up last night? So great was his obsession with this number, and so well known was his daily habit of running to look at it, that the correctional managers decided to have a bit of fun with him by changing the number. Monday morning was best because over the weekend there would likely have been some minor problems with drunks for instance.

As Dr. Doom marched briskly into the security office on Monday mornings, briefcase in hand, the correctional managers would move aside, looking deeply involved in thought. In reality they watched him move toward the count board. If the number in solitary confinement was thirty-one on Friday, a correctional manager might change it to thirty-five come Monday. Dr. Doom would see the new number, and his shoulders would sink. One day a younger correctional manager decided to up the ante. As Dr. Doom hurried in the front door, this man changed the first number instead of the second. Now instead of the number saying thirty as it had when he left on Friday afternoon, it read fifty.

When Dr. Doom entered the security office, everyone played busy while they waited for him to see the number. Dr. Doom stared as if in disbelief. He wasn't about to turn around and ask about this number, which might make him look foolish. His mind was no doubt reeling. How was it possible to have fifty prisoners in solitary confinement? How many prisoners was that to a cell? How many cells were there, anyway? I can only assume that once he was sure he hadn't read it wrong, and he hadn't driven to the wrong prison, he did the only obvious thing he could think of: he dropped his briefcase on the floor and yelled "Holy fuck!" at the top of his lungs.

The crisis did nothing to endear the management team to the staff, who were justifiably concerned about the lack of options for dealing with dangerous prisoners. If you have no room in solitary confinement, and the prisoners know it, they know they cannot be segregated if they misbehave. Moreover, the use of the prison's hospital cells for this purpose had somehow drawn public attention to our plight. As I recall, the mother of a young man who was among those languishing in a cell not designed for long-term stays, and certainly not meant to be shared by three people, may have spoken up.

One day I was in my office reading parole officer reports when I heard the voice of Don Head, who was acting deputy warden, my boss, in the outer area. (He is currently the commissioner of Correctional Services Canada.) It would have been more common for me to be invited over to the deputy warden's office than for him to come to me. We made small talk for a minute, and then he closed the door. He told me the overcrowding in Joyceville's solitary-confinement unit had been brought up in the House of Commons during question period. National headquarters had issued a directive for the situation to be corrected — before the issue could be raised during the next question period, the following Tuesday. In simple terms, we knew that by next Tuesday the hospital cells at Joyceville could not contain a single prisoner. We also had to find a way to take pressure off the area designed for isolating prisoners. Don told me the warden, the deputy commissioner, and those higher up agreed the best option available was to convert 1A Range in my unit to solitary confinement.

Although Don caught me off guard, the idea was not the least likely solution that might have been proposed; 1A has a history of being converted for special purposes and had once been the newcomer range. It is the shortest range at Joyceville, with only twenty-two cells, and it is located near the outside area where vehicles transfer solitary-confinement prisoners in and out of solitary confinement.

The plan required a number of factors to go right for it to have any chance of success, and we had to be up and running within days. We would have to move the twenty-two prisoners presently living on 1A Range; this would not be easy. Once many prisoners get settled and, more importantly, feel safe where they live, they are understandably reluctant to move — ever. The advanced age and infirmity of the prisoners on this particular range complicated the plan still further. The disruption of prisoners being placed in a cell on another range, possibly in another unit, has significant consequences. The man who has been uprooted has to get along with thirty new roommates, some of them dangerous, some of them paranoid, and some of them both and more. Very few of us know what it is like to live in real fear.

The next day, the morning operations meeting ran longer than usual. The main topic on everyone's agenda for the next several days was, of course, the conversion of 1A. On paper, the plan was fairly straightforward. We'd prepare a communication strategy to advise the staff and then the prisoners. We at the operational end of things would deal with the prisoners and front-line staff concerns. The warden and deputy warden would deal with human resource issues and the prisoners' elected committee, and update the deputy commissioner and Ottawa on our progress.

We would first have to move all the 1A prisoners to other cells. Next, we would have to retrofit all the 1A Range cells to meet the security specifications of a solitary-confinement unit. The cell doors had a wooden panel on the front top-half that staff can easily remove. These could be punched out from the inside if a prisoner were angry, as long as he didn't hit the bars with his fist. We needed to replace these wooden panels with steel plating. As well, every cell door would have to be fitted with a food slot that could be closed and locked, and the beds in the cells would have to be bolted to the floor.

All these changes hinged on the success of the first part: if the prisoners on 1A Range decided not to move voluntarily, our problems could increase dramatically. We could end up with a new solitary-confinement range but have increased our numbers in solitary confinement to do it, and we would look foolish. We decided the best way to minimize the disruption would be to offer the prisoners on 1A Range the chance to stay in Unit 1, if possible, and then to take into consideration the prisoner's choice for a new cell location. We'd have to see how many vacancies we had in Unit 1 and forecast any vacancies that might occur through releases before next Tuesday. If any releases were coming available, we'd hold them for 1A guys. After that we would have to look at other vacancies in the prison.

One idea that came up was to offer prisoners in Unit 1 the opportunity to move to another unit. Historically, the prison system has frowned upon allowing prisoners to change units unless absolutely necessary. For one thing, a move usually means a change of parole officer. If a lot of time in a particular prisoner's release planning has been invested, the parole officer is often reluctant to hand the ball to someone else to run it across the goal line.

Hugh Nelson, Keith Dickson, and I walked over to our unit across the courtyard to explore the options. I learned a lot from both these men during times of crisis. Keith and Hugh began to review the names of every prisoner in our unit with the two officers on duty. I had known both officers since I started back in 1980; they had been around in the days when preparing to take a man out of his cell meant talking to him until he calmed down and realized maybe he just missed his kids and never really wanted to fight in the first place. I offered comment when I could, but it was clear I was not necessary. These guys had it in hand. While we reviewed every prisoner on the board, the few prisoners sitting in the common room fixed their eyes on us. Soon the prisoner-workers would head back to their units for lunch and a count. By this time, if all had gone according to plan, the union representatives would know what we were doing, and the prisoner committee would also soon be advised of the pending changes. We decided to wait until after the count to tell the prisoners on 1A Range. In the meantime, we would update the warden and wait for twelve o'clock to arrive.

For me, the quietest part of every day in prison was during the count. Before and after were all the sounds and smells and general pandemonium of several hundred unhappy people confined against their will. But it was almost always quiet at count time, as if we all took a few minutes from the parts we played in this surreal theatre to admit and accept where we were and why.

I remember having these feelings most intensely just after I became a living-unit officer. Once my role moved me to the cell-blocks, I could no longer hide from the fact that I was a holder of the key. At noon every day and three times more, I locked these men in their boxes and counted them like sheep. I counted Nicky and Jesse, I counted Hobo, and I counted Jeff. I counted people who treated me like their friend. And every time I counted them they looked up at the sound of me raising the little wooden slat and gave me a grin or some gesture. For all their flaws and the horrible things they had done, they treated me well from the time I first met them. I missed those days now.

When it was time to tell the prisoners, the prison grapevine had been activated: they knew. Keith, Hugh, and I headed to the 1A common room. Most of the prisoners were on their feet and looking at me expectantly. The TV was on with the sound turned down; apparently they had been having a meeting as well.

"Good afternoon, gentlemen," I began.

Before I could say another word, a little old man of about eighty years jumped up and began to shake his finger in my face: Hostage Simpson, who had been a fixture of Joyceville for as long as anyone could remember. He was very old and very crotchety. His first name was Jack, but he would bristle at anyone who used it. He referred to himself as Hostage Simpson to any and all, and he insisted every day of his sentence that he was innocent. Everyone treated him with a special leniency befitting his confusion. Today he was hopping mad. "I do not recognize your authority, Mr. Clark!" he shrieked.

Keith and Hugh smirked behind me as the verbal assault continued. Many of the prisoners in the common room were laughing as well, enjoying the show they knew I would have to endure in good humour. When Hostage Simpson exhausted himself, he settled on a chair and was quiet for the duration of the meeting. I began to explain to the men what was happening. I always made a point of speaking to prisoners sincerely, in the same way that I would anyone else. Consequently, prisoners I dealt with generally assumed I was telling the truth. To the best of my knowledge, I never knowingly betrayed that trust. I had a great advantage on this day: Keith and Hugh had even greater credibility than I did.

One of the younger prisoners, a lifer, began to rail at us about the problems of cell space and what the United Nations thought about the practice of double bunking. We listened. Most of the other prisoners listened, too, while four or five of the more outspoken berated us for uprooting them because of something we had caused. The others said very little beyond making random comments like, "Bullshit," directed at no one in particular.

Many people engaged in the effort to move so many prisoners in so little time with the fewest problems possible. All the parole officers were required to consult each other on reassigned cases and where each one was in terms of release planning and so on. Cells had to be cleaned out, and moves had to be recorded on the count board. The main kitchen would have to adjust its numbers and add meals to the food wagons going to the solitary-confinement unit. Mail would have to be rerouted. No one worked harder than Larry, the prison's welding instructor. He worked ten-hour days on Saturday and Sunday to make sure that every cell door was fitted with a steel security plate, every cell had a steel food slot installed, and every bed was bolted to the floor.

Some prisoners were understandably shaken. In certain cases, the men we were moving had not left the range for a very long time, for no other reason than a generalized fear about what might be out there. Now they were being uprooted against their will. A prisoner might also be going to a parole officer he did not know. This, too, could be stressful, especially if he had hopes of early release. When common sense prevails, as it did on this occasion, provisions can be made to avoid unnecessary hardship. If a prisoner had support for parole in my unit, we would keep jurisdiction until that part of the sentence had been played out, to whatever end.

By noon on Saturday all but one of the 1A prisoners had been moved. The fact that everyone was working on Saturday indicated the importance of this venture and the system's determination to deflect concerns away from the number of prisoners still in solitary confinement at Joyceville. Keith and Hugh did a masterful job of placing our prisoners in locations where they would have a good chance of integrating and not be victimized. Only time would tell, however. While all this upheaval took place, Hostage Simpson sat huddled in his cell, defiant and probably very frightened. If it were not for Keith, I don't know what would have happened to him. Of all the people who had ever worked at Joyceville, the only person to whom Hostage Simpson would speak, the only person he trusted, was Keith Dickson. I do not recall how or where Keith managed to move him, but move him he did. Hostage Simpson was the last man to leave 1A Range, though defiant to the end.

This was my first real experience with the politics of the prison service. In my mind, the real story was the number of prisoners seeking protective custody and what that said about the present atmosphere at Joyceville, the system, and how it worked. Removing the source of the concern from public scrutiny did not address the real problem. As I reflect on it now, I can't recall any discussion about the underlying reasons for the solitary-confinement unit's surge in numbers. The only direction I received was to make sure no prisoners were in the hospital cells on Tuesday. With the help of my dedicated colleagues, we did.

Not all problems in prison were the result of prisoners or staff. Sometimes the people above us — that is, at national headquarters — caused the biggest problems. Take, for example, corporate objectives.

In the 1990s the Correctional Service of Canada had several corporate objectives. These have since been replaced by priorities, probably to more accurately reflect a tough-on-crime agenda. A commissioner named Ole Ingstrup established the corporate objectives. A man of some vision, Ingstrup attempted to elevate Canada's prison service out of its warehouse mentality and into the modern world of rehabilitation. He created a mission statement for the Correctional Service that was widely known and, as well, established several corporate objectives that would help fulfil the mission statement.

The first of the corporate objectives, arguably the most important one to the commissioner, generally stated the Correctional Service believes that every person has the potential to live as a law-abiding citizen. This seemingly benign objective would soon cause some wardens so much stress that they verged on nervous breakdowns.

According to friends working in Ottawa, Commissioner Ingstrup contended that Canada's federal prisons were somehow overlooking prisoners who were safe to release and keeping them in custody unnecessarily. He asserted that if the service met its duty in meeting Corporate Objective No. 1, roughly half the prisoners would be under supervision in the community. What followed was an unprecedented push by the Correctional Service to release more prisoners on parole than it had ever done in its history.

Ingstrup's analysis changed the very nature of risk assessment for would-be parolees. Previously, when parole officers felt a prisoner was ready for release back to the community, they would begin to prepare the prisoner's case for the parole board. A prisoner's parole eligibility date is only a guideline. The parole officers must evaluate each case carefully to assess the overall risk to the community a prisoner's release poses. It is by no means an exact science.

Each prison began holding mandatory monthly meetings to measure its progress in meeting Corporate Objective No. 1. Unit managers, like me, reported the status of all parole cases in their particular unit. Joyceville's warden would be visibly pale during these meetings. He, in turn, had to report on Joyceville's progress at meetings of the regional management committee (RMC). Colleagues who worked on the same floor as the warden remarked that he looked particularly red-faced and tense as RMC meeting dates drew closer. Joyceville was not distinguishing itself. We were considered the "soft medium," but our parole release numbers were humble. There were logical explanations for this. Commissioner Ingstrup ordered that prisoners whose criminal patterns had identifiable social origins receive appropriate rehabilitation programs. The National Parole

Board, in turn, increasingly insisted that prisoners complete their programs in advance of coming before them. The number of prisoners waiting for rehabilitation programs surpassed the system's ability to deliver, creating a bottleneck. Although the problem wasn't unique to Joyceville, the backlog there on rehabilitation programs was so long that most prisoners started treatment only just before their statutory release date, which for most prisoners is automatic and comes after two-thirds of the sentence is served. This, of course, meant that few of Joyceville's prisoners were ready before their statutory release date.

Another significant impediment affected Joyceville's ability to meet Corporate Objective No. 1. In the wake of a public inquiry years earlier — one sparked by, I believe, a recent parolee's murder of a halfway-house employee — the National Parole Board typically required prisoners convicted of violent crimes to receive a psychological risk assessment from a certified psychologist or psychiatrist. This requisite created long wait lists (a second bottleneck) and led to missed parole hearings.

The procedure for postponing a prisoner's parole hearing had previously been quite straightforward. If it appeared that a prisoner's bid for parole was unlikely to succeed, the prisoner had the right to put off the review until a time of his choosing, typically after he had completed more rehabilitation programs or could demonstrate greater understanding of and remorse for his crimes. The prisoner filled out a waiver-of-review form to explain why he'd decided not to proceed (e.g., to complete substance abuse treatment). The parole officer signed the form, and I countersigned it, placed a copy in the prisoner's file, and sent it off to the parole board. But now, at the tense Corporate Objective No. 1 meetings, each unit manager had to defend each waiver. The deputy warden and warden, who lacked current case-management experience, regarded the waivers as obstructing the corporate objective. They expressed frustration and resistance but offered no solutions.

As if to punctuate the absurdity of the crisis, regional headquarters decided to relieve unit managers of the authority to sign-off on waivers of parole hearings. From now on, the unit managers would present each waiver to the deputy warden, with a recommendation, and the deputy warden would decide whether or not the case would appear before the parole board. The decision was apparently predicated on the belief that unit managers and parole officers were not trying hard enough to prepare prisoners for early release. The truth is that the parole officers I knew were doing their job and generally doing it well. Adding a layer of official sanction simply diminished upper management further in the eyes of staff and increased the deputy wardens' stress. Our own was at her wits' end, and the stress was beginning to show.

One day the deputy warden phoned me at work, sounding slightly harried. "I am preparing the warden's Corporate Objective No. 1 briefing for RMC. Rob, you have four prisoners on 1A Range who are far past their parole eligibility dates!"

"Yes, that's true."

"Well, I need to put something down for all of our cases that are past their dates. We need to show what we're doing on each case to prepare them for their parole hearing. The warden needs it for RMC."

We had had this discussion before. I had explained then that these four prisoners suffered from diminished capacity (Hostage Simpson among them) and were not likely to be granted parole any time soon. All four had been unemployed since their arrival. All four were on zero pay. They rarely showered. Three of the four never left the range. None of them had ever responded to requests by their parole officers, or others, to sit down and talk or to participate in something — anything. They were walking ghosts. But this information was of no use to the deputy warden, because it would be of no use to the warden when he spoke to the deputy commissioner, who in turn, would find no respite from the commissioner.

"You need to have your parole officers fill out a parole application for those guys and send it in to the parole board so the board will schedule a hearing," the deputy warden said.

"I don't think the parole officers would see much point in preparing the cases for prisoners who aren't motivated enough to fill out the form, or do anything at all, for that matter," I responded.

"Well, you'll just have to give them an order."

"What about halfway houses?" I asked. "These guys won't show up for the interview when the reps come to assess them."

I pushed back as far as I could, and hung up. I disregarded my supervisor's orders as unrealistic. I pondered how ridiculous the Correctional Service of Canada had become and noted my own cynicism setting in. I dismissed my conversation with the deputy warden from my thoughts, but I gradually replaced it with one I would have with myself for many years to come, which focused on an assessment of the true nature of the CSC. I had spent much time to that point singing the company song. Now the tune sounded hollow and fake; the conductor, an imposter.

My cynicism was validated when the media, somehow, got wind of the 50 per cent goal and reported that the CSC was releasing potentially dangerous offenders to meet a bureaucratic quota. Publicly, the Correctional Service denied outright any suggestion that it had the slightest interest in such numbers as anything more than a statistic. But the corporate objective meetings ended very abruptly. Why it took public exposure for the CSC to realize the foolishness of the plan continues to perplex me.

A new deputy warden arrived around that time, a man named Monty Bourke, who had, I believe, come up through the system via the parole officer route. Because most of his recent experience had been in the community parole office, he had little patience with the prison's usual malingering pace. He also had absolutely no tolerance for the blue wall or for anyone who subscribed to it. He was one of the first, and one of the very few, real leaders I met in this business. Some people did not adapt to his firm approach. If he formed a poor opinion of your work ethic, you could find it difficult to climb out of that hole. But I appreciated that I could speak plainly to him, and I looked up to him.

Monty Bourke's arrival signalled a new approach at Joyceville. Those who had previously used the same tired excuses for why prisoners from their unit languished in solitary got their ears clipped at meetings and elsewhere, sometimes in private, sometimes not. I'll admit that was fun to watch. Prisoners long overdue for transfers began to move. Staff who often strolled in for an eight a.m. shift at around eight thirty became more punctual.

Bourke summoned me to his office not long after he arrived to advise me that he and the warden had decided to ask me to take over the solitary-confinement unit. Dr. Doom was returning to regional headquarters. Because of my respect for Monty Bourke I agreed to leave Unit 1, where life was good, and move up to Unit 2 and the solitary-confinement unit. I made the decision so quickly that I did not first consult with Keith, Hugh, or the other Unit 1 staff.

The correctional managers in Unit 2, like Keith and Hugh, took pride in their work and were adept at dealing with the day-to-day issues that invariably arose. The uniformed staff were also good, with two notable exceptions, and the parole officers were motivated, experienced people who worked well together. Jackie, my new assistant, was another strong ally.

When I took over the solitary-confinement unit, one of the first changes I implemented was to run a side roster for an officer in charge of solitary confinement. Running a side roster was a fairly new idea at the time and involved hand-picking three guards to dedicate their time to this post. They would own it, and it was much easier to keep three people up to speed concerning the treatment of prisoners. I was able to effect this change because I had two capable correctional managers. The conversion of 1A Range to provide additional space for segregated prisoners gave us breathing room and made a big difference in our ability to improve the standard of operations.

One of my earliest experiences in my new unit was distressing and enlightening at the same time. I was in the security office when I received a phone call from one of the officers on my team, one of the two "unfortunate" exceptions. I didn't know him well, but already he didn't seem the type to work with the prisoners to solve problems. He'd come to Joyceville from Kingston Penitentiary, and he liked to talk about how they dealt with problems at his former institution. Apparently frontier justice still had a strong footing at some sites. This man, "the Sheriff," believed that he, and only he, knew how to run a prison properly; only he knew how to deal with "these fucking convicts," as he often put it.

"What's up?" I asked.

"The cons are refusing to go to work."

"Why is that?"

"Because we put one in the hole this morning after we searched. We found drugs in his cell, and we don't know what they are."

The Sheriff was well known; so great was his contempt for all prisoners that he often behaved in ways that shocked his uniformed colleagues — always, of course, when no managers were around. I would soon have the experience of other officers coming to see me on the pretext of getting leave approved, or some similar excuse, so they could privately report having witnessed the Sheriff verbally abuse the prisoners, or worse; some described appalling acts of racism directed at prisoners of colour. Staff knew, as did the prisoners, that if they wanted confidentiality, they had it with me. In these interviews, however, I always came up against the blue wall. They'd say they couldn't put their report in writing, and they'd deny it if it were repeated, but they wanted me to know what was happening.

In response to the Sheriff's phone call, I went over to the unit. By then, the prisoners who lived on 4B Range were gathered in the common room; it appeared they were having a range meeting. They watched me come up the stairs and head into the office. The Sheriff had his feet on the desk, crossed at the ankle.

"I better sign in," I said, picking up the logbook. Opening the book on the desk forced the Sheriff to reluctantly drop his feet to the floor. "What's up?" I asked.

"They're refusing to go to work."

"Tell me again," I said. "We put one in the hole, and these guys are mad. Is that it?"

"Yes," said the other officer, who seemed irritated at the Sheriff.

"So what happened, specifically?" I asked.

"We searched this range this morning, and we found some pills in Davidson's cell," the Sheriff answered. "We didn't know what they were so we phoned the keeper, and he said take him to the hole. If the pills turn out to be nothing, he can come back."

"Okay," I said. "Let's see what they want."

I walked into the common room and said a general hello to the gathered prisoners, just like we used to do when we were living-unit officers, just like I had done a thousand times before.

"What's going on?" I asked.

Howard, a man I did not yet know well, who looked to be in his thirties and was serving a life sentence for the murder of a high-ranking member of a rival motorcycle gang, stepped forward. He was the most powerful man in Joyceville at that time.

"Your guards took a guy to the hole today over his meds," he explained as the other prisoners crowded closer.

"I was told there were unknown drugs found in a cell this morning, and that was why this fellow was taken to the hole."

Exclamations of "Bullshit," and "That's not true," rumbled through the crowd.

"That guy they took, he's a bug," Howard said, using prison slang for someone with a mental illness. "He doesn't know where he is half the time, let alone where his meds are. Those guys know that."

He pointed toward the unit office. There were some nods and other disgruntled remarks from the onlookers.

I responded in the same way I always did, in the same way that caused most prisoners to believe me most of the time when I spoke: I told them the truth. "I'm brand new to Unit 2, as you know," I said to the group at large. "I don't know anyone up here yet, staff or prisoners, so I don't know how things work or how they've been running this unit. My name is Rob Clark, by the way." There was silence, so I continued. "As I said, my understanding is that we found some pills, and not knowing what they were, the officers decided to exercise caution until we could be sure."

I could see in the eyes of several prisoners, however, that they didn't believe the officers had simply made a mistake or were being cautious. To some of them, this was nothing more than some bored guards playing head games — not unheard of in this business, unfortunately, but not necessarily the case in this instance. I wasn't about to jump to conclusions. "What I plan to do is go over to the security office to look at the pills. If I can, I'll take them up to the prison hospital and ask the nurse what they are. If it turns out that the pills are nothing more than regular medication, I'll bring Mr. Davidson back to the unit myself. Not only that, I will apologize." The silence was palpable.

Howard spoke up. "How do we know you'll keep your word?"

"Anyone here who knows me, knows they can trust me. The rest of you men don't know me now, but over time you will, and when you do, you'll realize I don't always tell you what you want to hear, but I'll always tell you the truth." This was a speech I'd made before. I continued, "I've been around long enough to know that my word is all I have with the men here. If I break my word, I won't have any credibility. If that happens, it will get around the unit that I can't be trusted, and I won't be able to do my job."

A prisoner spoke from the rear of the group. "I trust him. I used to work for him." The sea of faces parted, and I saw Donnie, a man who worked for me in the gym many years earlier. Donnie was as solid a con as there ever was. He was also very bright. We had gotten along well, and many of my colleagues also liked him. Everybody looked back at me, and I could see I had earned points for entering the common room in the first place and having this discussion.

My position did not require my patience or negotiation with prisoners who were questioning my authority in order to act in the best interests of running the prison. I could simply have given orders to lock these prisoners in their cells for disrupting the facility's routine. The Sheriff would have liked nothing better than to see all of them dealt with by force. If I chose, I could have caused a great deal of activity simply by picking up the phone and stating, "We have a problem over here." But I knew exercising my authority in this situation would create far more trouble than was necessary to obtain my real objective, which was to keep the prison running smoothly. I had to deal with this, and every other problem I needed to solve, without causing greater disruption. I believed fervently in managing every situation with reason and professionalism, and to me this meant exhausting less forceful measures first, so the use of tactics like pepper spray, shields, and batons are not deployed if they can possibly be avoided.

In this case, it became clear to me, and should have been clear to anyone with experience, that these prisoners simply wanted to be heard. They didn't expect to come out on top — they knew that almost never happened — but they wanted to be heard. They had managed to secure a face-to-face interview with the unit manager, and the manager agreed to check into their concerns and to get back to them. Perhaps I rewarded their refusal to report to work, but I also showed these men that they could behave reasonably and talk to me about their concerns. Many among this group of prisoners had no experience with someone in authority listening to them. Had one of the leaders said something like, "These guys are screwing with us! Let's teach them a lesson," some of the men staring at me that day in the common room would have gladly started a riot. Once those unmistakable signs begin — the sound of shattering windows, the faint smell of smoke — it's difficult to stay the breach. That was the case a few years earlier, when what started as questionable judgment in dealing with a few drunks became a full-scale riot.

After securing a promise from the prisoners to go to work, I said I would see them all again at three thirty when they returned to the range. The Sheriff did not look happy.

I took the plastic bag containing Davidson's seized pills up to the prison hospital where Donna Dixon, the very astute chief of health care, confirmed they were prescribed medication and had no value as a recreational drug. I was less than surprised. The officers who found the pills could have picked up the phone and called Donna's office. Instead, a prisoner was in the hole for nothing more than popping his meds out of a blister pack in a moment of boredom and leaving the loose pills on his desk — surely another sign they weren't illegal drugs. Some in the prison service would have left Davidson in the hole just to save face, just to remind all the other prisoners who was in charge. But in this case, he was returned to his cell in Unit 2, and the charge written against him was withdrawn with my apologies to the men on 4B.

Monty Bourke's arrival at Joyceville gave me increasing opportunities to act as deputy warden in his absence, something I had done on occasion before he came on board. I began to feel as comfortable in the deputy warden's chair as I did my own. But I was beginning to feel irritated in general with the staff at Joyceville. Although many aspects of acting as the deputy warden suited me well, I was often called upon to deal with incredibly mundane issues. One day, an officer accosted me and demanded to know why the trucks that delivered photocopy paper had US licence plates. Why did Joyceville buy paper from the United States when Canadians were out of work?

It was time to move on. One day in the middle of summer, I picked up the phone, called Collins Bay Institution, and asked for my former colleague and good friend, Keith Speck. Of all the people I worked with in corrections, he was the most honest, and I would have chosen him as the role model for any new employee. After a brief chat concerning the state of affairs, Keith mentioned that one of the unit managers would be leaving Collins Bay for a one-year assignment at regional headquarters. This, of course, meant a vacancy, one I could fill on a voluntary secondment from Joyceville.

I went up to the deputy warden's office and closed the door.

8 Gladiator School

The presence of Keith Speck and a few other bright lights notwithstanding, I wasn't back at Collins Bay for long before I concluded that it had become one of the craziest places on earth. Perhaps that was why Keith and I came up with the absolutely terrible idea of taking on twice the workload and managing not one but two units each, simultaneously. I stayed only a year, and it nearly killed me.

Just prior to my arrival the manager of Unit 3, a man I had worked with previously at Millhaven, unexpectedly took a job at another facility, and the other unit manager was seconded to regional headquarters for one year. Having two vacancies posed a problem. If we took employees from our own ranks and promoted them temporarily to unit manager, we created vacancies elsewhere, and then Keith and I would have to watch over the temporary managers and shoulder much of the load. Any hope of finding somebody competent to come here quickly and stay put was equally unlikely, and if slackers, or worse, filled the positions, we would regret ever taking them. We decided to each run two units simultaneously.

The deputy warden looked at us over his glasses. "You're serious?" he asked. We explained that after lengthy discussion we concluded this was the best option for a limited time. A broad smile crossed his face.

Once the dust had settled, it was decided Keith, who already managed Unit 4, would take on Unit 2. I would take Units 1 and 3. Unit 1 was, of course, Collins Bay's notorious gladiator school.

I had heard the stories about this unit. Its prisoners were reputedly among the worst and most dangerous in the Ontario region. The name "gladiator school" likely came about because historically Collins Bay was a high-medium-security prison and, as such, was the first stop for most prisoners coming down from maximum security. If these prisoners adjusted well to Collins Bay, they could be considered for one of the regular-medium-security prisons. All maximum-security prisoners entering Collins Bay started in Unit 1. They could move to more desirable locations only after demonstrating the correct attitude. Some of the former maximum-security prisoners who did not succeed remained in Unit 1 indefinitely, and prisoners who caused the most trouble in the general population were moved back to Unit 1 as part of their punishment. Over time, Unit 1 became the home for only the very worst prisoners, and its occupants took pride in being the worst of the worst. The violence and anti-social behaviour of Unit 1 exceeded Collins Bay's other units combined and became legendary among prisoners and staff in Ontario.

The first thing I noticed about my new unit was that the officers had switched off all the lights in the unit office. As I entered the darkened room, I heard more than one pair of large boots shifted off the desk. I turned on the lights. I had crossed paths with all the Unit 1 officers before, and a few knew me well. To get them talking, I asked them to tell me what was working on the unit, and what wasn't. Some complained about prison management, some complained about the cons, and some just complained.

"The reason we keep the lights off, Rob," one officer explained, "is so we can see down the range better. You know, keep an eye on things."

I knew this was not true. In fact, turning off the lights signalled to the prisoners that the guards didn't want them coming to the door and asking stupid questions — or any questions, for that matter. But I pretended to believe him. I turned the light off and stepped farther into the darkness of the office. I looked down the range. You could have heard a pin drop. I remembered then my first night at Joyceville, standing in the pitch black of the canteen with prisoners. After looking around in several directions for an awkward minute or two, I flipped the lights back on.

"I think I'll take a walk on the ranges," I said.

A younger officer named Mike, clean-shaven and bright-eyed, caught up to me with the barrier key.

"Do you want someone to go with you?" he asked.

"No, that's okay. Just stand watch for me, Mike; that'll be good."

I headed for the lower range on the left and got my first real look at the gladiator school.

Garbage and rotting food lay strewn about. The cans overflowed. On the filthy, peeling wall at the far back of the range, about halfway up, a jelly doughnut clung to the paint. All the cells were open-faced, with bars, like you see in the movies. Most prisoners in other facilities had the privacy of solid doors, with a window for staff observation. An enormous brass wheel, a mechanical innovation that still worked well more than a century after its invention, could close or open all the cell doors simultaneously.

Many of the prisoners were unemployed and were lying in their beds as I walked quietly past them. Some, hearing movement that wasn't customary for this time of day, turned to look toward the door as I passed. In the common area down at the end of the range, I could see a prisoner at one of the tables. He had his feet up and was smoking, watching *The Price is Right* on the large black-and-white TV bolted to the wall. He was also watching me. I continued to walk slowly down the range, scanning the cells but not looking long enough to cause tension. I strolled casually, like I was in the park, hands clasped behind my back. As I approached the end of the range, the man watching TV looked up at me directly. I recognized him at once.

"How's it going, Steve?" I asked.

"Not bad, Rob. Long time."

Steve had worked for me on the rec gang at Joyceville when I first started. A short man with an uneven beard, he was covered in jailhouse tattoos, including a very large, dark one on his neck and chest. He was wearing sweatpants and flip-flops. His faded, sleeveless T-shirt revealed more tattoos, intermingled the numerous scars that come from a life of intravenous drug use. Steve, it turned out, was the range cleaner (although he did not appear particularly dedicated) as well as the range representative responsible for dealing with minor problems.

I could see Mike, standing at the range barrier behind me, key in hand. "I'll just be a second here," I called out. He nodded.

Steve drew on his cigarette. "What are you doin' in this hell hole, Rob?"

We spoke for a few minutes, a bit louder than necessary so the other prisoners could hear it was just prison small talk. I told Steve I'd become a manager, and he laughed. We reminisced about the rec gang at Joyceville and some of the funny stories. He admitted his part in a plan to make some brew (alcohol) and let it ferment in its hiding place, a dirt hole near the baseball diamond. Steve and his co-conspirators covered the hole with plywood and hid the plywood under dirt and sod. The prisoners watered this one patch of grass several times a day to keep it looking natural. Unfortunately, it became so much more green and lush than the rest of the turf that it gave away their secret. We both laughed at the memory.

I would spend a lot of time in Unit 1. I attended meetings of the cleaners and their supervisors, and the prisoners became accustomed to seeing me on the ranges. At times a prisoner would call out that I risked my life by coming on the range. This did not deter me, however. I knew that I'd receive no such warning if I were really in danger.

On one occasion I stood in front of the men to address them about the conditions they lived in. They told me they were not interested in my attempts to make a difference, and I would have to find other ways to impress the warden. I countered that I didn't care about what the warden liked or didn't like. "It just seems to me that you deserve so much better than this. You're human beings; you deserve to live in a way that befits human beings. I'm not going to hound you about it, because I don't have to live here. I just think you deserve better, that's all." The next time I went down, lo and behold, the garbage cans had been emptied and someone had even cleaned up around the hot plate. Small gains, but gains nonetheless.

I found Collins Bay Institution very much like Millhaven in the sense that personal friendships often compromised the relationship between the uniformed guards and their immediate supervisors, the correctional managers. Many correctional managers had been front-line guards with the same people they now supposedly supervised. As at Millhaven, the supervision was often too relaxed. Two of the four correctional managers who reported to me were very professional in the performance of their duties. Like their Millhaven counterparts, most of the guards at Collins Bay wanted nothing to do with casework responsibilities and preferred to see themselves as cops on the beat. Collins Bay was the sort of prison where the frontier-justice mentality was firmly rooted. While some of the uniformed staff managed the prisoners with humour and intelligence, many others were more retrogressive in their approach. The response of some staff when prisoners injured themselves serves as a telling example. "Another safe release!" a guard might say after a prisoner committed suicide. At Collins Bay I first heard the morbid joke: "What's the first thing you do when you find a con hanging himself in his cell? Swing from his feet!" This type of disparaging prison culture always leads to a high rate of conflicts, and our case was no exception.

Collins Bay's administration also proved challenging. The warden had come from outside the region; I believe he had spent several years at national headquarters, and he had also worked in institutions out West. The deputy warden was new to the job when I arrived, the kind of guy generally regarded as an up-and-comer. He hit the ground running and was becoming known for his quick, and sometimes puzzling, decisions. I had not been at Collins Bay long when I received, through the deputy warden, a directive from national headquarters about the equal distribution of visible minorities in federal prisons. It explained the importance of maintaining an environment of cultural diversity, especially in the living areas, and cited problems experienced in some institutions when a particular ethnic group took over ranges and even entire units. In some Prairie prisons, for example, Aboriginal gangs dominated, and members of Toronto's black gangs were starting to come to federal prison. The directive called for administrators to pay attention to the concentration levels of any one ethnic group within a particular living area. The deputy warden noted that Unit 3 had an imbalance of black prisoners in a single range, specifically four more than in any other range. Of the thirty prisoners living in Unit 3, nine were black. The deputy warden ordered me to move two of them to another unit. He did not say which black prisoners to move; it did not matter.

The directive I had just been given seemed ill advised and potentially problematic. To prisoners, personal safety is paramount in a dangerous environment. Once prisoners find a cell on a range where they feel secure, they are reluctant to move. Because many prisoners considered Collins Bay a particularly dangerous place, the idea of moving to unknown territory would have been out of the question for some. And most were unlikely to move without a fight, which could inspire other prisoners to come to their defence. Just as when 1A Range at Joyceville became a solitary-confinement unit, relocating prisoners in Collins Bay could mean putting their lives in danger.

Many prisoners have perceived enemies in other units, stemming from any one of countless possibilities. The staff couldn't begin to keep track of the intrigues and conflicts among the prisoners that played out each day. Of course, the best option was to find two men who actually wanted to move, but no one in Unit 3 had made such a request, let alone two black men. Unit 3 was considered one of the two desirable units, having solid doors and relatively modern washrooms.

I promptly emailed the deputy warden about my concerns with possible repercussions and offered a number of alternatives. One was to factor race into the assignment of new prisoners. If new admissions were assigned to ensure equal distribution of visible minorities, it wouldn't take long to rectify any imbalances. Every week, new prisoners arrived and existing prisoners were released. My suggestions were rejected. The warden wanted the matter corrected that day, not later.

Okay, I thought, *he's the boss.*

I forwarded the email chain to the correctional managers and some other parties who would have to be in the know, advising them to find two black prisoners to move to Unit 2 or 4, whichever one Keith Speck decided. Keith and I also informed the prisoner committee of the plan, hoping to enlist the members' help. The problems we knew were likely to occur did. All the prisoners had been in their present digs for months or more, and none wanted to change units. The two prisoners who were eventually picked to move declared they would go to the hole if they were forced from their present cells. One wanted to call his lawyer. The prisoner committee was no help. Not surprisingly, we were called racist for moving black prisoners around instead of white prisoners. It was just one of those days.

In the end, these two prisoners did not move, not for any of the reasons I have cited. Because the officers in Units 2 and 3 didn't want these two prisoners moved, they dragged their feet. As well, the two black prisoners refused to pack up their belongings for the move, which meant the officers would have the tedious job of packing up the cell contents and documenting each and every item they touched. As a result, the moves were not completed that day, much to the frustration of some. The following day was a Friday, and it brought its own host of challenges, as Fridays in prison always seemed to do, including trying to move prisoners out of the hole to create space for the inevitable drunks and victims of assaults who would require solitary confinement over the weekend. By the following Monday, the deputy warden had stopped asking about it. He and the warden had moved on to the next directive from Ottawa.

This was my first experience working for a warden whose management style was to issue edicts instead of seeking input from the people paid to run the cellblocks. Never before had I felt so undervalued. The warden appeared to regard the ups and downs as inevitable. He was the first warden I knew who didn't attend the morning operations meeting; he held a separate, concurrent meeting in his office with the deputy warden and two assistant wardens. Keith and I were also welcome, but we had to choose between the wardens' meeting and the operations meeting, and we almost always felt the operations meeting was the more relevant option. The wardens' meeting did not focus on the current state of the prison but on whatever new directions were emerging from Ottawa, and my limited experience with them led me to conclude that all meetings in the Correctional Service were events where hours are lost, but minutes are kept, a variation on a popular notion.

Early one morning I sat in my office with a colleague, an older manager I knew to be above reproach. We were drinking coffee and watching the rain through the window. Most of the prisoners were still asleep. My colleague started to tell me a story about two Collins Bay unit managers, one responsible for the solitary-confinement unit.

An incident in the solitary-confinement unit resulted in physical injuries to a prisoner. Policy stipulated that the prison investigate and make recommendations to prevent similar incidents from happening in the future. The warden announced he was assigning one of the other unit managers to conduct the investigation. This meant a unit manager would be investigating a fellow unit manager, in the same prison where both worked. The problem should have been painfully obvious; maybe it was. The first tenet of investigations is detached objectivity. These two were of equal rank and would still be working closely together every day.

The unit manager completed the investigation and submitted it to the warden's office, with recommended improvements to existing practices. A couple of days later, he received a call from the warden's office, asking for an electronic copy.

The unit manager met the request. Sometime later, he received another call asking him to come up to the warden's office to sign the investigation, which was odd. The investigation had been signed and submitted about ten days before. According to my colleague, the unit manager asked what had happened to the hard copy he'd already signed and submitted. He was told only that the warden had printed off a new copy. He needed to sign it so the warden's office could send it to regional headquarters.

In the warden's office, a copy of the investigation was sitting on his assistant's desk, opened to the back of the report, ready for signing. The unit manager was no fool: over the protests of the warden's assistant, he picked up the report and started flipping through it, looking for changes to his text. It didn't take him long. A new recommendation had been inserted that urged the replacement of the current manager of the solitary-confinement unit.

I know a number of prison managers who would have signed that report. But this man refused. When the warden heard of the unit manager's refusal, he summoned him to his office and, allegedly, told him he would order him to sign it. The unit manager reportedly refused such an order. When he emerged, the document had still not been signed, and he was no longer a unit manager at Collins Bay. In fact, I was his replacement.

Sometime later, I happened to be having a beer with my friend Bob MacLean. We were talking about work, and he mentioned he was in the process of setting up an investigations branch at regional headquarters; it would be called performance assurance. Bob was bringing in some managers to work as full-time investigators. The chosen candidates would go to Ottawa to receive comprehensive training in the lawful conduct of investigations before assuming their duties. This could be what I was looking for. I was wearying of the day-to-day responsibilities of prison life. Running two units at once meant twice as many grievances (staff and prisoners), twice as many unit meetings, twice as many parole officer reports to read and quality control, twice as many problems, twice as many prisoners who needed to speak to us, and, probably worst of all, twice as many emails. Keith and I worked tirelessly, and our high level of co-operation and the help of some very dedicated colleagues, including my unit assistant, Vicky Padley, allowed us to succeed most of the time. But I told Keith that I'd had enough. I was tired of running two units, but most of all, I was tired of working for this particular warden.

The next day, I went to the deputy warden's office and told him everything I thought Collins Bay was doing wrong. I also made suggestions for improving the warden's knowledge of how to run a prison effectively. The next time I saw the warden, it was clear he had heard of my constructive feedback. I was not concerned. The deputy commissioner had approved my appointment as one of the new performance assurance investigators. For the first time in my career, I was going to join the pie-chart crowd at regional headquarters, something I had sworn I would never do.

When I left Collins Bay after one year, that jelly doughnut was still on the wall, a symbol of the general state of affairs. The prospect of doing something entirely new and different exhilarated me. I would be working with talented people, many I already knew, who had come in from other sites to help get this new initiative off the ground. The deputy commissioner's frustration over late and poorly completed investigation reports from the various prisons had led him to create a centralized department to handle all investigations and nothing else. The training my colleagues and I received in Ottawa was first rate. I learned a great deal doing this specialized work. All of us had earned good reputations in the local prisons and were seen as professional and objective, which made our work easier. We would come in after the dust had settled and begin to analyze exactly what had gone wrong.

After a process of quality control, and the proper observation of all legal entitlements for those involved, we would present our findings to the deputy commissioner. The warden of the prison under investigation also attended our presentation. The written reports our small group completed were far superior to the usual fare, and our on-time completion rates were much higher. Once again, it appeared as if I had landed in a very cozy spot. I did not have prisoners or staff wanting to speak to me innumerable times a day. I was free to work uninterrupted, and to do it my way. I had a supervisor who respected me, and I was able to see how other prisons functioned in times of crisis and recommend improvements.

I was in the job for approximately ten months. I chaired many investigations that involved more than one investigator and two that included community board members, people outside the prison service. One concerned a serious assault during a major disturbance at Millhaven. The severity of the victim's injuries necessitated a three-person investigation board, one of whom was chief of health care in a local prison. She accessed and analyzed the medical records. The other member was someone from the community, a man with, I believe, a background in education. He proved his value almost immediately when, at our first meeting, he voiced a question that he said had nagged at his conscience since he first reviewed the preparatory materials.

"Rob, I am concerned about how long it took the officers to help the prisoner who had been stabbed." From the perspective of an ordinary citizen, it made sense to question something that seemed odd.

The timeline we had established showed the prisoner had been stabbed and was in medical distress for almost forty-five minutes before officers entered the range and removed him to safety and for medical assistance. The videotapes from the security cameras on the range showed that during those forty-five minutes, the other maximum-security prisoners had refused to enter their cells. Unless they could be convinced to do so, no one could safely enter the range to provide assistance to the injured prisoner. The stabbed prisoner made it into his cell, where he was presumably bleeding to death; he could not be seen in the video. The officers on the scene did everything humanly possible to get the other prisoners to co-operate. They made multiple attempts to reason with the unruly mob before finally, as a last resort, spraying the range with tear gas, which only seemed to make the prisoners more defiant. They pulled wet T-shirts over their mouths and noses and continued to walk the range and taunt the officers as though asking, *Is that all you got?* I knew from my time at Millhaven that spraying the prisoners with gas usually had this result. Fortunately, the injured prisoner made a complete recovery from his injuries. Our final report praised the officers for their patience and professionalism under near-impossible conditions; it was well earned.

Working as a full-time investigator was a much-needed respite from the pandemonium of prison life. But the truth was, once I was no longer tired, I began to feel restless again. I missed the prisoners and the staff, and the excitement. My office suddenly seemed too quiet. There were no angry people demanding to see me, no one asking for advice. I found it harder to feel enthusiasm for the investigations I was involved in. I began to notice a recurring theme in the resolution portion of these reviews, which left me questioning their true value to the system in its efforts to improve. No matter how glaring the missteps, the warden concerned would shrug or, in one particular case, tell a golf joke.

I arrived at regional headquarters one day, turned on my computer, called "Good morning" toward my colleagues' offices, and opened my email. A message caught my eye: notice of an impending shake-up of senior managers in the Ontario region. I read on. As I scanned the names, all persons I knew, I saw the name Monty Bourke. My former deputy warden from Joyceville was going to Kingston Penitentiary as the new warden. If what I had heard about Kingston Penitentiary was true, he was not going to be very happy with what he saw in his new prison. In fact, knowing him as I did, I almost gloated at the thought of him kicking butts and striking terror in the hearts of the lazy and indifferent. Now, that would be a real challenge. After all, I had my energy back. It was time to work with staff and prisoners again. It was what I was best at, and despite the headaches, I liked it better than any other job I'd held. I sent Monty Bourke an email with the subject line "In Search of Excellence," the title of a book we had both read and liked. I told him I was working at regional headquarters and needed a challenge. He took me up on my offer.

9 Kingston Penitentiary

Many considered Kingston Penitentiary the worst prison in the Ontario region, and possibly the whole country. In 1989 the warden became so frustrated with the unprofessionalism of the uniformed staff that he commissioned an inquiry. In 2013 Daniel Schwartz reported for CBC News that the commission described Kingston Pen as a "dumping ground for bad guards" where "some guards terrorize[ed] fellow staff and inmates." The commission apparently didn't have much effect, because the stories about Kingston endured. The stories convinced me that no sane person would willingly work at Kingston Pen.

Approximately four years before I arrived, an incident drew considerable public attention to the Correctional Service of Canada and this particular prison. On October 24, 1993, a twenty-three-year-old black prisoner named Robert Gentles died after five guards physically restrained him in his cell. On that day, Kingston Penitentiary was in a lockdown. As is often the case during lockdowns, many of the prisoners were acting out in various ways and attempting to disrupt the already difficult situation. On 3G Range Robert Gentles had his radio turned up to a high volume. Guards ordered him three times to turn the volume down; he ignored them. Someone decided to send Gentles to the hole as punishment. First, guards sprayed him with mace three times, and then five guards entered the cell. The only people who really know what happened that day are those five guards. Gentles died, and a coroner's inquest found that he died of "asphyxia associated with multiple factors, including the effects of Freon 113 (the mace), restraint in a prone position, chest compression, and suffocation."

The coroner ruled Gentles's death accidental. I believe the coroner's verdict was right, but that does not mean Gentles's death was unavoidable. Many of the inquest recommendations, published in "Gentles, Robert Wayne: Inquest, March 30th-June 24th, 1999," spoke to the systemic cultural issues identified in this book: the use of force, the abuse of power, and the blue wall. Among other things, the coroner's jury recommended, "new officers, after initial in-class training, be on-the-job trained on an ongoing basis during their first year of work. They should be brought back frequently for training during their first year with respect to ethical dilemmas experienced on the job." The jurors hoped that training in ethical dilemmas would address the problem of "the officer's code," where guards, who might in other context report aberrant behaviour, succumbed to the pressure to protect one another. The jury further recommended that the union "encourage its members to report any illegal acts or harassment," noting "their obligations as peace officers should take priority over labour solidarity." According to one of the coroner's comments in the inquest, if the labour union helped or protected members from harassment by other members, the "ratting norm might be weakened."

The inquest's findings also noted the five guards who entered Robert Gentles's cell that fatal day had conferred with one another before they wrote their situation reports, in contravention of a 1991 directive that required employees to write these reports independently. The inquest jury recommended that situation reports have an attention box added to warn officers to fill out reports independently and that reports should be completed in a supervised room.

The jurors also called for representatives from CSC, the Ministry of the Solicitor General, and independent community members to form a committee to review the use of Kingston Penitentiary. Both management and staff raised "serious concerns" about the "working environment" at the prison. "In particular," the coroner wrote, "because of its austere and ancient architecture, we were told that Kingston Penitentiary is not conducive to good correctional practices. It was recommended, in fact, that the utilization of the Penitentiary be reviewed."

Finally, the coroner's jury recommended increased independent civilian oversight. The coroner noted the Arbour Report had made a similar recommendation, which the Solicitor General at the time had rejected.

This was the context in which I found myself when I arrived, willingly, in late 1997. I would find it a far worse prison to work in than I could have imagined. Kingston Pen first opened in 1835. Despite the prison having adopted the various titles and departments of modern-day corrections, I did not see a shred of evidence to suggest the day-to-day operations had evolved beyond whatever their original goals were. I do not intend to disparage those who preceded me at Kingston. I, too, would find this prison a greater challenge than any of the jobs I had previously held. I arrived as part of a team of new faces: a new warden, a new deputy warden, and two new unit managers, including me. Our arrival drew much attention, as it was understood we were going into a very hostile environment — and we were going to try to clean it up.

When we arrived, no one seemed truly invested in the daily supervision of this very dangerous prison. Current staff had apparently adopted a get-in-and-get-out-quick approach to surviving their "time." Many of the correctional managers were former front-line officers who had moved up. This meant they were friends with the guards they supervised, although I use the word "supervised" loosely. The presence of a new management team seemingly did nothing to encourage these correctional managers to regain control of the guards. On the contrary, my impression was that a few actively worked against us. Perhaps not surprisingly, many staff took offence to the notion of someone coming into the institution they had worked in for years, determined to clean it up. They had seen this before, more than once. Each of the new brooms eventually left, and conditions returned to their natural state. I couldn't blame them if they believed no one could change Kingston Penitentiary.

My team members were familiar to me. The new warden, of course, was Monty Bourke. My high opinion of him and his leadership had led me to Canada's most notorious prison. The new deputy warden, my direct supervisor, and the other new unit manager were men I knew from Joyceville. Another man I had known at Joyceville was going to oversee the general security operations of the prison. He was reputedly a tireless worker, and he had worked at Kingston Penitentiary in his younger days; thus, we had a field expert to help us find our way in this new environment where we might not get much help from the current staff. The third and final unit manager, already on staff, was a gregarious woman who had spent much of her career in uniform. When she was promoted to the level of unit manager, she brought along the same crude mannerisms that made her popular with some staff and prisoners at the beginning of her career. I had known her for a while, and I sometimes smiled at her outlandish behaviour and the effect it had on those around her.

Our first order of business was to divide the prison between the three unit managers. This, of course, meant dividing the cellblocks, the prisoners and the uniformed guards, the parole officers, the correctional managers, the clerical staff, and so on. The other new unit manager was assigned to run the temporary detention unit for prisoners returning to custody and one of the maximum-security ranges, Upper E. The gregarious woman asked to continue running the solitary-confinement unit, a particularly nasty corner of an out-dated and filthy place. I was asked for my preferences and expressed none. I felt confident that my approach to dealing with prisoners and officers would seem new to many, and I had high hopes for a favourable reaction. I was made the unit manager of the four-range maximum-security unit: lower and upper F and G, containing approximately 120 prisoners. The parole officers assigned to my unit were experienced and smart. My assistant, Irene, was kind, insightful, and dedicated.

In the first few weeks, the new management team made considerable efforts to be visible around the prison. I spent a lot of time on the ranges, talking to the officers and the prisoners, if they felt like stopping me for a question. I walked every range and looked in every cell. I could not believe the disregard for the rules. Most of the prisoners had hung blankets on the fronts of their cells, blocking them from view. Prisoners' cells housed stolen office chairs and office supplies, one had a sixty-six-centimetre TV on a wheeled stand — obviously taken from the prison school. Another had a twenty-five-metre extension cord. Others had homemade headboards and tables — Ty Conn, of course, would use just such a headboard in his escape from Kingston. Nobody seemed to care.

The reason for this complete lack of engagement was immediately obvious to me. The previous administration had approved a work schedule for the uniformed staff, including the correctional managers, which had them working very few days a month but extraordinarily long hours when they did. This roster was called two-fours, and it required the uniformed guards and their supervisors to work two consecutive sixteen-hour shifts. After working these two shifts, officers would be off-duty for four or five days. The officers and their supervisors were so exhausted from the duration of their shifts that they had little energy to engage with prisoners about rule violations, contraband in their cells, or anything else. Even if they were motivated, the long breaks between shifts made it difficult for them to know what was going on in the prison; they had no sense of continuity.

The fact that none of the correctional managers, except one, was processing prisoner charges submitted by the staff simply exacerbated the problem. Staff members who experienced prisoner threats or verbal abuse or who observed a breach of the rules were expected to submit a written charge. The correctional manager with jurisdiction was supposed to conduct a minor court proceeding that included interviewing the prisoner and make a finding of guilt or innocence. Prisoners found guilty faced sanctions, such as financial penalties or loss of privileges. An accumulation of institutional charges could cause a prisoner to lose support from his parole officer or a coveted job. As the only method that front-line guards had of exerting their authority, processing prisoner charges was crucial to the smooth running of the prison. But at Kingston, prisoners learned quickly they could get away with a lot.

Perhaps the officers felt that writing charges was a complete waste of time because nobody would read their reports. The solitary-confinement cell space was at such a premium that even if they had reported glaring misconducts, such as taunting officers and ignoring orders, the prisoners would go unpunished. Many guards simply turned a blind eye to the rule infractions they saw every day. They became reluctant to go on the ranges, fearing verbal threats and challenges to their authority. In short, the prison was a free-for-all, with one exception: vigilante justice. Prisoners who were unfortunate enough to be removed from their range and taken to the hole were at times subjected to unofficial sanctions such as rough treatment and verbal threats.

Not surprisingly, then, the participation of uniformed officers in case planning with the prisoners assigned to them was non-existent. Too many of these officers simply rode out the two consecutive sixteen-hour shifts with as little effort as possible and then enjoyed their four days off—longer if they worked in a sick day or two. One of the first things we had to do was remove this now very popular roster. This change put us into immediate conflict with the union, but we had no alternative. We replaced the favoured roster with a conventional schedule containing more days and shorter hours of work. The guards' reaction was, for the most part, predictably negative. A flurry of staff grievances intended to make our lives difficult ensued, and many officers used their sick leave to exacerbate the challenges we faced in trying to improve the day-to-day operations of this volatile environment.

As the manager of the maximum-security unit, I soon discovered that little to no communication occurred between the prisoners and many of the guards. Communication is the conduit that prevents bigger problems from developing, so this was a particularly dangerous situation. In most prisons range representatives are often used to resolve problems before they escalate. This was the case at Joyceville when the Sherriff locked a prisoner in the hole unjustly and the other prisoners refused to go to work without seeing me first. At Kingston Pen, however, this same problem was potentially much more perilous. Many of the men in my unit were extremely damaged, suffering from mental illness and prone to explosive behaviour — another reason the guards had adopted the habit of remaining in the control post whenever problems started.

One of the first new things I did was to begin visiting the ranges regularly and talking to the guards and prisoners. Their reactions made it clear to me that they were not used to having a manager to talk to, face to face, about the ongoing problems. Prisoners who used to submit a written grievance on everything began to wait for my regular visits to plead their cases. Many of the more explosive prisoners consumed much of my time. Talking to someone in authority who was willing to listen when they were losing control often mollified them. The officers began calling my office to see if I could drop by the unit, which I always did. But it became painfully obvious that the dysfunctional culture of Kingston Pen was too deeply entrenched for my efforts to have much impact. As well, the prisoners' volatile natures made it difficult to practise dynamic security. Some were so unpredictable that it was often more like managing a mental health unit. Despite anti-psychotic medication, Wilson, for example, would scream at and threaten the officers at the slightest provocation. He was repeatedly transferred to the Regional Treatment Centre, the system's mental health unit, before returning to Kingston a few days later, calm and composed until the cycle began again.

I remember being called down to the unit one day because a young prisoner named Ben was freaking out and threatening to kill the officers who had just searched his cell. He accused them of tearing up a picture of his grandmother. I entered the range alone and the prisoner in question flew at me, screaming and waving a torn black-and-white photograph in my face. Tears streamed from his eyes, and he was alarmingly close to striking me. I maintained my composure and assured him I would get to the bottom of the matter.

Both officers denied any knowledge of the photo or how it had been destroyed. The other prisoners were coming back for lunch and the noon count. They headed in groups up the stairs and through the barrier. I spotted the chair of the prisoner committee, a fellow named Jason I had known at Joyceville many years before. I pulled him aside and explained the situation. I couldn't believe that the guards would tear up the picture, and yet here was this prisoner going berserk and holding the torn picture for all to see.

When I told Jason which prisoner was making the allegation, I could see in his eyes that Ben and his antics were not new to him.

"Give me a minute with him on his range, and then I'll come and see you," Jason said.

Jason took Ben into his cell for about two minutes before coming back outside the barrier and motioning me toward the stairs. In a low voice he told me Ben had just admitted that he himself had torn the picture in a moment of rage, after finding out his cell had been searched. Realizing he had destroyed the only picture he had of his grandmother, Ben was now in a full-blown meltdown. Jason suggested we leave Ben in his cell for the afternoon, and I thanked him for his help. Despite having a few successes like this one, the prison remained random and chaotic whenever good managers were not around.

Perhaps the most tragic figure in my unit was a young prisoner, Mitchell, who was serving a life sentence. His unpredictable behaviour made it difficult for him to find and hold a prison job. This meant that he had no money to buy cigarettes, so other inmates paid him in cash or tobacco to hold their drugs or weapons or collect their debts. I was called to the unit late one afternoon. During the four o'clock count, a prisoner requested solitary confinement for protection. When he was taken to the hole and strip-searched, guards found two stab wounds in his lower abdomen. He was taken to the health-care unit, where he admitted someone had stabbed him. He also told the nurse who treated him that another prisoner on the range had been stabbed, one who probably would not come forward on his own. By this time, the count was completed and the prisoners had been released from their cells, according to routine, and with all of them out on the range none of the officers wanted to venture inside the barrier to look for the other victim.

I went on the range to explain to the men, wondering why recreation hadn't started, that an injured prisoner might be in their midst. I asked them to return to their cells for a visual inspection, promising that we'd resume the usual routine as soon as possible. After much grumbling, they complied. Because two officers were in health care with the injured prisoner, I offered to do the range walk with the remaining officer so we could visually inspect each prisoner for any injuries consistent with an assault or stabbing. I took the upper tier. At each cell I asked the occupant to show me his hands, front and back. Then I asked him to lift his shirt and turn around. I only made it about one-third of the way down the cells before I came to a prisoner, about five feet tall. When he lifted his shirt, I could see abrasions on his ribs and what looked like a single puncture wound to his side. He held my gaze, saying nothing. I moved on to the next cell without speaking and continued to the end of the tier to avoid identifying him to other prisoners as having co-operated with me.

With everyone still locked up, we removed this prisoner, and he, too, went to health care. He told us that Mitchell had stabbed them both. I walked down to Mitchell's cell and asked if he would come off the range and talk to me outside the barrier, in private. Mitchell was highly agitated. He said he would not leave his cell unless I promised him he could come back after we talked. By this time the warden and the deputy warden had caught wind of the trouble and were on the landing outside the unit area. I went out to bring them up to speed.

"I think I know who the perpetrator is," I said. "I was just talking to him, and he has agreed to come out and talk to me."

"That's good," the deputy warden responded. "If you can convince him to come off the range I'll have some officers waiting to grab him and take him to the hole."

"I'd rather not do that yet," I said. "I've given him my word that I'll allow him to return to his cell if he comes out to talk to me. I said this in front of the whole range. Right now he's like a coiled spring, and I would rather try to calm him down before we grab him — if that's what we decide to do." Both men looked at me. "If I give him my word to get him out here and then have officers waiting to jump him, my credibility with these men will be gone," I explained. "We could find ourselves with even bigger problems than we're facing right now, if the others react." As always, my objective was to ensure the safe running of the prison.

The warden agreed. I went down to open Mitchell's cell door, and he followed me off the range, all the while yelling to the other prisoners that Rob Clark had given his word not to "guzzle" him, a prisoner term for guards seizing and restraining a prisoner without warning. His vocal exit convinced me within minutes that Mitchell was the perpetrator. True to my word, I walked him back to his cell and locked the door. Then I informed him that we would have to place him in the hole until we completed our investigation. As I expected, he didn't take the news well.

When I returned with several officers a short while later, I told him he needed to co-operate but I would stay with him for the duration, so he had nothing to fear. I urged him to stay calm and gave him my word that if he hadn't been involved in the stabbings, I would return him to his cell and apologize. He agreed to be handcuffed and removed. He demanded to take his tobacco, and I agreed. I suspect he presumed his two victims would not rat on him and that he had a good chance of getting away with the stabbings.

While I negotiated with Mitchell, I had the sense someone was watching me. I turned and noticed that Ty Conn, who was still a prisoner at the time, was standing in the middle of his cell, staring at me. I nodded to him. He continued to stare. In retrospect, I wonder if he had already begun hiding escape paraphernalia in his cell and was terrified by the possibility that we might decide to search all the cells on the range.

When we got to the hole, Mitchell placed his tobacco on a chair and complied with the procedure of a strip search. I informed him of his rights while in solitary confinement and that he could call a lawyer. It seemed we'd managed the whole transfer without any violence when Mitchell's eyes grew big.

"Rob," he demanded, "where's my fucking tobacco, man?" I looked at the chair where he'd placed it. It had vanished.

None of the guards who were present would meet my eyes. They stood silent, glaring at Mitchell.

"Who picked up the tobacco?" I asked. No one answered me. In fact, they acted as if they had not heard me. And then I knew: they wanted a piece of this deranged young man. They knew Mitchell, and they knew that if his tobacco disappeared he was likely to freak out. If he freaked out, they would have to use force on him — lots of force.

"Listen to me," I said to Mitchell, who was beginning to vibrate with rage. "Go in the cell. Don't cause any problems, because you can't win. I'll see the range rep when I go back to the unit. I'm sure he'll be able to collect some tobacco for you."

Mitchell dropped his head and entered the cell without a word.

I thought I had seen it all, but the possibility of officers taking tobacco to provoke a mentally ill patient and seemingly justify a potential beating was more than I could fathom. I later learned from a staff informant that one of the officers in my unit was in the habit of planting homemade weapons to find in a search of the cells of prisoners he didn't like. Once a prisoner was found in possession of a lethal weapon the outcome was always the same: long-term solitary confinement, which could only lead to further mental and emotional deterioration. Needless to say, a prisoner's accusation that guards had set him up would not be taken seriously by anyone.

I would run into Mitchell several years later, after I had left Kingston but returned to complete an investigation. In the intervening years, he tried unsuccessfully to hang himself in his cell. He had permanent ligature marks on his neck and behind his ears. The lack of oxygen to his brain made his eyes permanently and severely blood shot, and slowed his speech. Listlessness and a lack of comprehension about where and even who he was supplanted his former volatility.

I moved on from my position managing the maximum-security unit at Kingston Pen not long after I rejected the plan to transfer Ty Conn to medium security. My attempts to bring sanity to an insane environment were exhausting me. Working long hours trying to improve the status quo in such an establishment began to take a toll; stressed, I got in the habit of having a few drinks at night to help me get to sleep. I decided to take a period of extended leave to recharge my batteries.

As I embarked on my leave, I remembered a day not long after I had first arrived at Kingston Pen. I was walking around the penitentiary, visiting all the security posts. I'd learned this was the best way to see how the place actually ran, and it was a good way to meet the officers. Many staff, especially guards, were not used to managers coming around for no other reason than to say hi and check in, and they appreciated the effort. When I arrived at the security control post for lower G Range that day, one female officer, in her late twenties or early thirties, unlocked the door and let me into the control post, which overlooked the entire range from a central, raised position. I shook her hand and introduced myself as the new unit manager.

Even though this was our first meeting, this officer probably knew I was part of the new management that headquarters believed Kingston sorely needed. She seemed friendly and happy to talk about the challenges of her job. As was my habit, I listened more than I talked. When it seemed appropriate, I offered my own view on things. I wanted her to know I had first-hand experience with her job and appreciated it was difficult. I asked her what she thought would help Kingston Penitentiary to run better; I had asked others the same question.

Instead of naming one of innumerable flaws, the officer replied, "I was going to transfer out of KP, but I've decided to wait six months to see if anything changes around here."

"What changes?" I asked.

She simply shrugged. "Everything!"

On that day, I left Kingston Pen and went to see my family doctor. He took one look at me and could see that I was not the same man who normally showed up for his yearly physical. We talked for about thirty minutes and he indicated that he was going to place me on six months' medical leave. As I left his office he offered one more piece of advice: "I don't want you even driving by that place!"

When I finally did return, I don't recall that I saw that same female officer again.

10 Correct Zero

I returned to Kingston Penitentiary from six months' leave as the assistant warden responsible for correctional programs and was given a large office just down the hall from the warden. My new assignment put me in charge of the prison school, library, gym, and yard; the various social programs, including Alcoholics Anonymous, the Black Prisoners and Friends Association, and the John Howard Society; the prison chapel; and, of course, the rehabilitation programs department: substance abuse, anger management, and cognitive skills training, to name a few.

I spent much of my first few weeks touring around, meeting all the staff who worked under the correctional programs umbrella. With the weight of running the maximum-security unit lifted off my shoulders, I met some talented and hard-working employees I had never known existed. The officers who delivered the rehabilitation programs at Kingston Pen were among the best and most dedicated employees it was my privilege to work with, and my new assistant, Carol, made taking over the correctional programs portfolio relatively easy.

Corrections Canada tries to encourage prisoners to maintain family contact, among other things, and this includes the opportunity to participate in private family visits. Approved family members are admitted to spend the weekend, typically seventy-two hours, in a setting away from the usual running of the main prison. In some prisons, these visits take place in mobile homes, while other institutions have built permanent cottage-like dwellings separate from the main institution. All potential visitors are security cleared first, and their criminal records and any previous history of drug use or trafficking are reviewed prior to approval. It is as close to a normal home environment as can be expected under the circumstances. Staff regularly conduct visual inspections of all participants in a family visit, and the prisoners must exit the unit for every routine prisoner count. Each unit contains a telephone linked directly to the main security office, and any family member can summon assistance at any time, should the need arise. In my experience, these visits were largely problem-free and of tremendous benefit to the prisoners, their families, and the smooth running of the institution.

Not all applications are approved. For instance, a prisoner with a history of domestic violence is unlikely to secure approval for a private family visit, even if his spouse is willing. But notorious prisoners like Paul Bernardo are eligible to apply, and Bernardo's parents regularly visited their son in Kingston Pen. Eventually he applied for a private family visit, and his application was approved. A date was scheduled.

Prisoners whose family visit requests are approved can order specialty foods for the visit, if they have the money in their institutional accounts. They can also select DVDs to have available in the trailer, including kids' videos for any children who might come. Most prisoners purchase a disposable camera from the prisoner canteen so they can record whatever memories are created over the three days. When the visit is over, the camera is turned over to social development staff, who arrange to have the film printed at the prisoner's expense. Staff examine the pictures to ensure that nothing inappropriate was photographed. Sexually explicit pictures of one's girlfriend may well be precious keepsakes to a prisoner, but perhaps a sign of something else to the prison psychologist, depending on the prisoner's criminal history.

Shortly after Bernardo had his private family visit, the warden summoned me to his office. After a brief chat concerning the state of affairs in the prison, Monty opened his desk drawer and removed a small envelope of developed photos. He pushed the folder across the desk. "Have you seen these?"

I had not. Inside were pictures of Paul Bernardo and his parents, taken during his private family visit. I began to flip through them.

"Let me know what you think," the warden said.

I came to the one I knew I was supposed to catch. The picture showed one of the most heinous criminals in Canadian history in a seemingly typical domestic setting, eating dinner with his parents, smirking and making a rude gesture at the camera. I looked at the picture for a moment longer before finishing my perusal of the stack.

Monty gave me a familiar knowing look. "What's your opinion?"

"My opinion is that the media would love to get its hands on that picture."

"I think so, too." He rested his hands on his desk in front of him. "I need you to do something for me."

Monty told me he had grave reservations about permitting Bernardo to keep the photographs in his cell. Only a few years before, someone at Kingston Penitentiary had provided a videotape of Bernardo in his cell to Global News, likely for a price. The network featured the unauthorized tape on its six p.m. national broadcast. Everyone — including Bernardo himself — believed they know who sold it, but the Correctional Service of Canada could never actually hold this employee accountable for what was a dismissible offence. Even though management, too, had no doubt as to the culprit's identity, not one person was willing to say, on record, "Yes, I saw him."

"I'd like you to meet with Bernardo," the warden said. "You need to convince him it's not in his best interests to have these pictures in his cell. I'm afraid one of them could be found in a search, and someone might think it would be worth money to the media."

I had to agree. It would not be good for the Canadian public to see this widely hated serial murderer and rapist enjoying time with his parents in prison, especially when the families of Leslie Mahaffy, Kristen French, and Tammy Homolka would forever feel the pain of an absence at their tables. "I'll look after it," I said.

Corrections Canada was very concerned about keeping Paul Bernardo safe and alive for the duration of his sentence. He could not be removed from his cell and taken outside the solitary-confinement unit, unless every prisoner in the entire penitentiary was locked up. I had to send an email to a number of people who needed to know of my plan to speak with Bernardo so they could adjust their schedules, if necessary, to accommodate the interview. It made sense for the interview to take place at a time when all prisoners would customarily be locked in their cells, and the meeting was accordingly scheduled for the following day, during the noon count. My colleagues advised me that meetings with Bernardo normally took place in the security boardroom, a rarely used room close to the solitary-confinement unit, and thus a shorter (and safer) walk for Bernardo.

The next day I waited in the security boardroom at a quarter to twelve, the package of photographs on the table. The security division offices nearby were empty, everyone having gone to lunch. I had never spoken to Paul Bernardo before, and I felt somewhat anxious about how I might handle seeing him face to face and having a difficult conversation with him. I knew about the unconscionable crimes he committed with his wife. In fact, I knew someone who had served on Bernardo's jury and who, despite professional help, never fully recovered his peace of mind after the trial. Treating Bernardo fairly, as I would any other prisoner, would severely test my professional objectivity, but to behave otherwise would betray my values.

I heard the unmistakable sound of the large door at the end of the hall opening and officers' voices I recognized. The sound of heavy boot steps grew closer. There was a brief silence and then a knock on the door. It opened and an officer named Craig greeted me with a big smile.

"Hey, Rob, you waiting for Bernardo?"

I could see past Craig — to a blond man with a young, almost boyish face, looking intently at me over Craig's shoulder. Behind Bernardo was another officer I knew and liked. Craig stepped aside, and both officers came into the boardroom with Bernardo. He was in handcuffs, like anyone else being escorted outside of the solitary-confinement unit. The officers removed the cuffs and said they would hang around outside. Once the door was closed, I introduced myself as assistant warden of correctional programs and gestured for Bernardo to sit. I sat opposite him at the large table. He looked around but not for long; he had been in this room before, sometimes interviewed by police detectives. He noticed the photographs on the table.

"Are those my pictures?" he asked.

"Yes, they are. That's what I want to talk to you about."

"Can I see them?"

I nodded, and he removed them from the package, going through them one by one. I waited silently. I had already decided that convincing him to leave the pictures with me would have a much better chance of success if he looked at each of them to his satisfaction. After about five minutes he put them back in the package. He gazed at me more closely now. Perhaps he recognized me as one of the managers who visited solitary.

"What do you want to see me about?"

"The warden asked me to speak to you." I leaned back a bit in my chair. I generally did this to make my authority less explicit and create a more relaxed atmosphere when speaking with prisoners, especially if I was trying to persuade them to go along with something I thought they might oppose. In my experience, many prisoners would co-operate as long as they felt they had a genuine say in the matter. This is a more time-consuming approach, of course, than simply declaring, for instance, "I'm going to keep your pictures."

Every prison employee who deals directly with prisoners has a reputation. My own, I am told, was one of fairness, at least in the eyes of most, so the idea of trying to bully Paul Bernardo into giving up his pictures (to which all prisoners have a right) had not occurred to me. I explained the conversation between the warden and me, expressing my own concern that someone could take his pictures and sell them to the media, even though I genuinely believed that 99 per cent of officers wouldn't consider such a thing.

Bernardo resisted the idea. He, too, adopted a relaxed posture as he argued with me about his rights and his pictures. I suspected he had decided this chat in the boardroom with me was a pleasant change from his cramped cell, to which he would return as soon as the interview was over. Eventually, our discussion came around to the Global News caper; Bernardo brought it up.

"You guys didn't hear me complaining when…sold that tape to Global News!" (He named the officer rumoured to be responsible.)

In truth, I don't recall much of the actual words we exchanged that day, but I do know the interview lasted about an hour. And in the end, Paul Bernardo reluctantly handed me the package with his family pictures inside. I promised him that I would take them to the warden's office, where they would go into the safe, and that the next time his parents came to the institution, I would bring the photos down for his parents to take with them when they left.

Later that evening at home, I reflected upon the events of the day and the interview with Bernardo. I had always prided myself on my objectivity, and I took particular satisfaction in maintaining my professionalism, even with the most reprehensible prisoners. As I contemplated, I looked at my children. My son caught my eye and made a funny face. My daughter was doing her homework. She looked up and smiled. I couldn't help but think of the parents of Leslie Mahaffy, Kristen French, and Tammy Homolka. Their love for their children would be no less than my own. I thought about the other women Bernardo had raped and the irreparable harm he had inflicted on all these people.

I considered how I would I feel about a person who had killed my child. I knew the truth, and the hypocrisy of my views struck me. I always preached detached compassion as the best way to manage a prison environment safely, but suddenly I was at a loss to justify the moral superiority I took to work every day.

This was the beginning of another especially difficult time in my career. During my year as assistant warden, I learned a great deal about correctional programs and the people who do this very important work. Ted McKay, a shop instructor, never wavered in his composure and friendly, easygoing persona, despite having worked for over thirty years in an environment like Kingston Penitentiary. He made a positive difference every day inside the prison. But if Ted McKay inspired me, many other staff members did not.

One evening, a meeting of the prison's John Howard Society went awry. Meetings of the various self-help groups were usually well organized, and civic-minded people from the community often volunteered their involvement. The prisoners who participated did so on their own time.

The day following the fumbled meeting, the supervisor of recreation came to my office as soon as I arrived at work. A big man with glasses and an infectious good nature, he always seemed a bit apologetic when he came to see me, which was often. He was carrying a sign-up sheet for one of the groups. He plunked down in my chair with his usual look of resignation.

"What's up?" I asked.

He removed his glasses and began cleaning them on his shirt. "Last night we had a problem with the John Howard meeting. Have a look at this."

As soon as I looked at the sign-up sheet, I realized it had far too many prisoners' names on it. He raised his hand as if to halt my questions.

"Here's what happened, according to the guys I talked to this morning," he said.

It started out as a routine evening. Some prisoners were in the gym, others in their cells or on the ranges. One of the evening's scheduled activities was a meeting of the prison's John Howard Society group. This particular meeting was going to be special: outside guests were coming in, and coffee and doughnuts would be provided. A list of approved prisoner attendees had been compiled, because there had been incidents of more aggressive prisoners crashing the party if they saw coffee and doughnuts. On this particular evening, however, another drawing card was that the outside guests included two female Queen's University students, new volunteers at the John Howard Society offices in Kingston. A crowd of onlookers began to form outside the meeting-room window.

A prisoner used cigarettes to bribe the opportunistic staff member on duty in exchange for admission to the meeting. Having witnessed this ploy, other prisoners stepped forward, cigarettes in hand. The meeting fell into disarray. The new arrivals helped themselves to coffee and then moved in to monopolize the conversations with the female visitors. The new volunteers, not knowing any better, were only too happy to chat with anyone who appeared in need of a sympathetic ear.

In spite of my best efforts, and the efforts of others, Kingston Penitentiary did not change much. We instituted some new policies and made ourselves more visible than many previous management teams, but in the end, it was still Kingston Pen. I once jokingly remarked to the warden over a beer that the best solution would be to remove the people and blow up the building.

"There is genuine evil in the mortar that's holding the blocks together," I said. "I sometimes feel like we're on a galley ship with three hundred other slaves, but only about ten of us are rowing. Every time I look at the others they start rowing, but as soon as I look away, they stop again and just sit and watch us."

Toward the end of my tenure as the assistant warden of correctional programs, Monty Bourke asked me to investigate allegations that the chair of the prisoner committee, a prisoner named Hunter, sexually assaulted prisoners. Kingston Pen had recently acquired a new deputy warden who was anxious to reduce the number of prisoners seeking the protection of the solitary-confinement unit, and he had involved Hunter in discussions on how to reverse the trend.

Hunter had suggested placing some of the protective-custody prisoners on or near his range, where they would be safe under his protection; his profile was sufficient to discourage other prisoners from hurting these vulnerable men. Several prisoners were convinced to leave the relative safety of the hole. For a while it seemed they were going to be all right. Before long, however, first one, and then two, and then more asked to return to the hole. In exchange for a guaranteed transfer out of Kingston Penitentiary, one of these prisoners made a statement that prompted the investigation.

The deputy warden had allowed Hunter to speak privately with prisoners while they were still in protective custody, which was when he allegedly threatened their lives and the lives of their family members if they didn't agree to leave solitary confinement. He convinced them the guards were in his hip pocket and would murder them if Hunter asked. Once the prisoners were out of protective custody and accessible to Hunter, he sexually assaulted them. Hunter's cell was at the far end of the range, out of the staff's view. One prisoner told me that Hunter forced him and others to attend his cell to perform oral sex.

When I asked these prisoners why they believed Hunter's claim to wield such power over the guards that he could have prisoners murdered, they told me Hunter knew everything about them — even the addresses of their family members. A prisoner named David told me that Hunter actually showed him a report from David's own file that contained his offences and the home address of his grandmother, David's only surviving relative. David alleged that Hunter threatened to send guards to kill her if he did not comply with Hunter's sexual demands. I can recall David's trembling hands, a cigarette between his fingers, as he shared his story in a whisper, so convinced was he that staff were listening and planning to hurt him.

Another prisoner agreed to talk to me only after Hunter had been placed in solitary confinement, and he made identical allegations, including that Hunter had shown him documents from his own file, convincing him of Hunter's power within the prison. This man, too, quivered as he spoke to me, and he looked around furtively the entire time we were in my office. "I've been here too long, Rob," he said at one point, teary-eyed. "People know I'm up here. I'm afraid I'm going to be killed for talking to you."

What I heard during this investigation astonished me. How could one prisoner get hard copies of the confidential files of other prisoners? I came to the realization that something very dangerous, with ominous implications, was going on. When I wanted to report what I'd learned directly to Monty Bourke, in confidence, he was attending a meeting at regional headquarters. I walked the fifteen minutes from Kingston Pen to headquarters so I could talk to him. I opened the door to the meeting room, just wide enough to catch Monty's eye. One look at me was all it took to prompt him to come out to talk.

In spite of all I knew and heard about Kingston Penitentiary, I was sure Monty would tell me the prisoners' allegations couldn't possibly be right. Instead, he looked at me steadily without the slightest hint of surprise. When I had finished, he told me to return to the prison and go straight to the office of Rick Rogers, the prison's security intelligence officer. "Tell him exactly what you told me," Monty said. "Don't speak of this to anyone else under any circumstances."

It would take several more months, but many other dark secrets about the inner workings of Kingston Penitentiary were exposed by a covert police investigation of the prison, known as Correct Zero. The investigation revealed what could only be called an extensive criminal conspiracy. By then I had left Kingston Pen to work at the minimum-security Pittsburgh Institution, convinced I would never again set foot inside the penitentiary's walls. But when Monty asked me to assist with an internal inquiry related to Correct Zero late in 2000, I accepted the assignment. Monty had treated me very well, and I knew he'd demonstrated a strong commitment to making Kingston a better institution. I was also conscious of the many good employees who were stuck there in a cesspool not of their making. While the police were conducting a formal investigation of criminal wrongdoing by some staff, we would investigate lesser internal alleged breaches of discipline that had come to light during the police investigation, which began in March 1999.

I reported to regional headquarters for an initial debriefing. I arrived to a room full of other managers from around the province summoned for the same task. I noted that everyone was of the assistant warden rank or its equivalent, and everyone held a good reputation. We gathered around a large conference table. A long scroll of paper was unfurled before us. It was an intricate bubble chart of prisoner names and employee names, connected by lines into an expansive web. Beside each name was a list of alleged involvement in things like drug dealing, money laundering, extortion, assaults, and the sale of confidential information by staff to prisoners like Hunter. The size of the chart and the number of people implicated shocked me. I noted with dismay that some of the staff were indeed people I had supervised, people I had trusted. Even one of my fellow managers was listed as having warned certain prisoners that their phone calls were monitored.

We were divided into investigation teams of two managers each. My partner and I completed three separate investigations, two of which remain vivid in my memory. The first concerned a young male officer who only ever worked the three-to-eleven shift, and who always worked alone in the solitary-confinement unit. After four p.m. each day only one officer worked in solitary confinement, because all the cells were locked. This particular officer liked this shift because, as he admitted when questioned, he worked as a bouncer in a nightclub after his shift ended at eleven o'clock. He worked at the nightclub until three a.m., headed home to sleep, and returned to Kingston for the next day's shift. The problem was that he slept while he was on duty in solitary confinement, and another staff member finally made a confidential report.

He would close the main door to the unit so he could not be seen from the entrance. Anyone who approached the barrier would have to call out for him to open the door, so they could not surprise him. The officer allegedly took a second, more alarming precaution. He would let the prisoner who worked as the unit's cleaner out of his cell to stand guard for him while he slept his shift away. This was obviously a very serious breach. The prisoner could have overpowered the sleeping guard and gained control of the keys. He could have opened all the cells. Our source further alleged the officer supplied the prisoner with cigarettes to gain his compliance. Worst of all, he allegedly paid the prisoner ally to assault other prisoners whom he found difficult.

As an experienced investigator, I knew we were unlikely to find independent corroboration. We needed an admission from the officer himself. I recall clearly how he swaggered into the interview room, his union representative in tow, and leaned back in his chair, grinning broadly. Odd behaviour for someone purportedly falsely accused of professional misconduct, I thought. His too-small shirt emphasized his enormous biceps, and he gave long, rambling explanations in which he dismissed the allegations against him as ridiculous. My investigation partner questioned him first while I listened and made notes. Although he denied ever breaking any rule himself, this officer acknowledged having witnessed many instances of other officers' wrongdoing. Indeed, I thought he was playing us in his attempts to seem forthright while deflecting our attention away from the interview's purpose — the allegations against him.

After about ten minutes, my partner looked at me and said, "That's all I have."

The officer turned to me, smiling and clearly feeling confident. He tipped his chair back, raising the front legs off the floor.

Instead of speaking, I began to read over my notes. I flipped backwards and forward several times, pretending to study the words on the pages, and looked perplexed. The silence began to grow; tension permeated the room. I could feel everyone's eyes on me. Finally I looked up and regarded the officer, whose smile was now slightly askew.

"What have you seen other officers do?" I asked.

"What?" he asked, surprised.

"You said you've seen a lot of other officers breaking the rules. I'm just looking for some examples of what you've seen other staff doing wrong."

His face changed dramatically. The union representative looked uncomfortable.

"I don't know what you're getting at," he finally said. "What do you want me to say?"

"You said you've never broken the rules, but you've seen lots of other staff breaking the rules. I'm just looking for some examples of what you've seen happen. You say you're here to be honest and that you want to help us in our investigation. So give me an example of something you've seen, even just one."

The officer was no longer smiling. In fact, he looked increasingly uncomfortable. "I don't know what I've seen! I've just seen things!"

"Let me explain something," I said. "You've told me that you're here to co-operate with this investigation. You've said you're innocent of the allegations against you and you wish to help us. You say you've seen other staff breaking the rules. I'm trying to ascertain how truthful you are and how reliable a witness you are. Just give me one incident where you've seen other staff breaking the rules."

The officer began to stammer and sputter. He couldn't remember any particular incidents. I suggested he was adhering to the code of silence. I continued to press him for a single example, and he continued to feign poor memory. I advised the interview was concluded. He muttered expletives as he exited the room. Predictably, our findings remained inconclusive, but my gut feelings about him were less ambiguous.

The other investigation concerned an officer alleged to be delivering bank debit cards to influential prisoners inside the prison. During the course of this investigation, however, another alleged breach was brought to our attention quite by accident. It concerned the Correctional Service's attempt to use part-time guards to reduce overtime costs. These officers were trained and outfitted with the understanding that they would be employed only to cover staff shortages. This meant full-time guards had far fewer opportunities to work overtime, which did not go over well. We heard allegations that full-time guards paid prisoners to harass and threaten the part-time guards. We had to interview a prisoner I knew, who was now in solitary confinement long term. He didn't want to meet with us in an interview room, so we went down to his cell door.

The prisoner asked me to keep my voice down as we spoke through the food slot. I put a pad of paper on the tile floor to kneel on as we talked. The prisoner had worked in the gymnasium at Kingston during the time I was in charge of that area as the assistant warden of correctional programs. In a whisper, he told me he was afraid for his life, as he was now known to be talking to investigators about what had been happening at the prison. He felt safe talking to me because he knew my reputation. He said officers had paid him in cigarettes and cash to harass and threaten what regular staff identified as "part-time scabs." He would spit at them, throw bodily fluids, and threaten their families, among other things, and in return he was promised that any charges laid would be caught and shredded. Unfortunately for him, not all the charges were caught and destroyed. Those classified as major charges were indeed processed. He now found himself in long-term solitary confinement.

"Mr. Clark, I don't expect you to believe me," he said. "I'm just a con. I know that. But if you check my file, you'll see that I don't have a lot of charges. And I sure don't have charges for threatening staff. All my charges are for being drunk or stoned. And even then I don't hassle the screws. Check my file. That's all I'm asking."

I reviewed his file. It showed a consistent history of intoxication-related offences up to a certain point in time. Following this was a spate of institutional charges for threatening staff. The file didn't conflict with the prisoner's version of events, but we didn't have enough evidence to proceed with formal discipline. I can say, however, that following the police investigation, some of the officers this prisoner identified were found culpable in other transgressions that ended their association with the Correctional Service of Canada.

Operation Correct Zero shook Kingston Penitentiary and the CSC to their very foundations. Several guards were suspended. Five guards were terminated after the RCMP found they had committed various criminal offences, such as drug dealing. Three others committed suicide once the investigation began. Two, a married couple, left a note explaining that the "music is getting too loud, and we can't face it anymore." Warden Monty Bourke issued a statement, printed in the *Globe and Mail* following the guards' firing, to acknowledge the CSC had "no tolerance for staff wrongdoing, no matter what form it takes, because it jeopardizes the safety of the institution and puts colleagues and offenders at risk." In June 2001, a report from the CBC described Kingston Pen as "an out-of-control drug-dealing centre run by gangs of prisoners and a number of corrupt staff." According to the same article, prisoners told the media that "guards regularly flout the law" and "gangs of prisoners control many parts of the prison."

By the end of my involvement in the internal inquiry, I was happy to return to my duties at minimum-security Pittsburgh, where life was not nearly so dark and bleak.

11 Pittsburgh

Pittsburgh Institution is located on the same tract of government land as Joyceville and holds only 230 low-risk prisoners. Originally built in 1963 and designed as a farm annex, Pittsburgh produced root vegetables and beef products, among other agricultural products, in the earliest years of its existence. The prisoners provided the labour, and ate the food they produced.

The prison farm operations were among the very best correctional modalities that CSC has ever had. For the first time in their lives, many prisoners enjoyed and took pride in working for wages. The opportunities to work with animals and to learn skills associated with farming simultaneously cultivated what was, for many, their first encounter with self-worth. I have known prisoners so intensely angry at the system that they seemed beyond any hope of redemption, but something about assisting with the birth of a calf can make anyone feel better. Prisoners commonly named the newborns and identified animals as their particular favourite. Men who had previously resisted co-operating in any fashion returned from the fields and the barns each day tired, sweaty, and sunburned. Many were too tired to do much besides eat and fall into bed, the alarm set for five a.m., exhausted but proud of what their hard work had accomplished.

Not surprisingly, then, many people were dismayed when the federal government shut down the prison farms in 2010. To sensible people, the therapeutic benefits that accompany this type of honest work are priceless, especially for those unfortunate souls who have never known any form of success in their lives. To worsen matters, the federal government justified the closure of the prison farms on the grounds that prisoners were unlikely to find employment in the agriculture sector. This simplistic analysis was absurd and insulting to anyone intelligent enough to understand what was being achieved on a more meaningful level than the mere acquisition of employable skills.

Not so long before closure, however, Pittsburgh was rebuilt in the 1990s and looked much different than in its early days. Approximately thirty-five units, akin to townhouses, were set up for five or six prisoners, who would live together and share responsibility for the general order and upkeep of their dwelling. All the tenants needed to get along and do their share. The prisoners who earned the privilege of serving their sentences in this much more humane environment were those the system had evaluated as posing very low risk to the public. Many prisoners who end up in minimum security are old, infirm, close to release, or far into their lengthy sentences.

I was still at Kingston Penitentiary when I initially heard rumours that some unit managers would be deployed from the major sites to work in Ontario's three minimum-security prisons, the first time unit managers would work in the minimums. Interested unit managers were to submit their names to regional headquarters. I considered what it would be like to work in minimum security. A prison with no fence seemed odd. Then I compared it to where I was and knew I was ready for a change.

Pittsburgh was looking for two unit managers who would each run half of the prison. Each unit manager would be responsible for around 115 prisoners, with a much higher ratio of prisoners to staff than in a higher-security prison. Pittsburgh relied heavily on the good behaviour expected in such an open environment.

Arriving at Pittsburgh was a welcome relief from the day-to-day battles at Kingston Pen, but to say I experienced culture shock is to put it mildly. At Kingston Penitentiary, I would sign a stack of forms every morning, mostly prisoner charges and use-of-force reports. At Pittsburgh, I might be required to sign a birthday card for one of the staff. The morning operations meeting would go on until ten a.m. at Kingston Pen, whereas at Pittsburgh Institution it lasted ten minutes. At Kingston Pen, I would read officers' written reports describing a brawl in the gym followed by a suicide attempt that required an ambulance to take a prisoner to an outside hospital. Another report might detail prisoners assaulting an officer by throwing bodily fluids at him, while still one more described a prisoner's assault on another, resulting in stab wounds. At Pittsburgh, the operations meeting dealt with its own life-and-death issues: where should we put the handicap parking spot? Do we have enough charcoal for the prisoner barbeque this weekend? It took me a long time to get my head around this much less stressful environment. In fact, for about six months, I did not adjust well. For the first time in my career, I began to think the prisoners had it pretty easy — maybe too easy.

The staff and the prisoners at Kingston Pen always seemed on the verge of conflict, but at Pittsburgh, prisoners and staff interacted more like regular people. This raised a very interesting philosophical question for me: was this more civilized and respectful environment a reflection of a more civilized prisoner clientele whose members earned their way to this low level of security, or was it possible that a more civilized and respectful environment created a correctional institution instead of a prison? In other words, did the prisoners produce the environment, or did the environment produce the prisoners?

Based on my first-hand observations, and those of other interested people, the environment in which prisoners live is a major determinant of whether a prison is dangerous and chaotic or calm, at least by prison standards. Just as with the living-unit system formerly at Joyceville, prisoners and staff at Pittsburgh spent large amounts of time in direct contact with each other. As a general principle, the more face-to-face contact there is between the two groups, the more opportunities for staff to intervene when problems can still be easily fixed. The interventions are many and relatively painless as opposed to random, faceless, illogical, and excessive, as is often the case in a maximum-security environment. In my experience, the more the prisoners feel they are being treated like human beings, the more readily they follow orders from staff.

Because I moved around so much in my work, I came to know hundreds of prisoners and hundreds of staff. In my travels, I crossed paths with the same prisoners in different prisons; when this happened, there was usually a friendly greeting on my part. Because my rapport with prisoners was generally very good, many reunions of this kind took place in my office with the door closed, where the "chair" was situated. Once the door was closed, men who had their guard up with everybody else finally relaxed. Sometimes I got each of us a bottle of water, and we just talked. I saw some men at all three levels of security while serving the same sentence.

One of them was Hobo, whom I first met as a boyish-looking prisoner at Millhaven in 1978. When I got to Pittsburgh, Hobo was there, having earned his way from maximum security to minimum. It was about twenty years since we had first met, but he did not look or seem much different. He still had massive arms and all the same signs of a life lived in battle, but he was essentially the same person. The only difference I could see was that when the system turned down the security, he responded in kind. This same man who used to expect to fight for his life every time he left his cell was now being scolded by the secretaries in the case management building for hanging around the front door. These ladies were petite, their glasses on a chain, but they could terrify Hobo with just a look.

My assistant would often say, laughing, "If I have to tell him once more, Rob, about hanging around that door, I'll kick him in the arse!"

I would think, *If you only knew him like I know him.*

I also met some of these prisoners after their release. Two of them, like Hobo, started their sentences at maximum-security Millhaven. One of them had the gladiator school on his record. These very tough individuals had seen it all. What happens when we open the prison gate and send them out to live among unsuspecting civilized people? Knowing what we do about how badly they behaved in maximum security, with more than one incident of disrespectful and threatening behaviour, one might assume it would not take long for these angry men to wreak havoc. But it usually doesn't happen that way — almost never, in fact.

Once released, most of these men adjust. These same prisoners spend much of their lives among us, although we do not notice them. They do not explode every time they have to wait in line at Tim Hortons, and they do not rob every store they go into. I have met men in a grocery store years later, pushing a cart and shopping with their wife and daughter. If our relationship in prison was good, they may introduce me to their family. I am always extremely respectful. While it is true that most ex-prisoners will experience adjustment problems and some will fail, many will not. As well, the vast majority of these failures are termed "technical violations," such as failing a urine test or quitting a job without first consulting a parole officer.

When I arrived at Pittsburgh, perhaps the most pleasant surprise of all was the parole officers who were assigned to me. I never stopped finding the life stories of prisoners — all the hardships, all the mistakes — intriguing. Helping people turn their lives around is, in my view, one of the most rewarding experiences a prison worker can have, and it is not always the parole officer who makes the difference. Sometimes a work instructor or a teacher, a chaplain, or a uniformed guard plays a transformative role. Inevitably, however, it will come down to the parole officer to make it all happen. No one else can do this very important part in the reintegration process.

At Pittsburgh, like other minimum-security prisons, most of the prisoners were eligible for release, and just as many had made sufficient strides at rehabilitation to keep the parole officers busy preparing cases for the parole board hearings. The number of parole hearings held in one month at a minimum-security facility far exceeds the number at higher levels of security. The quality of the parole officers at Pittsburgh was a major factor in how well the prison ran. It did not take me long to realize I had hit the jackpot. I was in charge of Unit 2, and the four parole officers I worked with — Heather O'Brien, Doug Roantree, John Van Luven, and Judie Cornell — were knowledgeable, professional, and self-motivated.

Unlike many parole officers, these people knew the importance of their job and the value of understanding the prisoners they dealt with. They read the entire file of each prisoner on their caseloads. Prisoners serving long sentences often have very lengthy files; a complete file review for a prisoner serving a life sentence can take several days and is nothing short of exhausting. The best parole officers start on page one, at the bottom of the file, and work their way through the reports from the date the sentence commenced up to the present. They also have long conversations with prisoners, to afford them the opportunity merely to talk and ask questions. Most prisoners have many questions, and most prisoners have a great deal to say.

Sadly, these two practices are almost extinct. Many of today's parole officers read only the most recent reports placed in the electronic file, and many do not interview the prisoners unless a legislated event, such as an eligibility date for some form of release, requires it. Many won't make the effort to visit the solitary-confinement area of the prison, even if one of their clients finds themselves in the worst possible situation. They tell themselves (and others) they are too busy; they have too many reports to write, even if writing the reports involves simply cutting and pasting information from previous reports — a technique betrayed by the same errors and spelling mistakes repeated for months, or years. The parole officer's supervisor is supposed to review each and every report for its quality, thoroughness, and factual accuracy, but many supervisors have no experience in case management and thus no idea what these reports should or should not contain.

It should come as no surprise, then, that I was utterly giddy to find myself among the parole officers in Unit 2 at Pittsburgh. When we held unit board meetings at Pittsburgh, these four good friends would strongly challenge each other's handling of the cases being presented. Sometimes the debate would take a policy turn that would extend the argument through a cigarette break outside. Extreme cases would force us to reconvene after lunch. This almost always occurred in such a professional and intellectually detached manner, it was a pleasure to be involved.

John and Doug both had over twenty years' experience in this field. Whenever John presented a case, he would act out the crime, playing all the characters and giving each a different voice. He'd run around the boardroom, pretending to hold a gun and taunt the police who were hot on his trail, and then play the role of the police officer in pursuit. Doug, on the other hand, presented in a calm, laid-back drawl that seemed to add even more validity to his compelling intellectual arguments. Heather was a skilled risk analyst known as the Policy Queen for her knowledge of even the most obscure rules governing the release of prisoners. Judie was younger and less experienced but discerning and self-confident. Judie once presented a case for release of an older prisoner, Donald. John and Doug had both had Donald on their caseloads during previous sentences and from memory were able to recount his endless failures. Judie stood her ground and answered all the challenges of her colleagues. Donald may still be living on the outside today.

Of everything I saw and experienced during my career, the memories of those parole officers and the conversations we had still evoke pride in what we accomplished and how we did it. I lost count of the number of times they presented a case of a new arrival from higher security and convincingly argued that no-fence Pittsburgh was a poor fit. Their arguments were always based on file information the previous case-management team had either not seen or not considered. In one instance, we received a prisoner from medium-security Joyceville, right next door. After being briefed on the errors in the case, I shared with the Joyceville unit manager our concerns that this particular prisoner was an escape risk. I received a less than respectful response for questioning the judgment of the staff involved in the recommendation. We reviewed the case again but remained convinced of our assessment, and Pittsburgh's warden ordered the prisoner returned to higher security. A flurry of childish emails from Joyceville ensued, and then Joyceville transferred the prisoner to Frontenac, another minimum-security prison. He escaped the same week he arrived.

No perimeter fences surround the minimum-security prisons, so it is not surprising that from time to time prisoners do escape. If the missing prisoner happens to be a violent offender, the media often focuses on that aspect of the case, but prisoners make it to minimum security because they are a low risk to the public. Not long after I arrived at Pittsburgh, when I entered the main security office early one morning to sign in, I learned we were short one prisoner. At around eight o'clock the night before, a young kid named Howard had vanished from Unit 2 — my unit. Having spent my whole career to this point in medium- and maximum-security prisons, the word "escape" had a career-ending ring to it, and I wasn't entirely sure what steps or protocols followed an escape from minimum security.

Howard's prisoner ID card lay on the counter. Presumably it had been picked up and examined many times since eight o'clock last night. His face was young looking, a man in his mid-twenties, if I had to guess. His convictions were for non-violent, property-related offences, and he was not serving a long sentence. In fact, he was getting out in six months. Why would he escape? I posed this question to the assembled officers. The responses were predictable and noncommittal: he must have owed money, he had a beef with someone in his house, et cetera. The more I read the information on the little card and looked at the boyish face in the picture, the more I was baffled as to what could have driven this young man to make such a terrible mistake. I decided to search for more information on this kid before that morning's operations meeting.

The case-management building was in partial darkness when I went to my office, at the rear. I made coffee and pulled Howard's file up on my computer. As I sat reading, the relatively innocuous nature of his criminal history struck me. In comparison to many files I had reviewed, this one was a bedtime story. Going over the various reports, I noticed that Howard, like many of our prisoners, had been participating in the private family visiting program. His approved visitors were with his mother and his sister. He'd had two such visits in the past seven months, and the author of the report believed both had strengthened his family ties. I read this and thought to myself, *We'll see how your family ties are after your mom finds out you escaped.*

I read a few more reports, biding the early hour, until people began shuffling by on their way to various offices and departments, where they, too, would flip on lights and coffee makers. At 8:20 I left my office, greeted the two administrative assistants, and headed to the operations meeting. We'd have more to discuss than birthday cards today. When I arrived, the warden and deputy warden had already seated themselves; a correctional manager followed me in. He had been on duty the night before. As per protocol, as soon as staff had detected the escape, he had implemented the prison's step-by-step contingency plan. He had already notified the Kingston Police and the Ontario Provincial Police before calling the warden at home; she had reminded him to call the duty officer at national headquarters. A prison representative was now heading to the local public school, less than a kilometre away, to advise of the escape and provide a picture of the missing prisoner.

Clearly my colleagues had dealt with escapes before, and I was happy to just listen and learn something new. Throughout the meeting, the correctional manager held a piece of paper in his hands, turning it over, folding and unfolding it. As we got up to leave at the meeting's end, having agreed what each of us would do, I noticed he took the paper with him. In the outer hallway, I asked him what it was.

"The kid's prison visiting records," he replied. "We send a copy to the cops, in case they want to check his contacts."

It made sense: if a prisoner escapes, he has to go somewhere, and he would need help. The only people likely to involve themselves in aiding an escapee would be people who cared a lot about him. I asked if this tactic usually worked.

"I'm not sure the police even check it out," he said. "It's a small thing to them compared to all the active investigations and so on. Besides, this guy isn't violent, and he's doing short time. They won't bust their butts."

The visiting records were, of course, in the visiting department I managed. So I dropped in to talk to the staff, who were, I'd quickly learned, unfailingly professional and conscientious. The two visiting officers were sitting at their desks, sipping coffee and opening prisoner mail with steel letter openers, visually inspecting the contents of each envelope to ensure it contained only paper. Senders of prisoner correspondence will often attempt to include things like drugs in the envelope. Perhaps the most ingenious case I ever saw at Pittsburgh was a letter with cute little cartoons on the back of the stationery — lots and lots of cartoons. Curious, the inspecting officer pulled the paper from the envelope and looked more closely at the images. They were identical, even rows covering the back of each sheet. Each cartoon turned out to be an individual dose of LSD. This could have had serious consequences for a prison where locking doors was not an option, and we had no fences to keep people in.

We weren't always as vigilant as we should have been. We had a prisoner in his late seventies, a curmudgeon whose claim to fame was a fraud he said had made international headlines, although no one had ever heard of him. He was well liked and had been at Pittsburgh long enough to be part of the woodwork. On the occasion of yet another birthday, his family travelled a great distance by bus, as always, and brought with them a beautiful cake. Owing to the relaxed atmosphere, the cake entered uninspected and was enjoyed under the watch of staff working in the visiting room. Unbeknownst to them, everyone who sang "Happy Birthday" that day knew which part of the cake not to eat. As visiting hours drew to a close, the unfinished cake, according to prison policy, should have been given to the visitors to take home or tossed into the garbage, but the staff was in a good mood, and the birthday boy took the leftovers to share with his housemates. They gathered around the kitchen table as he broke apart the remainder of his cake. There was no need for secrecy; the officers were involved in shift change. These prisoners would not see any staff members until the four p.m. count. Inside the cake was a bag of pills. I never ceased to be astounded at the ingenuity of some of the prisoners under our charge.

In the visiting office, I requested to see Howard's visiting card, and one of the officers retrieved it for me. Howard's mother had made the majority of visits. Back in my office, I typed into my computer the name and number of the escapee and scanned his file, noting where he had been and how he had come to be in a federal penitentiary. The more I read, the more I was convinced this young man was not a career criminal. Rather, he appeared to be an impetuous and foolish youth who could still be turned around. Under contacts and next of kin, I found his mother's name, address, and phone number. I had little doubt that he would call her at some point to let her know he was okay; he wouldn't want her to worry. But why escape? The more I studied the file, the more I thought it had to be an impulsive decision, the variety that had landed him in trouble in the past. I speculated he had not thought through his escape beyond the decision to leave. Now, having gathered his wits, he might be wondering how he could have done something so foolish. His mother had been visiting weekly, so they probably had a good relationship. He would eventually have to tell her what he had done, I reasoned, otherwise, she was going to think he was still at the prison. She would also expect to visit again this week. The clock on the wall read quarter to ten. I picked up the phone and dialled her number.

I had never done anything like this before. As it occurred to me that I might be outside my legal authority in revealing a prisoner's escape to his family, a woman answered the phone.

I had not thought through what I was going to say. I knew from experience it was always best to say less rather than more when speaking of matters that could upset a prisoner's family. I tried to keep my voice friendly and unconcerned as I explained the purpose of my call, before I identified myself, so she wouldn't immediately assume I was calling with terrible news about her son's well-being. Many families worry about their loved ones surviving in prison.

"I'm terribly sorry to trouble you, but I'm calling to get some advice in dealing with your son Howie. My name is Robert Clark, and I work at Pittsburgh Institution. I hope I'm not calling at a bad time."

"No, Mr. Clark, not at all. Is Howie in trouble of some kind?"

I needed to be careful here in what I said and how I said it. "I don't want to alarm you, but it appears he left the institution last night without permission. We haven't heard from him, and he hasn't returned."

"Oh my goodness, Mr. Clark! I can't believe it!" Her voice rose. "But Howie is getting out soon!"

I could tell from her voice that I had done the right thing. This woman was very concerned about her son and wanted to help him in any way she could — like most mothers. I explained that I thought her son had made a bad decision and probably regretted it. I said that he could still minimize the damage he had done in terms of finishing his sentence if he turned himself in. The sooner he did this, the better; the longer he was gone, the higher his chances of getting into further trouble with the law. His mother listened and said she felt certain Howard would be in touch with her sooner or later.

I gave her my home and business phone numbers and asked her to tell Howard that he could call me collect if he wished. If he turned himself in, I promised to write him a letter to show the judge, which could help his case.

"You would do that, Mr. Clark?"

"Absolutely. If Howie turns himself in, and he has not been involved in anything illegal, then I think the judge would take all of this into consideration."

"Oh my God, Mr. Clark, that would mean so much. I'll see if I can find him!"

By this point, she sounded more annoyed at her son than fearful for his well-being; I recognized that tone from my own childhood. When I hung up, I felt reassured. It was nice to speak with a regular person, a parent with her share of headaches. Hers, in fact, were bigger than most.

My offer to write a letter had been sincere, and it was not the first or last time I would write such a letter. I had seen lives changed for the better or worse by nothing more than the stroke of a pen. The words "not approved" or "not recommended" above my signature could be devastating to prisoners and their families. I never took this responsibility lightly, and I developed the habit of writing letters of praise for prisoners when I felt it was deserved. Often these letters would be the only positive piece of paper in an otherwise highly negative life narrative, simply because almost all the day-to-day written observations that find their way into a prisoner's file are negative. This is more a reflection of a system focused on secure custody than on the authors of these reports.

One time I wrote such a letter for a prisoner at Joyceville. I had copied the letter to the National Parole Board, the arresting police service, and the prisoner's attorneys. The parole officer handling the case, who did not support the prisoner's application, showed it to her unit manager, my colleague at the time. He was one of the guard-managers and was in truth a much kinder man than he looked, at an imposing six foot two and with a shaved head. Unfortunately, like most guards who became unit managers, his knowledge of parole work was non-existent. In a crowded Corporate Objective No. 1 meeting, he had challenged me about my letter, telling those assembled that it would just "confuse the parole board." I knew he was one of those managers who signed everything put in front of him by his parole officers without reading it; he had told me so himself.

I simply said, "What is in that letter is true. If the truth is confusing to the National Parole Board, then we have a much bigger problem than these statistics." I thought this was a rather funny comeback, however true, but in a security crowd, my humour had no audience.

So, certainly, I was prepared to write just such a letter on Howie's behalf. The rest of the day following Howard's escape was taken up with administrative duties. When I got home that night, I began my usual routine. The kids were doing their homework, and I was making dinner. The phone rang. I picked it up without looking at the call display.

"I can't believe you phoned my mom!" a male caller said incredulously. "Are you allowed to do that?"

"I really don't know." I paused. My son was dipping a blue crayon in his glass of milk. "I'm really glad you phoned me. You did the right thing."

"Well, I kind of fucked up." He sounded more tired than hostile, and I decided he probably needed advice more than a sympathetic ear.

"The fact that you've called me is good. Like I told your mother, if you turn yourself in, I am prepared to write something for you to take to court." I waited for him to respond.

"I don't have a ride..." he started to say. I could hear him talking with someone in the background. He came back on the line. "Sorry,

Mr. Clark. Um, if I come back to the institution, what's going to happen to me?"

I told him the truth. "If you turn yourself in to me, I'll have to place you in solitary confinement at Joyceville. After that, we will have to recommend that you go back to medium security. You will probably be released from there, because it's unlikely, with the time left in your sentence, that you'd be able to earn your way back to minimum security."

"Can you hold on?"

I could faintly hear more discussion. When he came back on the line, he told me he'd report to Pittsburgh in two days, the earliest he could get a ride. His sister was going to drive him back to Kingston.

Now I was in a bind. If I said yes, was I giving him authority to remain at large from prison? What if he committed a crime in the next twenty-four hours? I decided to hedge my bets.

"I cannot tell you what to do at this moment, but I strongly advise you to lay low until Wednesday. According to the law, I should encourage you to report to the closest police station as soon as possible and turn yourself in."

He gave that some thought. "I realize that, but I'm not going into the bucket," he finally said, using slang for provincial custody. "I'd rather turn myself in to you."

Okay, I thought, *this is as good as I'm going to get.* To allow myself a moment to consider his plan, I looked over to see what the kids were doing. Stephanie was marking her chore chart on the fridge to record that she'd set the table, although she had yet to do so. *She'd make a good bureaucrat,* I smiled to myself. I confirmed with Howard that he'd report to Pittsburgh on Wednesday at one p.m.

Just before we hung up, he blurted once more, "I cannot believe you phoned my mom!"

At Wednesday morning's operations meeting, the warden, whom I'd already brought up to speed, congratulated me on my apparent success. I just hoped Howard would show up as promised. He had, after all, disappointed his own mother more than once. Who was I? In the end, he did show. As I anticipated, he landed in solitary confinement until we could make arrangements for his official transfer to increased security. The warden presented me with a seventy-five dollar gift certificate to a favourite restaurant once Howard returned to the official count board. If I recall correctly, she reported my solution to regional headquarters.

I used the same manoeuvre twice more at Pittsburgh. In both cases, I called the mothers, having looked at the visiting cards to verify they were among the active visitors. In both cases, they attempted to intervene.

One mother called me back a week after my call. "Mr. Clark? I wanted you to know I spoke to Michael. He is in the Ottawa Detention Centre." As with Howard — and, indeed, most escapes I was aware of — Michael's flight was an impulsive, poorly thought-out enterprise, so ill-conceived that the fugitive soon wished he hadn't had the idea.

I would say this strategy is worth trying in every escape, although the contact person may be a wife, sibling, or close friend rather than a parent. As far as I know, no one ever considered adding it to the existing protocol for escaped prisoners. It would not be the first or last time, however, that CSC failed to try a new idea to solve an old problem.

At Pittsburgh Institution, I found I had more free time than I ever had at higher levels of security, thanks to the relatively co-operative nature of the prisoners. I picked up the habit of doing extra duty when required, filling in for the other unit manager while doing my own job. One of the positions I was asked to take over was the institution's victim services coordinator. Awareness of the rights of crime victims in Canada had increased tremendously, resulting in important legislation. One result was that CSC began to consider the victims' perspectives when making decisions about prisoners' release and to keep victims informed of significant changes to prisoners' sentences. Crime victims were increasingly likely to exercise their right to attend National Parole Board hearings. I attended hearings of this type many times and can attest from my still vivid memories they can be heart-wrenching, even overwhelming.

One of these hearings concerned a prisoner serving a life sentence for second-degree murder. I knew this man when we were both at Millhaven. Our paths crossed again, years later, at Joyceville. The act that landed him in the system had occurred many years earlier. High on drugs and armed with a knife, this man decided to confront his ex-girlfriend and her new boyfriend. When he arrived at the ex-girlfriend's home, her next-door neighbour, a woman with four young children, attempted to intervene. She died on her front lawn, her children clustered around her.

Now, almost twenty years to the day I had first met him, he was in minimum security and going in front of the National Parole Board. He wanted permission to spend forty-eight hours at the home of his wife in Kingston. If he received permission, he would be required to stop in at the Kingston Police station twice during those forty-eight hours of freedom. Upon return to the prison, he would have to provide a urine sample to prove that he hadn't consumed any narcotics during his leave. The murder he committed generated much media coverage at the time, and several newspapers now ran stories about his parole hearing. The four grown children of the murder victim were going to attend this particular hearing; they would have an opportunity to read aloud victim-impact statements. The prisoner's wife would be by his side for moral support. After discussing the situation at the morning operations meeting the day before, we decided I would attend the hearing to try to ensure there were no disruptions in what would be, for those in attendance, a distressing experience.

I arrived at work early the next day and, having chatted briefly with the officers in the security building about what to expect, headed to the warden's boardroom. The most important feature of this particular room was its location at the furthest point from where the National Parole Board meetings were held, while still being on the same floor. The distance between these rooms ensured a significant distance between the victims and the prisoner. The prisoner and his wife would wait in the warden's boardroom until they were summoned. For the other attendees, a small room directly adjacent to the parole board's hearing room was set up with comfortable chairs and a coffee table; a box of tissues and bottled water within reach. I tried to envision the moment when the victims would see the man who had taken their mother's life. What would they be feeling at a moment they had probably imagined for so long? What would happen?

I'd greet the victims and escort them to the waiting room before focusing on the prisoner and his wife, while the prisoner's parole officer took charge of the victims. The prisoner's wife was expected to arrive early and, hopefully, avoid contact with the victims as they arrived. Staff in the security building were on the lookout for both groups, and staff in the visiting area were expecting the prisoner's wife. She would wait there for her husband, who would join her before they were summoned to the hearing room. I headed to the security building and noticed two TV vans, one of them from Global News. Having confirmed that everything was set according to plan, I returned to my office. For half an hour I checked the clock frequently, and then the phone rang.

When I answered, a familiar voice said, "I think they're here, Rob."

In the parking lot, I met three women and a man getting out of a car. They were putting on overcoats and looking around. Joyceville, with its high fences and forbidding towers, sits in plain view of Pittsburgh. I had seen this reaction in visitors before, a look that seems to convey, *Am I in trouble, too?* — just as some people are intimidated by the sight of police officers, even when they've done nothing wrong. I recognized one individual among them who had been interviewed about the case in a front-page newspaper account. I approached and extended my hand.

"Good morning. My name is Rob Clark."

Everyone shook my hand in turn. As I met their eyes, I could see they were feeling distraught. These people, who had already been through so much, looked like they suspected something bad was going to happen to them. I immediately found where I needed to be in my own mind if I was to help them as I hoped. The murder of their mother was a terrible loss. It was our job to make sure they felt respected and that their very difficult experience would be handled with compassion and decorum. We entered the security building as a group, and they each signed the register. I directed them toward the little room with the box of tissues.

By now, the rest of the institution had begun its various daily routines. Staff and prisoners were coming and going. In the visiting area, the prisoner and his wife sat quietly in a corner. They both looked up at me expectantly as I entered, and I could see that they, too, were deeply stressed by what awaited them. The prisoner knew he was asking for a great deal. A life sentence puts a prisoner in a special category. They will never be seen the same way again, not by anyone who knows about their crime and sentence. Today, this man would have to convince the National Parole Board that he was a different person than the out-of-control young man who had taken a life in anger many years ago and now capable of being outside prison without posing a danger to anyone. His wife, whom he had married after serving many years of his sentence, would hopefully indicate to the members of the parole board that he was "normal" — at least normal enough for someone else to care about. I talked briefly with the couple about what to expect. I advised the prisoner the victims of his crime were very upset and suggested that as he made his way to his seat, he avoid eye contact with them. We proceeded to the warden's boardroom to wait for the call to attend.

The seating arrangement in the hearing room had already been agreed upon and the parole officer in the case had assumed overall control. The victims would sit as a group behind and to the left of the seat designated for the prisoner. Once they were seated, I would bring in the prisoner and his wife. He would sit directly facing the parole board members.

The tension in the room was palpable, and it remained so. The members of the National Parole Board, in what was one of the most awkward situations I had ever witnessed, conducted themselves in an impressive manner. Still, I had difficulty following the proceedings, because I was so keenly aware that in this room, close enough to reach out and touch each other if they chose, now sat a killer and the four children of the woman he murdered.

When the time came for the victim-impact statements, I braced myself for what I was about to hear. I was, after all, in an official capacity and expected to maintain order and decorum, no matter how emotional the proceedings. With bowed heads, the prisoner and his wife listened as each statement was read. The room was silent, except for each individual's voice sharing how this crime had affected their lives. I can still hear them.

I do not recall much else of that day. The National Parole Board granted the prisoner's request. My views on rehabilitation and second chances for prisoners, especially violent offenders, were severely tested that day. It took some time before I recovered my professional detachment. And although I thought the victim-impact statements I heard that day would haunt me forever, the worst was yet to come. My temporary assignment as the victim services coordinator was going to cause me even greater heartache.

CSC had adopted the practice of advising victims in writing of any changes to a prisoner's status. On occasion, we'd phone to make sure a victim received adequate notice of a prisoner's participation in some form of release plan and then follow up with a letter. Many times while I was performing this job, I would get the answering machine, and I would leave a brief message, along with my name and number. On occasion, however, someone answered. This, of course, changed the delivery of such news dramatically. These people were not expecting a call from me, and they were not expecting all their terrible memories to surface in an instant. Usually, they had a great deal to talk about.

One of these calls plunged me into profound doubt about my beliefs on crime and punishment. I called a middle-aged woman whose older stepbrother had sexually abused her over a period of several years when they were children; the crimes only came to light years later. I was calling to advise that the warden had approved her stepbrother for a package of limited outings to attend church in the community. As I explained the reason for my call, there was silence on the other end.

When I finished, the woman asked, "Is he getting out?"

"No," I said. "As I explained, he will be attending church with some other prisoners. These passes are only four hours in duration, and are on Tuesday nights and Sunday mornings."

When the woman spoke again, there was a quiver in her voice, which seemed to have lost some of its strength. As I waited for an opportunity to assure her of her safety, she began to cry. "It started when my mom married his dad."

Before I could say another word, she poured out her feelings to me over the phone. She told me about the exact nature of the abuse, and her inability to defend against it. She told me things I cannot repeat, but they left me feeling numb for a long while after I hung up the phone.

For the first time in my career, I began to think that what had happened to the victims was far worse than the punishment of imprisonment, especially for those confined to a place like Pittsburgh, where working on a suntan and picking up charcoal for a barbeque were part of the routine. I thought about my children, Stephanie and Adam, and began to relate the victims' feelings to my own children. My heart grew cold, and I was suddenly overtaken by deep, overwhelming rage. I even permitted myself to imagine what forms of revenge I would exact against anyone who dared to hurt my children; I would be ruthless.

For a long time, I had to struggle to regain some semblance of balance in my professional demeanour. I eventually refocused myself on the task at hand — helping prisoners to turn their lives around — and eventually I was able to let go of those deeply troubling thoughts. What did not recede, though, was my growing restlessness. Once again, I wanted a new challenge.

One bright sunny morning, I opened my email and found an interesting staffing notice. Bath Institution, a low-medium-security prison on the same land as Millhaven, had a vacancy for a unit manager. I had come to believe that moving around so much had given me a far greater knowledge base than would have been possible working at only one or two prisons. I picked up the phone and called a friend who worked at Bath, a hard-working and intelligent manager named Scott Edwards. I told him of my interest in a change, and he promptly began praising Bath as the best-kept secret around. He assured me I would love to work there.

"Are other unit managers asking about it?"

"Only one that I know of. If you say the word, I'll let them know to expect your application."

After thanking him, I hung up the phone and gazed out the window. I had been at Pittsburgh for three years. There were great staff here, and if I left, I would walk away from a highly coveted post. I would leave something I knew well for something I did not, but I had done this often enough that I was not deterred.

12 Suicide in Solitary

For as long as I could remember, Bath Institution had been considered a good place to do your time if you were a staff member, and a good place to land if you were a warden. Bath was converted from minimum security to low-medium security in the 1990s. As with Millhaven, two high chain-link fences topped with razor wire surrounded Bath. Inside the fences, however, it was a much different story.

In 2004, when I joined the staff, Bath Institution had three units. Two were long hallways of individual cells, like most prisons, while the third consisted of individual houses, like Pittsburgh. The doors on the cells in these three units were like the doors inside a house, and we could not lock the prisoners in against their will. The prisoners had keys and could lock their doors when they left their cells. This meant that staff and prisoners interacted face to face much more frequently than in most medium-security prisons. In short, Bath still functioned very much like the minimum-security prison it was originally designed to be. And just like Pittsburgh, the day-to-day atmosphere between prisoners and officers was mutually respectful and co-operative. Bath also ran well because it had some of the best uniformed staff and correctional managers I ever worked with. So effective and professional were the two managers in my unit, Suzanne Fabio and Gerry Gillis, that I found myself somewhat superfluous.

One of the most interesting events to occur while I was at Bath happened outside of the facility. Sometime near the end of October, I received a call from Kingston Pen. The prison had recently had a prisoner suicide in its solitary-confinement unit. Any prisoner death from other than natural causes meant a full investigation by national headquarters. An unnatural prisoner death was bad news for any warden, and Ottawa's ensuing investigation would look to find weaknesses, operational or otherwise, that might have contributed to the death. The acting warden at Kingston Pen asked me to conduct a preliminary investigation. I would examine the same evidence as national headquarters' investigators. My findings would forearm the acting warden with knowledge of the aspects the official investigation would most likely criticize. The acting warden could begin implementing corrective measures with the hope of minimizing headquarters' criticisms. This manoeuvre is considered damage control, and I had seen it used before.

I was asked to conduct the investigation because of my experience in this area. For ten months I'd done nothing but conduct investigations at regional headquarters, during which I dealt with every breach imaginable. So I was not surprised I had received a call. The surprising part was to come.

When I arrived at Kingston Pen, the acting deputy warden warmly greeted me and thanked me for my help. He told me I would work on the investigation with one of the penitentiary's managers. At that moment, there was a knock on the door. A well-dressed, clean-shaven man I'll call Stan entered, smiling. After a few pleasantries, I told Stan I would be in touch and picked up a package of materials, the standard collection of documents provided for investigations, to take with me. At home that night I spread out the package's contents on the table, made myself some tea, and sat down to read.

The first documents I looked for were the officer's situation reports: handwritten, eyewitness accounts by the first staff on the scene, as well as those who were involved afterwards. In this case, all the officers on the scene had reported essentially the same information. A picture emerged from reading these reports. The prisoner was on moderate suicide watch in the solitary-confinement unit at Kingston Pen. The day before the event, a Saturday, the prison psychologist had seen him and made arrangements for him to see the prison doctor on Monday; he complained of pain from recent knee surgery, and he also felt that prison staff were conspiring against him, one of the symptoms of long-term isolation.

On Sunday, he covered the window to his cell. Even though solitary-confinement staff knew prisoners were prohibited from covering their cell windows, they allowed this practice. The window remained covered for hours. At approximately a quarter to seven that evening, officers finally opened the prisoner's cell. Their descriptions of what they saw read like something from a horror movie. He was, they said, lying face down in a large pool of blood, a note from his parole officer clutched in his hand. "Sorry to hear about the loss of your sister — glad you plan a visit with family," the note read.

All quickly concluded he had been dead for some time. This was confirmed when the first responders entered the cell and turned the body over. His hands remained fixed in their position at death; his arms remained bent, his hands sticking up in the air. Several of the officers included the term "rigor mortis" in their written observations. I was beginning to understand why the acting warden wanted to know how bad things might be. Prisoners on suicide watch are supposed to be monitored more frequently than other prisoners, for obvious reasons. In this case, it appeared that no one checked on this prisoner for an extended period of time. In addition, he had managed to sneak a disposable razor into his cell, likely following his shower, and used it to take his own life. I had no doubt: this was indeed bad.

I finished reading through the reports, but my thoughts kept returning to the vivid descriptions from the officers who were first on the scene. One officer would later tell us as part of her testimony that it was "the worst thing I have ever experienced in my life." I believed her.

Stan and I agreed to spend the rest of that week dealing with our regular duties and begin the investigation the following Monday. I arrived at Kingston Penitentiary at about eight thirty Monday morning, signed in as an official visitor, and headed toward the office of my new partner. We started the way people do in these situations, talking about the weather and making small talk for a few minutes, and he offered me a cup of coffee. I pulled my file folder out of my briefcase.

"So what do you think?" I asked Stan. "I've read the situation reports, and it looks pretty bad."

"Why does it look bad?" he asked.

Okay, I thought. *Maybe Stan doesn't have much exposure to operational matters, and why would he? There's no reason to expect he would know the rules in the solitary-confinement unit concerning the visual monitoring of prisoners on suicide watch.* I elaborated, "I guess one of my main concerns is how long the prisoner was dead before he was discovered. After all, he was in rigor mortis."

"What makes you say that?" Stan leaned forward, looking intently at me. Maybe he hadn't read the reports yet. Maybe he had been busy.

"All the officers said so in their situation reports." *That should do it,* I thought.

"The officers aren't medically trained. They don't know what rigor mortis is. They don't know anything about it."

My first instinct was to doubt myself. Maybe I didn't know what I was talking about when it came to rigor mortis. Maybe Stan knew that it's more complicated than most people think, and I had unwittingly shown my own ignorance on the subject.

"Do you think he wasn't in rigor mortis?" I asked.

"We'll have to wait and see what the coroner says, but don't go by what the officers said. They don't know." Another possibility struck me: maybe Stan wasn't looking forward to what might lie ahead.

Maybe he was an adherent of the blue wall. I began to wonder how he'd hold up if we had to find anyone responsible for the death.

Our investigation took us to the scene of the incident, the solitary-confinement unit. We called ahead to make sure we wouldn't show up during a time that might prevent the officers from talking to us. My normal practice was to obtain as much information as possible before doing any interviews, which positioned me to ask better questions. Stan and I entered the unit office where two uniformed officers were seated, and I showed them our convening order, the written authorization for the investigation.

As we chatted, I glanced around. I already knew quite a bit about what was expected of solitary-confinement unit officers of federal prisons; some things do not change much from site to site. These duties include making sure that each prisoner gets one hour of exercise in the fresh air once a day, allowing sufficient time for showers and access to phone calls on certain days as required, and, probably most important, making range patrols at least once an hour. The post order also says that prisoners in solitary confinement may not, at any time, cover their windows, preventing the officers from seeing in. Opening the food slot instead to look inside might result in a cup of urine flung in your face. At Millhaven I recall a prisoner borrowed a broom, on the pretence of cleaning his confines, set it on fire, and nearly thrust it down the throat of the officer who used the food slot to check inside the cell.

Looking down the range, I now noted that almost all the windows were covered. I did not say anything — yet. While Stan continued making apologetic small talk, I took the opportunity to pick up the solitary-confinement logbook, the record of relevant incidents or concerns. "Better sign in," I said and opened it to that day's date.

Inside I found what I expected. The officers had signed in as required and indicated that the keys, radio, and equipment were all okay when they took over the shift. So far, so good. What followed, however, was a long list of times written down the left-hand side of the ledger, from seven a.m. to three p.m., which were the officers' supposed patrol times to check on each of the prisoners. But these officers had already checked off all their patrols as completed. This could mean they intended to do their checks and had simply filled them in to save time later. But the other, much more serious possibility was that the officers didn't take this part of their jobs very seriously and wouldn't complete this duty in a professional manner, if at all. Based on what had happened to the prisoner whose death we were now investigating, the second scenario seemed more likely.

Experience told me that sometimes staff would allow a particular rule to slide if it proved unfair or impractical for the prisoners. A prisoner in a solitary-confinement unit with female officers on duty might cover his window if he was going to undress or use the toilet. If he was depressed or bored, he might cover his window just to get some attention from someone, anyone, to keep from going completely mad. This is how some long-standing breaches of policy begin. Over time, if unchecked, the "this is how we run things" phenomenon begins to take hold.

According to precedent, staff are also likely to ignore the rules if enforcing them is deemed too much work. During stand-up counts, every prisoner is expected to be on his feet, so officers can verify that every prisoner is alive and healthy at least once every twenty-four hours. It is supposed to prevent the staff from counting a dead body, sometimes more than once. Other counts do not have this requirement; prisoners may be sleeping while those counts are completed. When the stand-up count was first implemented, the prisoners reacted negatively, and many refused to stand. They received a prison charge for disobeying the rule. Officers who charge prisoners invest time in writing up the charge and then delivering a copy to a possibly irate prisoner. These charges mean the correctional manager must hold a small internal court hearing, complete with a written decision of the verdict and punishment, when applicable.

This process is required for each and every prisoner who receives a charge, so if three hundred prisoners refuse to stand, that results in three hundred charges and three hundred court proceedings.

It did not take long for correctional managers to decide they didn't want their officers enforcing the stand-up count. The officers themselves were unconvinced of its value when they could clearly see the prisoners sitting at their desks or watching TV, for instance. It was common knowledge there are easier ways to get a shift in. The problem created when staff rejected the stand-up count was clearly evident when Tyrone Conn fooled officers at Kingston with a dummy in his cell. And yet, here I was, standing in the solitary-confinement unit, where a man had covered his window to commit suicide, and today — two weeks later — all the windows were still covered. Apparently no one thought that might be a problem.

I turned my attention back to the others in the office. It seemed to me that Stan was almost effusive in his interactions with the officers and unconcerned with troubling details staring us in the face. I wondered if he wanted no part of this investigation. I was doing an investigation on matters I understood well, and when it was over I would return to my job at Bath. Stan, on the other hand, had been placed in the untenable position of investigating his fellow staff. Possibly, he was thinking about how his colleagues might treat him later if we turned in a scathing report.

When we finally commenced our interviews in the boardroom, our list consisted mainly of uniformed guards. As officers came in individually, I introduced myself and Stan and showed them a copy of the convening order. I already knew many of these officers, and the interviews went well. I always began the same way: I would explain plainly what we had been tasked to investigate, and then I would give them a copy of their situation report to review. When they felt ready, we would begin. I always found that staff appreciated feeling respected during this sometimes difficult process.

Despite the relatively positive and open tone of most of the interviews, however, Stan was growing visibly more anxious. Finally, after a witness had left the boardroom, he closed the door with a bang.

"What's wrong?" I asked.

"It's you! You're leading the witnesses to say what you want them to say!" He was pale, and he spoke with a raised voice. I might have been insulted, but I could tell Stan was under stress.

"What do you mean?"

"It's the way you ask the questions! You tell them he was already dead and in a state of rigor mortis. And then they agree because they're trying to please you and want to agree with whatever you say!"

I couldn't see how I had led any witness in the other interviews. I thought it unlikely that prison guards would prioritize pleasing a manager from another institution over concern for their own colleagues. Perhaps I had been right in thinking Stan was concerned about his status in the prison if our investigation resulted in formal discipline. If staff perceived him to have collaborated with management in finding a scapegoat, at least from their perspective, he would probably find working at Kingston impossible. The blue wall again.

"I didn't realize you felt that way," I said. "I don't want either of us to feel this is a witch hunt. It certainly isn't. I'm sorry if you think I've overstepped in how I've asked questions." This seemed to relax him. "From now I won't use the words 'rigor mortis,'" I continued, "no matter what."

"Okay. It's just that these officers don't have any medical training, and I think we need to be very careful about our language," Stan said.

The next witness, a female officer, came in. I started off on a new foot.

"So," I said, "your written report is similar to some of the other reports we've seen in that you noted that resuscitation was not attempted."

"That's right, Rob. He was already dead," she said.

I paused. "How did you know he was dead?"

"That's easy! Ask anyone who was there. He was in full rigor mortis!"

Stan's head dropped.

When we had finished all of our interviews, we briefed the acting warden and the acting deputy warden. My comments about the still-covered windows in the solitary-confinement unit appeared to give them both a start. Stan wrote up the report, and he did it quickly. By the time we were done, I had a bad taste in my mouth. The officer in charge of the solitary-confinement unit on that fateful day was one of the better officers on staff. He'd had his share of challenges and had simply cut a corner at the worst possible time. I was glad to get back to Bath.

The following year, I experienced the biggest change in my career in many years: I entered a job competition for the position of deputy warden. Up to that point, it had never crossed my mind to seek a higher position than unit manager. I had been a unit manager for about eighteen years in several different prisons, and I still believe that I was very good at it, better than most, in fact. The nature of the work suited me.

The main reason I had never wanted to be a deputy warden was that I felt it would take me too far away from down inside, where the face-to-face contact between staff and prisoners takes place. It is here that people like myself could solve many small problems every day and keep the prison running smoothly. I truly believe it was noble work. I would have happily remained a unit manager until the end of my career. Unfortunately, the Correctional Service of Canada was preparing to undergo a radical change in operational philosophy. Unit managers would no longer exist, at least not in the same sense.

The new version gave responsibility for the day-to-day operations, including for the uniformed staff, to new middle managers. This left unit managers in charge of a small group of parole officers and not much else.

After ruminating on this unexpected development, I decided I had no choice. I would have to enter the next deputy warden competition or be stuck in a new version of my old job, which looked to be very uninspiring indeed. So I competed and was successful. Not long after, I received notice that I was being sent to the Regional Treatment Centre. RTC, as it is called, was a 147-bed maximum-security mental health unit. At that time, it operated out of two large buildings located within the walls of Kingston Penitentiary. Much to my surprise, I was going back to Kingston Pen.

13 Deputy Warden

The Regional Treatment Centre was a prison within a prison, the central location for Ontario prisoners receiving mental health treatment. These prisoners could not function in the general prison population. The first thing that struck me about RTC was the presence of nurses working in the units with the uniformed officers, something I had never seen before and that I found amazing. The second significant difference was that RTC staff, including the uniformed officers, referred to these very needy prisoners as patients, which of course was accurate, and treated them accordingly. I would learn that this blend of benevolent care and soft security achieved some very positive results. Unfortunately, the RTC's capacity to provide timely care to all the prisoners in the region who needed its services was limited.

The staff at RTC included three psychiatrists and numerous psychologists, nursing supervisors, and occupational therapists. They had developed a sense of inclusiveness that I found impressive. Most of the patients were suffering from one or more severe mental illnesses. According to one of the psychiatrists, roughly 60 per cent were schizophrenic. They found the experience of confinement far more harrowing than most of those down inside. Many had begged for protection from the moment they got off the Blue Goose, the provincial bailiff's bus that transported federal prisoners to the

Millhaven Assessment Unit. Once prisoners enter solitary confinement as protective-custody prisoners, the system labels them, and the label sticks, making them the likely target of prisoner violence if they are put into the general population. Prisoners placed in solitary confinement for their own protection remain in solitary confinement until they are transferred to a prison where their status is either accepted or not known. In most cases this process is lengthy, fraught with bureaucratic delays, and often results in emotional and psychological damage to the prisoner.

Approximately 40 per cent of prisoners who enter federal penitentiaries suffer from at least one diagnosable mental illness. According to the *Annual Report of the Office of the Correctional Investigator 2010-2011*, "38.4% reported or were assessed at intake as showing symptoms associated with possible mental health problems that require follow-up assessment by a mental health professional." These included: "obsessive-compulsive (29.9%), depression (36.9%), anxiety (31.1%), paranoid ideation (30.6%), and psychoticism (51%)." The same report also noted, "mental illness is typically under-reported in the prison environment, due to stigma, fear and lack of detection or diagnosis."

This means that at least four of every ten have problems that will make their survival less likely. This is the group of prisoners with the highest potential to end up in solitary confinement on a long-term basis. Solitary confinement is widely overused in Canada's prisons as a solution to many, if not most, institutional problems, although it solves none.

Most of the patients arriving at RTC came to us from a solitary-confinement cell. In most of these cases, prisoners had been in solitary long enough to start exhibiting signs of increasing mental illness. Symptoms could become so acute as to render them a risk to themselves and the staff. If they arrived completely out of control, they went on the restraint bed. If not, they were placed in one of the solid-faced cells at the front of 1B Range until the next day, when a psychiatrist would see them. If prisoners aren't already suffering from mental illness when they enter solitary confinement, the experience can be traumatic enough to create it.

The 1996 Arbour Commission of Inquiry noted typical symptoms and potential consequences of long-term isolation and sensory deprivation associated with solitary confinement, as described by the prison psychologist at the time, which included the following:

> Perceptual distortions; auditory and visual hallucinations; flashbacks; increased sensitivity and startle response; concentration difficulties and subsequent effect on school work; emotional distress due to the extreme boredom and monotony; anxiety, particularly associated with leaving the cell or seg[regation] area; generalized emotional lability at times; fear that they are "going crazy" or "losing their minds" because of limited interaction with others, which results in lack of external frames of reference; low mood and generalized sense of hopelessness....
>
> If the current situation continues it will ultimately lead to some kind of crisis, including violence, suicide and self-injury. They will become desperate enough to use any means to assert some form of control of their lives. The constant demands to segregation staff [are] related to needs for external stimulation and some sense of control of their lives.

Patients at RTC were divided into two groups. Those deemed nonviolent and medication compliant lived in C7, known as psychosocial rehabilitation. The most acute cases, and thus the most dangerous prisoners, were housed on 1B Range. This range would dominate my time and my thoughts for the next eighteen months. The range contained seventeen cells. Thirteen had open bars on the front, and four had solid doors. Patients who might act out through the bars were confined to the solid-door cells. The office for 1B Range was a cramped affair with seventeen closed-circuit camera screens mounted on the walls above the main desk; these screens were illuminated most of the time. Each showed poor-quality black-and-white images of the cell's occupant and were critical to the observation of those who might harm themselves.

Approximately halfway down the range was a cell like no other. This cell was used only when a federal prisoner somewhere in Ontario required physical restraint to keep him from seriously hurting himself. Such a prisoner is someone who, for example, becomes so distraught that he bangs his head violently against the hard surfaces inside his cell, even after he is bleeding heavily and concussed. Such a prisoner might instead slash themselves, bite themselves, or chew razor blades. In all of these cases, a physician would sign a Form 1, a temporary involuntary placement in the restraint-bed cell. The restraint bed was equipped with leather straps and cuffs. Nursing staff remained present twenty-four hours a day. They kept detailed and meticulous records, and every four hours, the nurse on duty briefed the attending physician. The physicians themselves visited the patient at least once every twenty-four hours. Every hour the patient was permitted to use a bedpan, drink liquids, or take in food. The straps were adjusted to allow as much comfort as possible.

I never really got used to seeing patients in restraint. One night I was called in from home shortly before eight p.m. to authorize the use of physical force in placing a man on the restraint bed. The patient was a small, thin man around twenty years old. I sat in the office with the psychiatrist on duty. We watched the restraint cell on the security monitor. Thick leather straps bound the patient's wrists, ankles, and chest to the bed; a nurse and an officer were also in the cell.

I said to the psychiatrist, "If that was my child, I'd cry myself to sleep every night." He simply nodded, and we continued watching the young man on the screen.

I had served in the correctional field for about twenty-eight years at that point, and I thought I'd seen everything. I had not. As I watched uniformed guards adjust a pillow so the patient could sip from a straw, I recalled other employees in other prisons who sat with the lights off to avoid providing any assistance, even in the smallest way possible, to anyone. At RTC I witnessed guards counsel prisoners who were acting out and praise patients who were finally beginning to come around — a stark contrast to an officer at Kingston who yelled, "Get away from the window!" at any prisoner who tried to ask a question. It was apparent, however, that we could provide only temporary relief. As soon as a Form 1 patient began to show signs of improvement, they were returned to their parent institution. We needed to transfer them so that we could accept other prisoners in crisis. Unfortunately, the system did not alter the conditions of confinement that led to or exacerbated the patients' mental illness. In almost every instance, patients returned to solitary confinement, where they might languish for months or years. In many cases, they would return to the very same cell they had occupied previously, as if they had never left.

The patients who occupied the other sixteen cells of 1B were, in a word, unique. At the very end of the range, in the last cell, was the self-professed king of Scotland. At six foot two and 250 pounds, this patient had grey hair and a full grey beard. He was a strong man, very aggressive, and on occasion, violent. He suffered from an extreme psychosis and truly believed he was the king of Scotland. He spent most of his time lying on his bed, looking silently at whoever went by. He did not like the nurses, and he hated me, but he seemed to respond to the officers. Perhaps he respected the authority of the uniform. He was in the habit of firing staff when they did not follow his instructions or in some other way failed to impress him. He fired some employees at RTC twice in the same shift.

Closer to the front of the range was a patient named Donald. A small man at five foot one and painfully skinny with thinning hair,

Donald was schizophrenic. He also suffered from the uncontrollable urge to drink water, and lots of it. In fact, he drank so much that for medical reasons we had to keep the water to his cell turned off, including the toilet. Once an hour, a staff member would go down to Donald's cell and turn the water on long enough to flush the toilet, if required. We weighed Donald regularly to monitor his water intake. He was often heard talking or even screaming in his cell, alone. On other occasions we could hear him laughing and talking casually, as if the voices in his head were pleasant company.

For the king of Scotland, Donald, and others living on 1B, one event always provided some unwelcome excitement: needle day, when patients received their regular injection of whatever medication was strong enough to hold their symptoms at bay. The day typically began with verbal threats from the patients, who were usually resistant to their injections. Sometimes, the anti-social behaviour of one was enough to set off the patients in the adjacent cells. Staff would struggle to administer an injection to one hostile prisoner, without hurting him, only to find that the next one had removed all his clothes and covered his body with feces.

Many stringent legal requirements govern administering injections to patients against their will. Most of these involve terms like "duty of care" and "incapacity" and fall on the shoulders of the attending physician. Physical force to restrain a patient can only be used with the authority of the warden. I was required to make a video record explaining my reasons for using force on a non-compliant patient. I appeared on a great many of these videos, filmed by a uniformed officer, who was part of the highly trained institutional emergency response team, or IERT. As a small facility, RTC did not have its own IERT, so the squad came from Kingston Penitentiary next door when necessary.

The uniformed guards who worked on Kingston Pen's IERT at that time showed as much patience and compassion as the best of the living-unit officers back in the 1980s. Equipped with shields, batons, mace, and considerable specialized training, these officers could have easily restrained these patients in seconds, right after the first refusal to lie face down with their hands behind their backs and ankles crossed. Instead, they would stand at the cell door, sweating under their heavy equipment, talking, pleading, and negotiating until they were blue in the face. Most of the time, these protracted verbal negotiations were enough to gain compliance.

Although the clientele was challenging, I liked the year and a half I spent at RTC. After spending twenty-eight years trying to convince others to think and talk instead of react, I had finally found a prison where that was precisely what they did. I was often placed in the role of acting as warden, given the number of meetings the warden attended off-site. I should have been happy to finish my time here, but something was wrong; I just wasn't sure at the time what it was.

One day, a 1B officer named Larry Sharpe, a kind-hearted man who was wonderful with the patients, called me down to the range. He told me there was something I really needed to see. When I got to the range, he was waiting for me with a cell key in his hand.

"You aren't going to believe this, Rob," he said. He turned and began to head down the range, then stopped short in front of the first cell, one with a solid door. "This wasn't here an hour ago when I did my walk."

I stepped back to make room for him to open the cell door. Inside was a lone Aboriginal male wearing a heavy security gown. These gowns are almost indestructible so that patients can't tear the cloth and hang themselves. He was about twenty years old with long, thick, matted hair that covered his eyes. His forearms were covered in burns and scars. His head was lowered, his gaze fixed on the floor. The cell smelled heavily of urine and sweat. I guessed by the look of the floor that he had not been using the toilet. He moved aside to the corner of the cell as I entered. On the back wall was a painting, about a metre across and half a metre high. It was a nature scene: a tree, a mountain, and a stream; birds, clouds, and a sun. Every stroke was the same, thick, red, and with a drip at the end. This young man had painted the entire picture in his own blood. As a proficient "cutter" from way back, he had received only plastic cutlery — a spoon — with his breakfast that day. Unfortunately, he also received an individual serving of jam in a small plastic container with a sharp edge once the paper was peeled away.

"That's quite a picture," I ventured, at an utter loss.

He did not speak or look up. I could see I was not going to reach him, and perhaps nobody else would either. I left the cell, and Larry closed the door behind us. I remember that scene like it was yesterday. Something in me just shifted that day.

I went back upstairs to the warden's office. I closed the door and slumped down in the chair. I stared out the window at Lake Ontario, feeling stunned by what I had just seen. I briefly thought of turning on my computer and looking at the files of the young patient downstairs. I realized that I had not taken the time to get his name. I momentarily considered calling Larry back but dismissed the notion. What was the point? The longer I sat, the more depressed I felt. I began to look back over the past thirty years, at what I had become, not just in my work but also in my life. I was not the same man who had entered Millhaven in 1978 hoping to make a difference. I still needed a few drinks each night. Elaine and I had divorced many years earlier; we'd both remarried, and now this marriage was failing as well. I felt a mere shadow of my real self, a walking ghost. I began to think about retiring.

Just as I was considering retirement, Stephen Harper's Conservative government took a "tough-on-crime" stance, and commissioned a complete review of the prison system and its operations. The resulting report, *A Roadmap to Strengthening Public Safety*, argued that the prison system was too accommodating in its efforts to rehabilitate and allowed prisoners too many privileges, apparently mistaking these basic rights for privileges and predictably concluded that Canada needed to get tough on crime and criminals. It reached this conclusion despite overwhelming evidence that being tough on criminals has never proved an effective deterrent, nor has it ever made any prison a safer place. In fact, the most highly regarded experts in the world unanimously condemn such an archaic philosophy, pointing to evidence-based successes in countries where rehabilitation is the focus.

The Conservatives gambled that their position would resonate with voters, and the gradual and systemic abuse of prisoners' rights would attract little attention. Once the government received its commissioned report, it sprang into action with a speed that suggested it had been poised and ready for some time. A new vision, the Transformation Agenda, was conceived by the Correctional Service of Canada and unveiled in 2008. It called for a series of changes to the department's operations from top to bottom.

This tough-on-crime approach sought to alter or reverse several very important pieces of correctional legislation, including statutory release. No longer would prisoners serve the last third of their sentences in the community, under the supervision and guidance of parole staff and other professionals, adhering to curfews, attending meetings and counselling sessions, submitting to drug tests, and seeking employment. The work involved in helping prisoners successfully reintegrate in the community is crucial, but the Harper government proposed to curtail and even abolish the practice. Prisoners would serve their entire sentences behind bars and emerge with no supervision and no assistance. Many prisoners lack the capacity to find a foothold in the community without professional help. At least four out of ten will be suffering from a diagnosed mental illness, according to CSC's own numbers. The chances of recidivism are much greater. How could such a practice make Canadians safer?

If tougher punishment and what it entails were to become a reality felt inside of Canada's prisons, it follows that prisoners would be spending longer and longer periods in custody. Aboriginal prisoners and mentally ill prisoners would serve the longest portions of all, based on history. Since we know that this custody is fraught with problems, it should be all the more apparent that longer sentences and harsher treatment are not conducive to reducing crime. They are not conducive to rehabilitation, or making prisons safe to work or live in — not if we are being honest with ourselves. Far too much evidence to the contrary exists.

The response of the legal and human rights communities was immediate condemnation of the government's changes. A press release from the Correctional Investigator's Office in 2014 stated:

> More offenders are staying longer in higher security penitentiaries where access to programs is most restricted. The majority of offenders are now returned to the community by way of statutory release at two-thirds point of the sentence versus conditional release. Use of force interventions, inmate assaults, segregation placements, involuntary transfers and self-injurious incidents are trending upward leading to conditions of detention that are less conducive to safe reintegration.

The same press release includes correctional investigator Howard Sapers's critical remark:

> Returning offenders to the community who are embittered by their incarceration experience instead of provided opportunities for positive change is not in anyone's interest. We know that timely interventions followed by graduated and structured release is less costly and more successful than releasing an offender directly from prison with limited or no period of supervision.

The Harper government fired Howard Sapers, citing the need to find a more "suitable candidate."

As incredulous as I was that such ideas were discussed seriously, I was even more astonished that many of my management colleagues immediately embraced these new policies. The same people who supported Corporate Objective No. 1 to get prisoners out the door, now declared that in keeping prisoners behind bars longer we were embarking on a bold, new direction that would make the public safer.

I was personally offended by what I considered an abrupt and wrong turn in correctional philosophy. How do you spend twenty years following one set of beliefs, and then arbitrarily dismiss it outright? Everywhere I looked, I saw it happening. Perhaps I was naive. When I factored in my own feelings of disillusionment and dissatisfaction with my work, I concluded I could no longer work for CSC. In the fall of 2009, I left the Correctional Service of Canada for good.

Conclusion:
A Culture of Collective Indifference

Officially referred to as "segregation," solitary confinement means keeping a person locked in a small cell for up to twenty-three hours a day with very few or no privileges. The UN says that more than fifteen consecutive days of solitary confinement amounts to a form of torture.

— Lucas Powers, CBC News, July 2016

At a time when the rest of the world is scaling back the use of solitary confinement, Canada remains steadfast in its reliance on a broken and dangerous system.

— Carmen Chung, senior lawyer at the BC Civil Liberties Association, CBC News, March 2016

In the beginning, my experiences in CSC were largely positive. My interactions with prisoners were easy and natural, and I was not alone in this. My volunteer experience at Millhaven seemed to show that even the most dangerous prisoners would meet civility with civility. These men have not spent their entire lives in prison. One only has to walk down to the visiting area in any prison to see that the same prisoners who might be considered dangerous based on their crimes can also be deeply concerned for their family's welfare and happiness.

No human being is defined completely by a single act, no matter how extreme. Virtually all prisoners can behave very badly or very well, depending on the circumstances. What is the reason behind these dramatic shifts in behaviour? I believe the environment dictates how the prisoners behave in almost all instances. If the environment is conducive to civil behaviour, the prisoners respond in kind. If the environment is one of arbitrary harshness and indifference to their needs, they will, again, respond in kind.

Many years ago, I was working at Joyceville during a labour stoppage. During this particular strike, instead of doing my unit-manager job, I volunteered to run the recreation area for the evenings, just as I once had. One night I was walking around the area, the way I used to, but something was very different. I used to be able to make small talk with the prisoners and joke around a bit, but this was no longer the case. Then I ran into Dan, a prisoner I'd known since Millhaven.

"Why is everyone staring at me and gunning me off?" I asked.

"They're not used to seeing a copper walking around down here," he said. "It's not like the old days anymore. You're probably freaking them out a bit."

He was right, it wasn't like the old days. Instead of living-unit officers walking around, mingling with the prisoners, watching ball hockey and movies in the dark together, uniformed staff members sat inside a fortress-like control post with tinted glass a centimetre thick, waiting for shift change and hoping they didn't have to go out and deal with the prisoners. As a living-unit officer, I had sat on the gym floor, in the dark, with three hundred prisoners. In those days, we had not felt at risk, because we were not in danger; the living units created an environment of dynamic security.

On February 19, 1980, I took an oath to work professionally, ethically, and dispassionately to assist all prisoners to become law-abiding citizens. I pledged to set a good example every day and to accept that the prisoners under my charge came to prison with more deficits than gifts. Every new staff member still faces this challenge, and it ultimately forms the foundation on which they approach their work. These employees will look to those around them. If they see patience and understanding, as with most of the Pittsburgh, Bath, and RTC employees, they will adopt a benevolent day-to-day approach. If their first day on the job were in Millhaven's J Unit as I experienced it, they may believe that verbally abusing prisoners and constantly threatening them with negative consequences is acceptable.

Under our current system of justice, the vast majority of prisoners are, at some point, going to be released back into society. Most want to stay out of prison if they can. If rehabilitation is our primary objective, we must set aside our personal outrage at the nature of the crime and look at every prisoner as a unique human being in need of assistance to get their life back on track. Yet in my experience, only about one-third of CSC employees maintain this as an overriding principle in their day-to-day work.

I suspect many readers will remain unconvinced about which methods work best. It is not uncommon to hear people say, "If prison was tough enough, these criminals would stop committing crimes in order to avoid going back." Many hold this point of view, ranging from those grossly uninformed to some world leaders. There are indeed veteran prison employees who still believe we need "tighter security and fewer privileges." The use of force is always available to those who work inside prisons. It is only a phone call away. But to run a prison safely, force should only be used as a last resort. If the prisoners as a whole believe they are being abused instead of treated fairly, the temperature in the prison rises. If these grievances take hold among those who have not even been directly affected, prisoners begin to feed off each other's anger. If these feelings of resentment reach critical mass, you have the prime climate for a riot.

All prisoners are difficult in their own way, because they are unique human beings confined in conditions that do not meet their needs. The more often we can provide a symptom-specific response to the problems that arise in prison, the more often we will experience success in running our prisons safely and humanely. As long as solitary confinement continues to be the catch-all for every problem that arises, there can be no hope of any real change in correctional philosophy, or in its results.

I am not suggesting that Correctional Service of Canada would cease to have problems if it could simply maintain an atmosphere of benevolent therapy. I am suggesting, however, that the secret to this complex issue, the key to the lock if you will, is the environment we create.

One of the most potentially dangerous situations presently facing the Correctional Service is the rising numbers of prisoners it is currently holding, numbers increased by the previous Conservative government's tough-on-crime bills. As numbers rise, the prisoners have less room to live in. This leads to tension, which leads to anti-social behaviour — most often, in my experience, violence. This violence in turn causes more prisoners to seek protection in the form of solitary confinement. In the critical *Annual Report of the Office of the Correctional Investigator 2013-2014*, Howard Sapers delineated the rising numbers:

> During the reporting period, the daily federal incarcerated population count consistently topped 15,000 inmates, averaging 15,200 incarcerated (+10% increase in the last 5 years). In FY 2013-14, the national double-bunking rate (placing two inmates in a cell designed for one person) averaged 19.2% (+93% increase in the last 5 years). Through the reporting period, in-custody medium security counts were higher than rated cell capacities except for Pacific region. Across the country, there were 8,328 administrative segregation placements, with an average segregation count of 850 offenders on any given day (+6.4% increase in the last 5 years).

Solitary confinement, or administrative segregation, is arguably related to suicide rates in prisons. In 2014 correctional investigator Sapers released a report on suicide in prison, in which he noted: "Suicide is the leading cause of un-natural death among federal inmates, accounting for about 20% of all deaths in custody in any given year." Fourteen of the thirty suicides over a three-year period that his office reviewed occurred in solitary-confinement cells under conditions of close monitoring and supervision. In a September 2014 press release relating to this report, Sapers remarked, "I am concerned that the Correctional Service of Canada continues to rely on long-term segregation placements as a means to manage symptoms or behaviours associated with mental illness, suicidal ideation, or self-harming. This practice is unsafe and should be expressly prohibited."

Rarely, Sapers noted in his report, did CSC investigators examining deaths in custody "go the extra step to identify how the death *might* have been averted had staff acted or decided in a different manner." Sapers further observed, "Lessons learned from even a single suicide should have a lasting impact on the organization and its efforts to prevent and publicly account for deaths in custody." Sapers recommended that CSC reports on suicides routinely be made available to coroners and to designated family members of the prisoners involved.

In the case of the Kingston Pen prisoner whose suicide I was called in to investigate, I doubt very much that information about the circumstances were provided to the prisoner's brother, who sat quietly and listened while the prison chaplain informed him, in a phone call, that his brother had taken his own life. I do not believe the CSC would willingly admit that the prisoner had been lying in a huge pool of his own dried blood, that he had been dead long enough for rigor mortis to set in, or that he had a note about the death of his sister clutched in one of his hands when he died. I do not believe the CSC would have stated they had permitted him to cover his cell window, even though it was against the rules, and even though he was diagnosed as depressed and placed on moderate suicide watch.

All of these failures are egregious and, appallingly, they continue. On July 4, 2016, a thirty-year-old prisoner named Terry Baker at Grand Valley Institution in Kitchener, Ontario, hanged herself in a solitary-confinement cell. She had made previous attempts to end her life, and she was on suicide watch at the time of her death.

A little over a year earlier, Christopher Roy, a prisoner at Matsqui Institution in Abbotsford, British Columbia, committed suicide in his solitary-confinement cell. He was thirty-seven years old, the father of two daughters. Roy had been in solitary confinement for sixty days when he hanged himself. At the inquest into Roy's death, his institutional parole officer cried as he described this man's descent into madness and despair. According to the parole officer, Roy was prohibited from having reading and writing materials in his cell. The officer noticed that Roy was showing signs of mental deterioration and pleaded with his superiors to let the prisoner have at least a television set in his cell. This request was denied. Perhaps most importantly, Roy had no idea when the period of solitary confinement would end — if ever. In the days prior to his suicide, Roy began to act out, including covering his cell window. Perhaps the greatest irony in this tragedy is the fact that Christopher Roy was in a solitary-confinement cell because he turned himself in to the RCMP following a breach of his parole conditions. For those of us who truly understand the nature of this business, a prisoner who willingly returns to custody following a breach poses the least risk to others.

In a CBC News report by Angela Sterritt in July 2016, Roy's parents were quoted to say they "have been living a nightmare since his death." Roy's father has no doubt that his son committed suicide only because he was in solitary confinement for so long. "All I can say is that everybody who knows Chris knows that he has never been a suicidal human being," he told the CBC.

In 2010 Edward Snowshoe, a twenty-four-year-old federal prisoner with significant mental health concerns, hanged himself. He, too, was in solitary confinement. Snowshoe engaged in self-harm, covered his cell window, refused to speak to staff, and would not attend segregation review boards about his case. Instead of recognizing these actions as signs of increasing mental deterioration, staff ended up virtually ignoring him. At the time of his death, he had been in solitary confinement for 162 days.

Don Head, the commissioner of the Correctional Service of Canada (and a former colleague of mine), wrote a formal response to the Edward Snowshoe inquiry. Patrick White for the *Globe and Mail* reported that Head, in his report, "accuses the aboriginal inmate of continued 'aggressive behaviour'" — an assertion that contradicted testimony from front-line staff who stated that Snowshoe was "very quiet, kept to himself, didn't give us a lot of problems." To Howard Sapers, also quoted in the *Globe and Mail*, Head's response seemed "geared toward explaining the status quo rather than addressing the judge's recommendations.…'There is a defensiveness and really an unwillingness to acknowledge that things could have been better.'" His own conclusion, quoted the same article, was clear: "In reality, there are areas that could be and need to be improved."

Undoubtedly, the most reported prison suicide in Canada in recent years, and the one that should have marked an end to the use of solitary confinement by the CSC, is the case of Ashley Smith, a nineteen-year-old prisoner at Grand Valley Institution. In October 2007, she strangled herself with a strip of cloth while guards watched her on a video monitor and did nothing to intervene. Originally sentenced to serve one month in a youth custody centre for throwing crab apples at a letter carrier when she was fourteen, Smith's defiant behaviour immediately landed her in solitary confinement, and she was frequently violent and difficult to handle, which extended her one-month sentence. At the time of her death, Smith had spent more than one thousand days in solitary confinement.

In his 2008 report titled *A Preventable Death*, Howard Sapers described Smith's experience. She spent all her time in a security gown in a poorly lit cell, and her interactions with other people were limited to contact through the food slot. She had no shoes, no mattress, and no blanket and absolutely nothing to occupy her time. Toilet paper and deodorant were strictly rationed. She was not allowed to have any soap in her cell, and, the report noted, "while menstruating, she was not permitted underwear or sufficient sanitary products to meet her hygiene needs." She often slept on the floor. Although she had a history of expressing suicidal thoughts and tied ligatures around her neck, CSC officials instructed staff to ignore her, even when she was choking herself. Sapers's remarks were trenchant:

> What is most disturbing about the Correctional Service's use of this overly restrictive form of segregation is the fact that the Correctional Service was aware — from the outset — that Ms. Smith had spent extensive periods of time in isolation while incarcerated in the province of New Brunswick and that confinement had been noted as detrimental to her overall well-being. Despite this knowledge, the Correctional Service's response to Ashley Smith's significant needs was to do more of the same.

The first inquest into Smith's death, in 2011, ended in a mistrial. The second inquest ruled Smith's death a homicide and made 104 recommendations, including a ban on indefinite solitary confinement. Don Head was among many witnesses subpoenaed to testify at the inquest. As the man at the top, his attendance at the inquest would undoubtedly cast a very clear light on the nature of our penal system, and if anyone would be able to speak with authority on such matters as the use of solitary confinement, it would be Head. Unfortunately, this was not the case.

Writing for CBC News in September 2013, Maureen Brosnahan

reported Head tried secretly to get the coroner, Dr. John Carlisle, to disallow his summons to testify, arguing that he was not involved in Smith's day-to-day management and had been on French-language training for part of her incarceration. The Smith family lawyer reportedly accused Head of trying to hide. "Prime Minister Harper stood up before Canadians and promised Canadians that CSC would fully co-operate with this proceeding. Meanwhile, we have the top man at CSC going behind closed doors and trying to duck the inquest," he told CBC News. "It's shocking."

In the end, the coroner refused to withdraw the summons on the grounds that Head had valuable evidence, according to CBC News.

I watched Head's testimony at the Ashley Smith inquest. A CBC 2016 report by Kate Bueckert quoted Conservative senator Bob Runciman's observation that Head "looked like he had been out working in the back garden." And Runciman felt Head's physical appearance "was a very visible indication of his contempt for the process, you know, keep your nose out of my business approach and I think that's reflective of the whole approach to dealing with [the] mentally ill in the federal system."

Ashley Smith's death in 2007 represents one of the worst failures in the history of Canada's prison system and was one of the events that prompted me to question the true nature of my employer, the prevailing culture at CSC, and whether or not I could, in good conscience, remain part of the system. We might ask ourselves why, with everything we know about the harmful effects of solitary confinement, almost nothing has changed. Writing in the *Globe and Mail* in 2016, Debra Parkes, Chair in Feminist Legal Studies at the Allard School of Law at the University of British Columbia, notes:

> Each year, thousands of prisoners are held in a form of solitary confinement called administrative segregation. They are isolated in a small cell for 23 hours a day, not for punishment, but for some other reason — they are

suicidal or self-harming; they are at risk from other prisoners; or they are difficult to manage for any reason...

Despite its widespread use, there is nothing natural or
commonsensical about isolating people who are at risk,
acting out, or experiencing mental illness. Like slavery
was in its day, solitary confinement is a normalized,
inhumane practice, on which we will one day look back
and wonder why and how it was tolerated for so long.

In a 2016 CBC News report by Catharine Tunney, former Supreme
Court Justice Louise Arbour noted that, too often, solitary confinement is used as a convenient disciplinary tool in a resource-deprived
system. Arbour responded to the recent suicide of Terry Baker with
a call to end solitary confinement in Canada's prisons. She remarked
that a prison sentence is, ostensibly, the punishment for crime, "not
an opportunity for further abuse." She further observed that isolating
and sometimes restraining prisoners and depriving them of human
contact is cruel and "completely counterproductive in getting them
to integrate in the prisoner population and function."

I have my own opinion about why nothing has changed. I believe
solitary confinement endures because the use of and reliance on
it is part of a deeply ingrained culture of collective indifference in
Canada's prison system. In my thirty years down inside, I saw a great
deal that I would like to forget. I knew many prisoners who suffered
unspeakable ills as a result of long-term solitary confinement.

When I first left the prison service and began planning this book,
I wrote a letter to ten Members of Parliament, representatives of all
three major political parties, outlining my concerns with the Harper
government's tough-on-crime bills and what I believed would be
the very detrimental effects of draconian measures against some of
our country's most vulnerable and disenfranchised citizens. I also

wrote about the overuse of solitary confinement and the plight of the mentally ill in our federal prison system. As Senator Runciman was quoted in a CBC News report, "the only way we're going to see significant change is change of staffing at the senior levels in Correctional Service Canada, and at some point the government will have to step in."

I received only one response, from the youngest MP in the group. The respondent had clearly read my letter in detail and had taken the time to prepare a coherent and intelligent response in support of my concerns. The letter was signed, in blue ink, Justin Trudeau. CBC reported that soon after his election last fall, Prime Minister Trudeau "tasked key cabinet ministers with implementing recommendations from the Smith inquest, including better treatment for mentally ill inmates and tighter restrictions around the use of segregation." In March 2016, Trudeau's government announced the reinstatement of Howard Sapers as correctional investigator. In November 2016 Ontario Corrections minister David Orazietti announced the appointment of Howard Sapers to lead an independent review into the use of solitary confinement in Ontario jails.

I have no idea what lies in store for the Correctional Service of Canada. Although I would like to believe that significant positive changes are possible, I have my doubts. The culture of this organization is so deeply entrenched and so pervasive that I remain skeptical of its capacity for genuine introspection. The people I know who still work in this system tell me it's worse now than it was when I was around. The increasing reliance on closed-circuit security cameras and electronically operated doors has further eroded the human contact that is essential to humane treatment and ultimately the chances for rehabilitation.

Acknowledgements

I must express my gratitude to the many people without whom this book would not be. Maureen Garvie was the first literary professional to edit the original manuscript, and her advice was invaluable. I am eternally indebted to literary agent Robert Lecker. His comments led to major changes in the book's organization, and it is solely due to his support and guidance that Goose Lane Editions accepted *Down Inside*.

I give sincerest thanks to the people at Goose Lane who took a chance on me, and to my encouraging and generous editor, Jill Ainsley, who completed significant and necessary edits. Jill took the manuscript from a lengthy, rambling narrative to a finely tuned, well-paced series of stories with an important message. To Paula Sarson, who helped me to clean up various ambiguities and inconsistencies in the text, and who put the final sheen on the finished product, a sincere thank you.

I wish to acknowledge all the victims of crime who shared with me their personal stories of loss and heartache, which shook me to my core and allowed me to see the social dilemma of crime and punishment in all of its complexities.

Finally, I must acknowledge those dedicated men and women of Correctional Service of Canada. Although I wrote this book to bring public attention to the many shortcomings in our federal prison system, it also true that there are many heroes in Canada's prisons doing their best to make a difference every day. You know who you are, and you know my personal regard for you and the work you do. Many of you inspired me with your unflagging efforts to bring sanity to an insane environment. Perhaps we were trying to accomplish something that was in the end not yet possible. After all, I have heard accomplishing that which seems impossible always takes longer.

Index